Sport, Theory and Social Problems

A Critical Introduction

Eric Anderson

 Routledge
Taylor & Francis Group

LONDON AND NEW YORK

First edition published 2010
by Routledge
2 Park Square, Milton Park, Abingdon, Oxon, OX14 4RN

Simultaneously published in the USA and Canada
by Routledge
270 Madison Avenue, New York, NY 10016

Routledge is an imprint of the Taylor & Francis Group, an informa business

Typeset in Times New Roman by
Pindar NZ, Auckland, New Zealand
Printed and bound in Great Britain by
TJ International Ltd, Padstow, Cornwall

British Library Cataloguing in Publication Data
A catalogue record for this book is available from the British Library

Library of Congress Cataloging-in-Publication Data
Anderson, Eric.
Sport, theory, and social problems : a critical introduction / Eric Anderson.
    p. cm.
  Includes bibliographical references and index.
  1. Sports – Sociological aspects. I. Title.
  GV706.5.A57 2010
  306.4'83 – dc22   2009050203

ISBN13: 978-0-415-57125-8 (hbk)
ISBN13: 978-0-415-57126-5 (pbk)
ISBN13: 978-0-203-85743-4 (ebk)

Sport, Theory and Social Problems

What impact does sport have on the lives of ordinary people?

How does sport help to perpetuate inequalities in society?

What can social theory tell us about the role of sport in society?

At its origin, competitive sport was institutionalized in Western cultures for the privilege of white, heterosexual men. Over time, sport has become more open to categories of people traditionally marginalized in society: women; those from lower social classes; gay men; people of color; and those who are differently abled. However, focusing solely on increased social inclusion in sport masks significant problems with both the culture and structure of sport. This critical textbook examines social exclusion in sport and analyzes the socio-negative attributes associated with competitive, institutionalized sport, for all who play.

Focusing on sport at non-elite levels, this book explores the lives of everyday citizens who participate in sport and examines how inequality and social deviance are structured into the social and sporting systems. Each chapter uses one or more key social theories to address a particular social problem in sport, such as learned obedience to authority; the acceptance of pain and injury; the adoption of hyper-masculine, homophobic, and sexist attitudes; the teaching of in-group/out-group; and the use of sport as a false mechanism for social mobility. By concentrating on real sport, and through the use of evocative vignettes illustrating the experiences of real people, this textbook develops the critical senses, social conscience, and theoretical understanding of all students of sport and anybody for whom sport is part of their everyday life.

Eric Anderson is an American sociologist at the University of Bath, UK. He is well known for his research on sport, masculinities, sexualities, and homophobia. He has authored several books and peer-reviewed articles, including the award-winning *In the Game: Gay Athletes and the Cult of Masculinity*. Visit his website www.ericandersonphd.com.

Dedicated to Professor Judy Treas.
Thank you for teaching me to think like a sociologist.

Contents

Introduction

There is a good chance that you are reading this book because you love sport. If this is the case, you need to know that my aim is to help you divorce yourself from that love. First, I intend to introduce you to some valuable and easy-to-understand sociological theory. This is the easy part. However, I intend to use these theories (and evidence gained from sport sociologists), to change your mind about the so-called "good" (what I call the socio-positive) that you think sport brings to individuals and society. In this book, I highlight how damaging organized, competitive teamsport can be.

In order to do this I have to counter your thinking about sport (or at least the type of sport I discuss in this text). Eventually, even if I fail to swing you to see things the way I do, I hope to at least inspire you to think more critically about the role that sport plays in contemporary society. I hope that we will all agree that when we think critically about sport, we can at least suggest methods for improving it.

However, I must warn you: if you love sport, but have never thought critically about the problems associated with the way we structure, organize and "play" it, you might find this book a challenge, for I am sure to contest some of your deeply held beliefs. Few people appreciate having their deeply held beliefs questioned, and their cherished institutions or activities critiqued.

My critical perspective on sport in this text is intentional for two reasons. First, you have grown up in, and therefore been heavily socialized into, a sport-obsessed, sport-loving culture. You have been told (both directly and covertly) how "good" sport is. You have learned this from a number of people representing important institutions: education, the government, the health and fitness industry, religion and of course the extensive sport-media complex that maintains astounding influence in Western cultures.

Our obsession with sport – our collective belief that sport is a socially valuable enterprise – is so extreme that Varda Burstyn (1999) calls sport "a great secular masculine religion." She argues that sport maintains a privileged place in our society, a position that escapes significant scrutiny. But just because sport is highly esteemed, it does not necessarily mean that it is actually "all good." As with most institutions that are privileged (like religion), or as with most institutions that hold favor in our hearts (like the nuclear American family), they tend to escape critical scrutiny. Instead, scrutiny falls on all those who fail to meet the dominant model. Indeed, if you critically analyze cherished institutions (something I love to do), you are bound to get criticized yourself: this is a shoot the messenger type of phenomenon, and after making your way through a few chapters, some of you *will* want to shoot me.

As a general rule, we dislike having the things we strongly believe in questioned. Thus, and regardless of the evidence against our belief, when my students first encounter my arguments, they look for examples to justify their pro-sport beliefs, discounting those that contest it. When I present them with the same overwhelming empirical data and logical arguments against sport, they eventually slip from their entrenched position in favor of sport. They next step back to the defensive attitudinal position of, "Well, does it do more good than harm?" I find this very position somewhat ironic. First of all, how does a 51 percent threshold support the argument of "doing good"? We do not use this standard for medicine or education – 51 percent on my students' term papers would not be good. My answer to this basic question, "Does sport do more good than harm," is generally, "That's certainly hard to quantify, but no, I do not believe that it does." I also ask, "And is 51 percent effectiveness and 49 percent damage worth all the fuss? All the money?" I do recognize that there is some "good" to sport. I question however just how much good comes from it. Thus, in this book, my intentional omission of the "wonders" of sport is not to say that all sport is all bad all the time. Matters are never that simple. I will therefore begin this text by admitting that there is plenty to love about sport. My students, please take note. It is not often you will hear me say that.

I begin my confessional about the socio-positive of sport by admitting that I coached high school distance runners for eighteen years. They were (in many senses) absolutely wonderful years. This is for several reasons, but primarily, it is because sport allows us to identify with an organization that is larger than "us." Competitive, organized teams permit us to be part of a group, which is akin to the feeling of belonging to a close kinship group, a gang, or clan. We enjoy this group membership, and the identity it brings for many reasons. Some hope that their outstanding success in this membership category will bring them symbolic immortality (although for the vast majority, not even your own kids will care about your youthful sporting accomplishments). Others desire the social identity, as this legitimately helps us feel more connected to our friends and society, and it hyper-inflates our sense of importance of the group we belong to. Exemplifying this, when I coached, I had the "sense" that what I did, our wins and losses, were "oh so very, very important." However, in highlighting how absolutely unimportant they are to others, I engage you in reading them.

When I was 16, I won my first 800 meter track race, in a dual meet with another high school team. Later that year I won my league's sophomore 3,200 meter race. I continued to win the occasional race, once even winning a varsity match as a 16-year-old. By the time I was a junior I was my team's top runner. I won the Huntington Beach High School versus Marina High School 800 and 3,200 one day. Another meet, I won the 1,600 and 3,200 against Fountain Valley High School. In my senior year I won the Huntington Beach versus Edision dual meet in Cross Country, with a spectacular time of 15:31. Although I only came in third in the next invitational race, I lowered that time to 15:13 for the three mile race. But enough of my career (did I mention I came in the top 100 of the LA Marathon one year?), what about my coaching? Over the eighteen years I coached, I had countless wins. My freshman team won the Sunet League Championship meet in 1988, and again in 1989. My varsity team won in 1993, 1995, and 1996. Heck, we even won the Orange County Championship meet in 1995. Here, one of my athletes won the individual title for the boys, and another (who you will read about later) won for the girls (Jenny). We later went on to win the (how many of you are still reading this?) Central Park Invitational (I bet not many).

I bet you did not make it through that paragraph; you got the idea that I was elucidating upon countless, meaningless wins. Even if you did make it through, I bet you could not really care less. It highlights that, for the most part, nobody is interested in your sporting accomplishments – except you. Ultimately, the only people who care about those wins and losses (outside professional sport) are those in the event; and some of them are even smart enough to know that the outcome of the competition is absolutely unimportant.

Highlighting this, I remember once on my high school team, one of my team-mates was winning the "all-important league championship race." With only a quarter mile to go he was sure to win. Suddenly, he stopped. I passed him wondering what he was looking for in the dirt. I later learned that he had lost a contact lens and I couldn't rationalize how he could just stop a race in the end, one he was destined to win, in order to look for a contact lens. However, in those days, lenses were expensive, and he reasoned he best stop right there, because he could mark where it fell out. It was an informed choice that best enabled him to find the lens. It took me 25 years to understand that, to him, the race was not as important as it was to stay out of trouble with his parents for losing an expensive contact lens. While this runner had a sensible balance of the (un)importance of sport at 17 years of age, I did not.

Now that I have confessed my previous identity of loving youth sport, I will now admit that I can at least understand why many people also enjoy watching and "supporting" professional sport. Although it does not excite me today, at 14 years of age, I watched my home baseball team (the Anaheim Angels) battle for a spot at making the World Series. I sat alone in my living room, cheering, tensing my teeth from anxiety. I was fully absorbed in their plight – dearly hoping that they would qualify for the World Series. So I understand (or used to understand) what fanaticism is all about, and how fun (and painful) it can be to follow a professional team.

I understand that watching sport can bring you through an emotional roller coaster. It can do so in a way that does not happen with other forms of passive entertainment. I admit that as much as I love movies and theater, neither of these can get you shouting in ecstasy or anger as sport can. I also understand why people follow or support certain sports teams. After flipping through pages of bad news in the paper, the sports section gives one a 50 percent chance of reading something that makes them feel good. The fact that there is nothing new to the sports section, it offers nothing novel (one team wins, the other loses; one team thanks god, the other fails to blame god), reading about it, daily, is a type of reliable monotony that can add a sense of order to a chaotic life. Even after the horrible events of September 11, 2001, Americans found sport a way to bring normalcy back into our altered lives.

Today, however, I ask myself: what would happen if the average sports fan donated half the time he/she usually spent watching, reading about, and attending professional sports matches to a worthy charity? Today, I wonder if the average sports fan understands just how the co-option of sport has duped them into brand loyalty in a way that only Apple has otherwise been successful.

However, this book is not about *that* type of sport. This book does not discuss professional sport, the sport-media complex, or even the Olympics. In this text, I do not drone on endlessly about sport and "the body" or about other abstract matters that many of my friends/colleagues write about (in ways that not even I can understand). I also do not discuss much about the financial implications of sport and education, or about how sport sucks away badly needed public funds from more worthy causes. I do not discuss how sad it is that some of my students in England are given governmental funding so that they can sail their little boats, or kick their little balls, when their mothers, sisters and girlfriends are dying of breast cancer, yet are denied Herceptin because it is too expensive for the government.

Instead, I discuss sport at the level that most readers have played it. Thus, in this text, I provide a critical examination about participation in organized, competitive youth sport, high school sport, university sport, and other organized community levels of playing sport. I focus primarily on the damage caused on the field, mostly leaving for another project a discussion of the damage caused off the field.

I justify this limited focus accordingly. First, there is a divergence in sport sociology research. Much of the research relates to professional sport, and much relates to recreational and education-based sport. One reason many introductory textbooks are so large (and expensive) is that they attempt to cover both sets of research. Second, it is also important to remember that very few people play elite sport. For example, there exist only about 3,500 professional teamsport positions in the top four money-making sports in the United States (and a good portion of these positions are filled by foreign players). Conversely, there are tens of millions of people who play sport at other levels. Accordingly, this critical text (focused on the US, UK and Canada) examines social inclusion/exclusion, and the socio-negative implications of sport at the non-elite levels – the levels that you the reader have engaged with, personally. By removing focus from those professional issues, we can better examine the lives of everyday citizens who play sport, and better understand how social inequality and social deviance is structured by our current sporting system. In this text, I therefore examine how sport socializes deviance and over-complicity to authority into those who play it, how sport discriminates against women, children, gays and lesbians, the differently abled and those of color.

What This Book Examines

Because this text focuses on our common interaction with sport, I only examine the non-elite levels of play. More specifically, I focus on the types of sport that most of us have had formal interaction with or played. Certainly there are hundreds of different sports, but there remain a dozen or so that are thoroughly weaved into our youth, high school, communities, and university education systems. Thus, in this book, I am mostly discussing sports that are competitive, organized, coached, and institutionalized into either leagues, schools, or other administrative bodies. I am interested in these sports because millions of us play in them. In the United States it is estimated that over 41 million girls and boys play on organized teams (Hyman 2009), and almost half of these are in soccer. I focus therefore on organized, competitive sports that we commonly think of when we say "sport": baseball, football, American football, hockey, lacrosse, rugby. To a lesser extent, I include athletics, swimming, volleyball, tennis. I reserve my harshest critique for invasion sports (such as football and basketball) and to a lesser extent criticize the individual sports (running and swimming).

While some criticism might still apply, I do not mean to implicate eco-sports (surfing, sailing, hang gliding, and mountain climbing), games of skill (darts, ping pong) or board games (chess and scrabble) in my critiques. Also, to be clear, when I talk about sport throughout this book, I am not talking about taking the dog out to play catch with a Frisbee, going cross-country skiing, running an organized 10K race, doing yoga with friends, or even going out to kick the soccer ball around in a Saturday afternoon pick-up game with friends. Just the opposite, I maintain we need to divert sports monies into exercise and fitness programs like these.

In examining organized, competitive sport, I am looking for inequalities, power plays, and the use of sport to oppress people and/or distract us from greater social problems. In this book, I will help you see problems associated with not so much the act of sport, but the *way* we play it, and the problem of *how* we value it. I will however, mostly refer to individual sports as just "sport." I leave it to you to remember that I am not analyzing a Saturday afternoon game of ping-pong with your grandpa.

I may already have the competitive, organized teamsport folk silently protesting, "What is there to critique about playing high school or university sport? If these sports were so destructive why would we compel kids to play them as part of physical education?" However, before I engage the questions of why they value mainstream sport, and why I do not, let me first point out that it is not enough to simply state that sport is "good" because playing sport is fun. Nor is it enough to say that we live in a corpulent society and that sport rectifies this. There are plenty of activities that are fun that society condemns, and there are certainly much better methods for losing weight and gaining health (like hiking) than bashing one's head into an opponent. What I seek to examine in this text is why we play sport, why it is fun for some, at whose expense this fun comes, and who benefits from organized, competitive teamsport.

Culturally but Uncritically Valuing Organized, Competitive Sport

Various attributes are associated with organized, competitive sporting participation in Western cultures. For example, one longstanding notion (for boys) concerns indoctrinating men into manhood. Ray Raphael (1988) argues that without historic rites of passage, modern men are confused about what it means to be a man. He proposes that competitive sport helps fill this void. Others maintain that sport helps men (who they perceive to be naturally violent) vent their anger in an acceptable manner (cf. McCaughey 2007). They argue, however, that as women have increasingly gained cultural and institutional access to sport, cultural arguments for valuing sport have changed from models of masculinity-making, to character building; attributes that women can "benefit" from, too.

One of the more resilient myths (for boys and girls, men and women) is that teamsport teaches us how to work together, and get along with others (Miracle and Rees 1994). Some maintain that sport teaches kids to win and fail in public, perhaps letting them "learn" from their triumphs and tragedies in the process. Some extend this to maintain that failure (and its resultant public ostracization) even "builds character" in kids that I argue are too young to understand the rules of a game. More fancifully, some suggest that competitive teamsport is an effective solution to many of the social issues related to the social integration of racialized people (Girginov *et al.* 2006). Others, like Sage (1990), take a more political approach, suggesting (rightfully so) that sport permits governments to transmit dominant social and political values, the way religion once did. Whether one agrees with these values (like nationalism/patriotism) is a different matter.

If you ask my first-year university students why sport is "good," they repeat the lore of sport's mythical attributes: sport promotes teamwork, cooperation, fitness, and self-esteem. They suggest that sport helps minorities find employment out of ghettos; that sport promotes school attendance, decreases drug use, crime, and other forms of mischief; and that sport helps certain athletes earn scholarships to pay for the rising costs of university attendance. All will suggest that sport builds fitness (often overlooking the trail of their own broken bodies). All of these propositions will be analyzed in this text.

To me, however, one of the most fanciful beliefs is that sport serves as a social vessel for the acceptance of young kids into peer groups, and that it provides them with a system of adult support in growing up. Michener (1976: 19) for example, says "Young people need that experience of acceptance; it can come in a variety of ways ... but in the United States it is sports that have been elected primarily to fill this need."

While it is certainly true that most of us need to feel that we belong to something, and while sport certainly can and does fill that necessity for some, it seems to me a stretch to suggest that sport *is* that place, without problem. To me, all of this "fluff" about the virtues of sport can defined by the word "hyperbole." It seems to me that sport is a terrain where kids are evaluated according to their physical worth, where those who do not make the grade are cut, socially excluded and/or marginalized. Yet, I am initially pressed to get my new students to understand this.

The fact is, Anglo-American cultures (to which my students belong) do love sport (teamsport particularly), attributing to them a large number of socio-positive characteristics. Accordingly, studies of parents show that they believe that sport will teach their sons moral character, self-restraint, and a sense of fair play. For example, compared to the 6 percent of American parents who discourage athletic participation, 75 percent encourage it (Miller Lite report 1983). In the US, this is largely a fact of how sport intertwines with public education (Gerdy 2002). Accordingly, some American high schools report participation rates as high as 72 percent (Carlson *et al.* 2005). Thus, there exists great cultural and institutional pressure for youth to participate in sport. But even in the UK, where sport is less institutionalized in education, participation in sport is extraordinarily high. Here, teamsport participation is pressured by peers or made compulsory by parents or institutions of education. As a result, if there is any institution described as being all-encompassing in the lives of Western youths – it most certainly must be that of sport.

There is limited evidence for some of these socio-positive beliefs. Recall that I am not saying that sport is all bad, all the time. For example, researchers find that the most salient benefits of organized sport participation is found in elevated self-esteem, better school attendance, and educational aspirations, higher rates of university attendance and perhaps even post-schooling employment (Eccles and Barber 1999; Carlson *et al.* 2005; Jeziorski 1994; Marsh 1992, 1993; Sabo, Melnick and Vanfossen 1989). However, I maintain that these quantitative investigations are somewhat misleading. This is because these studies fail to examine whether the benefits associated with sporting participation are the result of something intrinsic to teamsport participation, or whether they simply reflect the physical, symbolic, and emotional dominance that a socially elite group of people exhibit over marginalized lesser-than-athletes in sport-loving cultures. In other words, do athletes have higher self-esteem because they score goals, or is this a statistical reflection of the lowering of non-athletes' self-esteem in response to being subordinated by athletes who are culturally and institutionally glorified (particularly in school systems)? The structuring of sport works to praise and champion those already more likely to succeed in life.

Furthermore, when most of these studies report to examine the socio-negative attributes of teamsport participation (Miller *et al.* 2005), they often examine variables that lend themselves to quantifiable analysis, like disciplinary referrals. Thus, they fail to examine the more important socio-negative variables (those that do not lend themselves to quantification), like the volitional and unintentional damage inflicted upon those who do not fit the athletic mold, or the emotional and physical damage that sport often brings. Nor do they examine (as I do in this book) the way sport is used to shape youth into a working-class ethic of hard work, sacrifice, and stoicism that benefits corporations, religion, and the military. These studies fail to examine how sport operates to break down an individual's sense of self, their agency, and restructure them as complicit to the orders of one (usually male) leader, the coach.

In other words, I reject most of these supposed socio-positive aspects of sport, instead believing them to be far more psychologically and socially damaging than they are beneficial. I maintain that sport has managed to escape critical scrutiny in our society. Sport has been given a "free pass," so that it can continue to manipulate and damage youth, with little social critique. I am not alone in thinking this. Brackenridge (1995) articulately writes:

… sport has held a special place in the affections of Western industrial societies for its supposed virtues and its potential as a tool of economic and social development. The special status of sport has also protected it from critical scrutiny and meant that social inequalities and other problems, such as sexual harassment and abuse, have all-too-often been ignored or tacitly condoned (p. 16).

Highlighting my overwhelmingly negative view on organized sport, I once argued for weeks with a number of graduate students in a coaching psychology course that I taught at Long Beach State. Here, I heard my students say, "Sport teaches kids to deal with loss," and "Kids need to learn to fail in life." So I decided to test their theory: *had sport taught them to deal with loss? Had it helped them learn to fail in public?*

Upon returning at midterm, I wrote on the board, "High score 97 percent, low score 23 percent, mean 57 percent." I then wrote down the top three exam scores on the blackboard and, next to this, the students' names who earned them. This was written under the heading of *winners*. I next wrote the heading *losers* and proceeded as if I were going to reveal the names of the failed students. The class collectively gawked. "You're not going to write the names of the three lowest scores are you?" I responded, "Sure I am. Youth sports have taught you how to accept public failure."

Yet, as athletes most of their lives (and purveyors of functionalist ideology), this group of coaches were unable to accept the exercise. They publicly protested the unfair nature of what I was about to do. One even proclaimed that it would be illegal for me to do such (he was right). After I pointed out that my intent was simply that of an exercise, they began to get the message: if they couldn't handle the public humiliation of a low test score at 25 years of age, how could a 9-year-old handle the public humiliation of losing a game for an entire team?

The uncritical mentality of my students helps elaborate the cultural power that sport maintain. It is not that my students are stupid; it is that they have never heard my type of message before. Letting something go unexamined often has the effect of rendering it to the status of untouchable. Accordingly, sport exacts socio-negatives while cloaked in the veneer of providing socio-positives: they are wrapped in multiple and robust myths that massively overgeneralize the potential for socio-positive effects, and ignore the socio-negative. I am sure that you recognize these myths; they occur in the few stories of sport and sportsmanship when players do acts that honor integrity. But I argue that the reason we remember these stories is because they are the exception, not the rule.

The media helps maintain sport's privileged place. This is because sport journalists are mostly failed athletes themselves. Those who get jobs writing about sport are not the fat kids who were picked last throughout their formative years and have learned to loathe sport. Instead, they are (mostly) men who desire more than anything to be "one of the boys" on the field. Sport journalists are, as Stan Eitzen (2001, IX) describes, "little more than … cheerleaders." Therefore, critical commentaries on sport (or a campaign of critical commentary) does not much exist in the media.

It is therefore not surprising that my graduate students had not actively challenged the myths of sport; that they had not learned the lessons that they so readily believed sport has to teach. Instead, my graduate students were previously merited by their sporting endeavors, and nobody challenged them on this. They probably never experienced the harassment of repeated public failure of those less gifted (those who far outnumber the gifted). As I will show in Chapter 4, the fact that these coaches were former athletes themselves has serious implications for the way they reproduce the system of abuse.

The socio-negative aspects of sport I highlight in this book are not solely because of the competitive nature, or the gender-segregated structure, on which sport is built. It also reflects the masculine ether in which most competitive sport swims. Sport is a unique cultural location where (again) mostly boys and men, but also girls and women, gather to bond over physical joy, pain and labor. For most men, the idea is to do this away from women. In sport, men relate in emotional and physical ways, not acceptable in other cultural spaces. Sure, women can play, bond and experience the joys of sisterhood as well. But what is the effect on women's progression toward cultural equality of doing this in separate sporting spaces? If sport teaches us to work well with one another, shouldn't we desire sport to teach boys and girls, men and women to work well together?

The gender-segregated nature of sport is the most salient one, but not the only way upon which sporting participation is divided. Sport is also intentionally divided by age and ability (or disability) status. Unintentionally, sport is often divided by race, class, sexuality, and religion. In this book, I ask, for example, how sport can teach our citizens to value diversity when organized sport so often lacks the presence of openly gay (male) athletes and those with differing abilities and/or disabilities? How does sport teach us to value others, when it is based on beating them?

Your Personal Relationship with Sport

With this introduction into viewing sport through a more critical lens, it is important to ask yourself how you have benefited (or not) through or because of sport. Your personal experience of sport is likely to cloud your judgments about the operation of it. In other words, you come to this book with a set of judgments, determinations and values about sport. The order for this generally runs from experience, which elicits a feeling, which is then justified with reason, which is supported by selectively picking data to support your position. This is called rationalization.

But in order to think more sociologically, we cannot let our experience determine our judgment. We must learn to make our judgments sociologically, not through our own feelings or experience. We can draw from our experience to give us some insight (particularly as to areas that we might further explore with sociological data and sociological reasoning), but we need to be cautious in proclaiming that sport is "all good" simply because one had a good experience with it.

Contrasting with the experience of an individual, the job of a sociologist is to examine all social arrangements with a critical eye. Questioning metanarratives, myths, stereotypes, and hegemonic processes of social matters enables sociologists to better comprehend sport and its relation to society, regardless of whatever the dominant culture's beliefs might be. Remember, sociology is the study of culture, the large pattern. Sociologists look at the big picture: we are interested in the forest, not an individual tree within that forest. This also gives us permission to generalize. In some sense, sociology is about making "good" generalizations. So when I say, "athletes get injured in sport," know that I understand that not all athletes do, but I imply that the vast majority do.

Unfortunately, sociologists are humans, with socialization patterns that also bias us. We are not immune from making judgments about sport according to our "feelings." As researchers, our perspectives are biased through the experiences we have with sport. It is not as easy for a social scientist to separate his or her "feelings" from the data as it is for one who works within the hard sciences. For example, two sociologists might read the same transcript of an interview with an athlete and have contradictory interpretations of it. Our framework of personal beliefs affects how we interpret data.

I (egotistically) maintain, however, that I am particularly well placed to study sport. This is because (as you will learn later in this chapter), I have a unique relationship with it in that I have come "full circle," from a position of believing that sport is a wonderful institution, to a position in which I would rather just see competitive, organized, adult-run, traditional sport removed from our planet altogether. In other words, I have come from a functionalist to a critical position.

Functionalist Orthodoxy and the Age of Critical Enlightenment

In addition to assessing the impact of organized, competitive teamsport on young men and women, it is equally important to analyze why we believe so strongly that sport is good. There are two dominant (overarching) theoretical frameworks for viewing the relation between sport and society, functionalist (functionalism) and conflict theories.

Functionalism is the belief that society operates in much the same way as our bodies operate. Here, functionalists maintain that if something exists, it must exist because it has a function to the normal operation of that body. A functionalist thinker would therefore suggest that our institutions are like organs, in that they all work together to produce the smooth running of society (our body). Accordingly, functionalists warn that even if you see a problem with one particular institution (organ), you should be careful in extracting it or modifying it; as doing so might negatively affect another institution (organ) that you did not intend to change. More succinctly stated, Giddens (2001) suggests that functionalism is a system that is organically related, intended to maintain equilibrium, adapting to the needs of a changing environment and predicated in a value of social consensus.

For example, the emergence of sport in Western culture is explained as an adaption of play in the modern, industrial era. Here, play was co-opted by structure (formalized by rules) in order to adapt to the increasing rules and regulations of a modernizing society (more on this in the next chapter). Thus, a functionalist might see sport as a social phenomenon that emerged in order to temper a change in the operation of society. Sport becomes the solution to an imbalance. Functionalist thinkers maintain that social change is only acceptable when it occurs very slowly. They maintain that if you push the system too quick, you will disrupt its equilibrium. Functionalist views are therefore used to slow the progress of women, racial minorities, and gays and lesbians in Western societies. They argue that permitting women to work, giving minorities freedom, or legalizing gay marriage fundamentally harms the family and the social structures that keep our society working – even though it never does. The functionalist idea concerning sport is that the severe regulation of sport is necessary in order to take care of people (indoctrinate them into a capitalist form of living) in a modern society. This is discussed in Chapter 4.

Conversely, conflict theorists (that's me) find this proposition to be part of the propaganda of those benefiting from the current status. My like-minded colleagues maintain a conflict paradigm, in that we are more rebellious in desiring rapid social change. Theorists from this position examine institutions for their faults, often with the political intent of changing institutions. We reject notions that it is dangerous to alter social beliefs. We do so because we view the current system as being designed to promote the power and wealth of a few, at the expense of the many.

Exemplifying this, a functionalist is likely to view the ancient Roman Games as functioning to appease an unruly Roman citizenship. They might describe these games as a unifying event, a sporting entertainment spectacle to please the masses and control a citizenry. Conversely, a scholar using a critical lens might view these same games as an exploitation of the lower classes, abuse to animals, reification of a patriarchal society (women were banned) and as genocide against the under or unprivileged (whom they labeled criminals).

Thus, someone from a functionalist perspective will look to see the value of sport and how it influences positive change in society, while someone from a conflict perspective is likely to examine how it causes social inequalities. But fear not, critical reflection upon it will not abolish sport altogether. It may help change sport in a positive direction, but our cultural esteem for sport is too strong for my wish to come true.

In case you have not figured out where I stand on this divide, I will make it clear: I am not just camped with the critical theorists in my field of sport sociology, I am as critical as any of them. I am *deeply* entrenched in critically examining sport, and I have no interest in presenting "a fair and balanced" approach. You will therefore think that I am quite biased. This is because I emphasize that sport has always been, and continues to be, a mechanism in which those with power re-establish, justify, and valorize themselves. Sport increases the gap of inequality between the haves and the have-nots. I maintain that all is not well with how we play and value sport, and in the final chapter I provide some solutions as to how we can increase the socio-positive output of sport.

However, I can understand if you are one who is already shaking your head, believing that sport can't be all that bad. Previously, I did not think so either. I had to come out in order to come to my senses.

Coming Out in Order to Come to My Senses

I came to study the relationship between sport and society by a circuitous route. Although I was never talented at sport that required coordination, body mass, or violence against an opponent, I did find incredible joy in the sport of distance running. As a high school runner, I found sport to be a place where I developed friendships, and maintained contact with a valuable role model (my coach). However, I also used cross-country running to escape the mandatory participation in sport through the abusive institution that we call Physical Education. This was a sporting culture that I was highly intimidated by. Most of my intimidation came because of the association of sport with masculinity and heterosexuality.

Since I was six years old I found boys cute, wanting to be close to them. In 1976, aged eight, I attended the opening day of *Star Wars*. Before the curtain rose, I spotted a boy a few aisles down and a couple of seats over. I was attracted to him, and my eyes fixed upon him. I longed to be with him, to sit next to him, to press my body to his. I was envious of the friend he had sitting with him. The feeling was not alien to me. I had had similar feelings before.

I realized that I was staring at him for an unacceptable period of time. Aware that my actions could alert others to my secret desires, I looked for an excuse for my excessive staring, "Mom," I said, "I want my hair cut like his." At this age, I already knew how to hide my true identity. Though I did not know my actions had a label, I was "passing" at age eight. In other words, not only was I aware I was gay, but I also understood that society condemned it.

I was not very athletic back then; actually, I was more of a motor-moron. To make matters worse, I never learned the rules and practices of formal sport. By the time I was old enough to realize I didn't know how to play baseball, football, or basketball, I was too embarrassed to ask my friends or father to show me. Thus, sport that involved balls, or contact, intimidated me. Neither my mother nor father were particularly interested in sport; they were academically, not athletically minded. Nonetheless, it would have been nice to know how to play the games, so I wouldn't have been socially ostracized. For when a kid fails in the classroom, the failure is known only to the student, the teacher, and perhaps the parent. When a kid fails on the athletic field, however, it is failure open for all to see and discuss (this is something known as the fishbowl phenomenon).

The paranoid fear of being thought gay (which of course I was) and feeling inferior to other boys, were hallmarks of my youth. I felt frustrated, scared, intimidated, and alone in my attraction to boys. Complicating matters, I was in high school during the extreme AIDS phobia and homophobia that characterized the years 1982–1987. To be gay in the mid-1980s was detestable: there could be nothing worse. This, combined with the paranoia of being discovered, the frustration of being vexed by what I considered (at that time) "this damn desire," and the solitude I felt, brought on thoughts of suicide. Alone, and in despair, suicide seemed a reasonable answer.

Sport was perhaps one of the only things that saved me from the intense cultural and internalized homophobia. As I grew more competitive as a runner, my self-esteem improved. Because of my leadership role in sport, I began to feel confident that I could speak to, lead, and influence others. Thus, when I graduated from high school, I returned there to coach. Here, the better my athletes did, the more my own self-esteem grew. I learned to love the acquisition of knowledge that helped me win. I began to read books related to running, health, psychology, and the hard sciences – all topics that would make me a better coach. I occupied my days with studying, writing, and coaching. All of these diversions were good for me, they not only gave me confidence and knowledge, but they also provided me an excuse for not dating.

I remained in the closet into my 20s. At this point, I had built my career on being a good coach, and I knew sport was not the place to come out. Aged 25, I had earned an MA in Sport Psychology, written two distance-running books, and coached some of the best runners in the state of California. However, my body (psychosomatically) began to spite me. I began to develop migraine headaches, stomach pains, and the symptoms of an ulcer. I was ailing. I knew that in order to be me, in order to be truly free (and healthy), I had to come out of the closet. So, in the summer of 1993, I came out of the closet as an openly gay high school and cross-country coach (Anderson 2000). It was this event that began my journey from sport functionalist, to critical theorist.

Over the following years, the knowledge of my sexuality spread through the school. Homophobia increased at my school and reached its peak in 1995, when a football player brutally assaulted one of my heterosexual athletes who he assumed to be gay simply because he was on my team. The brutal attack saw the football player knock my runner to the ground, where he sat atop him and began pounding at his face. The assailant even tried to gauge my athlete's eyes out. When a bystander begged him to stop the beating he proclaimed, "It ain't over until the faggot's dead." My runner knew that he had to escape.

Although his vision was obscured by blood, he managed to squirm from beneath the large football player, and run away. He climbed a fence that the pursuing football player was too large to scale, and got away. He was left with four broken facial bones, and for the rest of his life he will have two screws through his palate. The police department reported the incident as "mutual combat" – *not* a hate crime or aggravated assault, and the assailant received no time behind bars. Essentially, he got away with it.

It was clear to me that the incident did not "just happen": the beating was influenced by various factors, people, perhaps even institutions (Anderson 2000). Immediately I suspected that his actions were covertly encouraged by what seemed a lack of administrative action against those who previously displayed hostility toward my team. In their inaction, the high school administration sent an institutional message of support for the continuation of violence against my team.

Such homophobia is, of course, not surprising, especially when one considers that the assailant had been socialized into the homophobic language of masculinity embedded in combative teamsport like American football. Perhaps his training served as a powerful socialization into the norm of violent masculinity. It is this socialization, and our blind obsession for sport, that I maintain is responsible for *most* of our social ills. Masculinity, I maintain, is a public health crisis (Anderson 2005a).

In addition to a predictable anger that lingered for years, I was also left with an intellectual angst over not fully understanding how such intense homophobia could develop within an individual, and how educated people (like the school principal) could dismiss such violence as "simply a fight." I was not satisfied with the "boys will be boys" or "people hate what they don't understand" rationalizations. I sensed the matter was much more complicated. I sensed that the beating was attributable to the manner in which the assailant was socialized into masculinity; the value of physical brutality he learned in sport; and the culmination of many years of growing aggression and hostility that largely went uncontested by the school administration. Essentially, I was clear in understanding why he assaulted my runner; what I was less clear about was why the school's administration had been so unwilling to stop the harassment before it got to the point of serious bodily injury.

My Masters in Sport Psychology had equipped me to understand how to help athletes negotiate psychological problems in society, but it failed to explain the origins of social problems in the first place. For example, I had been trained to help athletes negotiate the pressures of competition, but not to examine our cultural addiction to competition. Realizing that my training was insufficient to fully understand the social dynamics that culminated in this beating, I returned to school to earn a doctorate in sociology at the University of California, Irvine.

As a sociologist, I now better understand the near-seamless manner in which groups of people can maintain power by policing ideologies through the threat of force and the willing compliance of those oppressed; a process we call hegemony. I have grown to understand the complex role that sport plays in society, particularly in the production of a violent, homophobic, femphobic, and sexist form of masculinity. I understand the role sport plays in teaching its participants to accept risk, to out-group others, and to use violence in order to gain athletic capital. I began to understand that sport was responsible for producing much of that cultural homophobia in the first place. And while sport may have provided me with a self-esteem activity when I was in the closet, it also produced an athlete who brutally assaulted one of my runners (Anderson 2000). In other words, sport is both good and bad. Or, perhaps sport is mostly bad, but we view it as mostly good. This is because sport only ostensibly solves a problem it created in the first place. When one considers sport from this complex perspective, it can put you into a mental state of what social psychologists call "cognitive dissonance."

Cognitive Dissonance Theory

Cognitive dissonance is a valuable tool for helping you to understand the process of what happens when your logic no longer aligns with your emotions. When we think one way about a topic, but feel opposite to the way we think, we are said to be in a state of cognitive dissonance. For example, when I was closeted I desperately wanted gay sex (emotionally and somatically), but I was socialized to hate homosexuality and I did not want to be gay. Thus, I both wanted and did not want something at the same time.

You might also have cognitive dissonance by maintaining two opposing beliefs about the same topic. Some of you might love and hate a friend at the same time. You might love and hate sport at the same time, too. Accordingly, cognitive dissonance is one way of saying that things are complicated, or that you are unsure, conflicted.

Cognitive dissonance theory is useful, not only because it explains how this state of mind emerges, but it also predicts what you will do once you enter a state of cognitive dissonance. Thus, cognitive dissonance theory is a proven tool for analyzing the contrast between two or more varying and incompatible cognitions – and predicting what behaviors might emerge from an individual's dissonance (Aronson 1969; Bem 1967; Festinger 1957).

Traditionally, studies using cognitive dissonance theory inflict (normally under lab conditions) a gap between two disparate wants or beliefs. The result is that people normally end up aligning their beliefs to whatever *society* maintains. I, for example, am intrigued by how German citizens viewed Adolf Hitler and his policies in the build up to Second World War. Many of his policies were thought to be good for Germany, but then his racial policies and anti-Semitism did not align with the personal beliefs of most. Because Hitler, through his Ministry of Propaganda, was skilled at swaying public opinion, many people rectified their dissonance by going along with the cultural norm, praising Hitler.

I discuss cognitive dissonance theory here in order to help you make sense of how you deal with this book. Cognitive dissonance theory will help you understand how we deal with the tension caused by the variance of how you *think* logically about sport, compared to how you *feel* about sport. This is important because society largely maintains that sport is good, and in this book I am going to show you another side of sport.

If you experience this material in the same manner that most of my students do, there is a predictable pattern you will follow. Most of my students have had successful athletic careers before coming to my university to earn a degree in the Coaching Education Program that I teach on at the University of Bath, in England. Because they have had successful careers, it necessarily means that they do not represent the average sporting narrative; instead, they represent the elite of men and women who were good at sport, praised for it, and they therefore built their identities as athletes. Highlighting this, as part of a pre-evaluation, the day my students arrive at our university I ask them to fill out a questionnaire. I ask them to describe themselves, saying "please fill out the blank." The blank is preceded by the words "I am," so it looks like "I am _____." This is the first question on the survey, so they do not know what the rest of the survey will be about (thus biasing them) before they fill out this response. Yet nearly 70 percent of the students respond, with something like "a football player." This highlights that their master identity, the top identity (or group membership) upon which they judge themselves, is that of an athlete.

When they then begin to hear my logical and empirically supported arguments against sport as a socio-positive institution, they find themselves entering cognitive dissonance. Their first step is to attempt to rationalize, logically, their dissonance by denying the critical side of their thoughts. Usually this involves pointing to the pro-sport rationalizations that they were taught as they grew up. I hear, "Sport teaches you to apply yourself to academic work," to which I respond, "Can't you just do more academic work to teach yourself to do it?" They argue, "Sport teaches you to be competitive, and you will need that in the work world." I respond, "Can't you just get a summer job, or an internship, and learn the work world directly?"

Eventually, I break down (or debunk) their socio-positive arguments to the point in which they find themselves saying that sport is good because, "it just is." "It just is?" I ask. "Is that an argument, or is that the reflection that you feel it is, but can't argue the case that it is?" Now, nobody likes to be told that they are wrong, or that their feelings are invalid. So, rather than my students taking the exercise as an opportunity to collect data to support their feelings, they instead attack the messenger (that's me). By discrediting the messenger, they can re-credit themselves for believing what they feel without having to make an intellectual argument as to why they think that standpoint is correct. In other words, when we get into cognitive dissonance, we rarely change our minds outright or immediately. Instead, we fight, struggle, and point fingers.

I remember one class I taught in California. I made my opening arguments to the class of 400, and as the lecture ended someone went outside and yelled, "What does he know about sport, he's a faggot!" The beginning of the next lecture I wrote on the board, "What do I know, I'm just a faggot." I then said, "Gay I am, yes. But if you're going to master this material, if you are going to beat me in a debate, you will need to learn to do more than insult – you will need to think in logical ways." I challenge you to do the same: if you plan to contest me (in your head or in your classroom discussions) you will *need* to do the same.

All of this struggle is made in an attempt to hold onto our precious sense of what is right and what is wrong. But what is "right" is determined by our culture, often independent of critical analysis. What is "right" is often based on history, tradition, or in the case of America, one particularly zealous sense of religious fundamentalism. However, what is "right" also changes; although this change occurs too slow for my taste. For the only thing you can truly count on is that matters *will* change. What was considered right years ago (slavery for example) is now considered morally disgraceful.

With this book, I promise to place you into some cognitive dissonance. The question then becomes, "What will you do once you are there?" I hope you engage with the dissonance, revel in feeling different about sport – it is then that you are learning to think. Ultimately, even if you determine that sport is a wonderful enterprise, I hope to at least plant seeds of doubt in your mind. But even if I fail in my endeavor, even if you read this book and come away more secure in your feelings that sport is a socio-positive institution, I hope you will have come away learning about the utility of social theory. For this book is as much about using sport to teach you social theory as it is about using social theory to teach you about sport.

Understanding Social Theory

Social theory attempts to explain a phenomenon, or set of phenomena. However, social theory did not come easy to me. It took me seven years of graduate school before I began to understand what theory was, and how it is used. Why did it take me so long? Nobody explained to me the key to understanding theory: the key is that nobody really knows what theory is.

First, theory can be divided into two domains, one is used in the empirical (tangible and measurable) sciences (both natural and social), and the other is found in more abstract disciplines: fields of study that do not nicely lend themselves to quantification or testing, like philosophy, logic, and the humanities. Thus, a theorist of math will develop wordless equations; a theorist of philosophy will discuss untestable ideas about humanity; a theorist of politics will develop an ethical theory about the purpose of law and government; and a theorist of science will develop theories that are testable in the lab. In my field, sociology, we use both types of theories; those that are testable and those that are not.

Furthermore, there is considerable difference, and often vicious (and boring) academic disputes across academic disciplines, as to the proper usage of theory. Some academics spend a great deal of time arguing over what these mostly white (usually dead) men actually "meant." In doing so, they sound like members of various faiths arguing over biblical interpretation.

Another reason theory is difficult to define is because it is confused and/or conflated with a hypothesis, which is one's guess at the outcome of events. If a hypothesis proves true, it may become a theory; but if it cannot explain enough phenomena, it might not.

All of this makes trying to label what a theory is rather difficult. One's theory is another's philosophy, is another's hypothesis, is another's guess, is another's head-scratching jumble of inaccessible language. Highlighting this, some sociologists use "configurational theory," and many sport sociology textbooks discuss it, too. But I have absolutely no idea whatsoever what it is, what it is for, or why anyone cares about it. Even in the most basic introductory textbooks, I cannot understand it. I suspect many other PhDs, including the authors of those textbooks, cannot either.

This points to another problem with the social sciences; many social theorists frequently write about their theories in academically inaccessible language. This, sadly, is mostly intentional. For the most part, academics are quite concerned with being perceived as intelligent. One way to accomplish this is to write in ways that are difficult for others to understand. The latent effect of this is that it permits various people to interpret the theory differently, and perhaps contributes to the life and utility of a theory because, ultimately, it cannot be totally proved or disproved. Because of this (and as much as my colleagues might bark at me for saying this), I do not recommend that students read volumes of social theory. Wikipedia is a rather good place to start, and in many places, it is all you need to know. If you like and can digest what you read there, then feel free to engage yourself by reading about it on other websites. Ultimately you may wish to read a book about that theory.

For me, a sociologist who is more concerned with writing something that is meaningful and understandable than impressing my academic peers, I loathe this highbrow, overly erudite written posturing. This is one reason you will not find post-structural theories discussed in this book; they are mostly just posturing. They are often espoused by intellectual but out-of-touch academics that have nothing real to add to the knowledge of sport and society.

Instead, in this book, I desire to explicate useful theories, and I will describe them and show you how to apply them in an easy-to-understand manner, so that you will understand exactly what the theory means. You may then determine whether you find the theory useful.

When theory is useful, it is very helpful. For example, independent scholars might notice that ice caps are melting, while others find rising carbon dioxide in our atmosphere, and still others find a bleaching (dying) of coral in the Great Barrier Reef. All of these findings can be united under the umbrella of a theory of global warming. This helps us understand the interconnectedness of events.

In social sciences, a good theory helps us understand the social world on a larger scale. For me, however, it is necessary that a theory be somewhat testable, or at least observable. As public intellectual Christopher Hitchens stated at a recent lecture I attended, "What can be asserted without proof can also be dismissed without proof." Evidence and accessibility are key requirements for good sociology.

There is little dispute that the field of social sciences (in Western cultures) began in the 1800s and grew throughout the 1900s. It began with the theoretical work of Marx, Weber, Durkheim, and Freud. These men challenged us to consider why humans do what they do, instead of simply attributing things to god. Enlightenment age thinkers asked why we organize ourselves as we do, and how matters can change in order to relieve the oppression of those stratified at the bottom.

However, it is impossible for me to thoroughly explain each of the theories I use in this book. Most of these thinkers have written volumes of work. What I attempt to do, however, is pull out a particularly salient theory (or part of a theory) and apply it to sport. In doing so, I show you how the theory helps us understand more about what the sporting process means. I do not however want you to think that there can only be one theory to make sense of one social situation. Indeed, two scholars can look at the same subject with varying theoretical lenses, and come up with the same conclusion. Thus, the theory one uses is partially up to preference for the style of the theory. Ultimately, I hope to use theory in this book in a way that helps you realize that you too can understand, utilize, and comment on social theory. In doing so, I hope you feel less intimidated about the word "theory."

Chapter Structure

This book is designed to facilitate the critical focus I apply to sport. Traditionally, texts spend a great deal of time reporting on the specifics of what research has found, alternating between socio-positive and socio-negative outcomes. But bearing in mind the critical approach of this book, each chapter will be constructed as follows:

1 Each chapter begins with a sport-related vignette – a true story of an athlete, to capture your attention.
2 Each vignette is reflected in an introductory level discussion of relevant social theory.
3 Each theoretical discussion is related to sport.
4 Finally, major research findings are addressed, particularly relating to how sport continues to reproduce socio-negative attributes.

I hope that you find that this unique structure provides the significant bonus of making this text as much about the utility of sociological theory, as it is about the specific findings of sport sociology.

1 Why We Overly Value Organized, Competitive Teamsport

Jeff's Story

"I never thought I would be a cheerleader," Jeff tells me during a National Collegiate Cheerleading Championship meet in Daytona Beach, Florida. "I grew up in a very conservative family in a very conservative state," he says as he reaches for yet another beer. There are other heterosexual male cheerleaders in this hotel room, too. Many of them seem to relate to Jeff's story.

Jeff was raised in a highly devout Christian household. He describes his dad as being stereotypically macho. Accordingly, playing any sport other than American football was never a choice for him. "My dad wanted me to play," he says. "My mom wanted me to play, too." Although Jeff wanted to be in his elementary school's band, his father would not permit it. "I remember him saying, 'my son will not turn out to be a faggot, you will play football like boys are supposed to.'" Thus, Jeff's father forced him into football, believing it would make him into a "real man": one who is emotionless, yet prone to rage; in control, yet trained to follow; physically robust, yet willing to risk health; ostensibly heterosexual, yet unable to prove it. "I was trained to be the all-American, red blooded boy. You know, American pride, apple pie, churchgoing, the whole bit."

Then, through the tragedy of talent, his football abilities brought him attention from the local high school coach, who approached his father to arrange for Jeff to play for his team. This forced him into football in high school, although the deal was arranged without Jeff's consent. Jeff's masculinization in sport, it would seem, strongly influenced him to live between the narrow sheets of masculine acceptability. "You have to understand, I loved football, but I didn't want to be all that macho. But by the time I got to high school, I was something of a local superstar. Everybody knew me in high school. I was 'Jeff the football player.'"

But things changed for Jeff in college. He attended a big university, with a competitive football program. And, for the first time in his life, he was unable to make the team. "I had been a football player all my life," he says. "Everything revolved around it. I thought I'd play in college, but I didn't make it. I couldn't believe it. I didn't know what to do. I desperately needed to be part of something again; anything."

The "anything" Jeff refers to is collegiate cheerleading. Competitive cheerleading in the US (and increasingly in other Western countries) has morphed from simply supporting other athletic teams (with sideline cheering), to a competitive sport in its own right. Today's cheerleaders also compete in complex dancing and stunting routines where a number of judged criteria determine success. Despite this evolution, however, men who cheer are still stigmatized as gay. Accordingly, few try out for collegiate cheerleading without persuasion (Anderson 2005b; 2008c; Hanson 1995).

To recruit men to cheer, existing cheerleaders use a variety of tactics, including sexualizing female cheerleaders and the heterosexualizing and masculinizing of male cheerleaders. While doing research on cheerleading, I found one university's cheerleading recruitment poster (hung near the men's gym) highlighted all of these methods. Featuring an illustration of a bikini-clad woman sliding into a pool of water it read, "Want strong muscles? Want to toss girls? Our Cheer Team needs stunt men!! No experience needed."

Ex-football players, like Jeff, are somewhat receptive to these recruitment efforts. After failing to make their university football teams, most of these men clarify that they miss being associated with an athletic identity and/or being part of a team, and they judge cheerleading as an acceptable final effort to return to teamsport (Anderson 2005b). "So I'm not on the field now, but it's better than being in the bleachers," Jeff says.

Jeff's story is particularly interesting because he used to bully male cheerleaders. "Yeah, my teammates and I used to call cheerleader guys fags." The tone of his voice turned to something of a confessional. "I'm ashamed about it now. But you have got to understand, it wasn't that I was homophobic. I had to call [male] cheerleaders fags, because if I didn't, the guys on my team might think I was gay. So, basically, I had to call them fags, or fear being called one myself."

As we continued to talk, it became apparent to me that Jeff has spent his life attempting to live up to the expectations of other (heterosexual) men (cf. Kimmel 1994). This is not to say that he did not enjoy football. He certainly enjoyed the fame it brought him, but it is to suggest that the masculine culture of football, and the desire to be thought heteromasculine by his parents and friends, led him into a sport that was known for valuing the most conservative, violent, and homophobic form of masculinity in American sport. This was odd, I thought. The more I hung out with Jeff, the more I thought he was just a super-nice guy.

The reason I thought Jeff was a nice guy, perhaps, is because he tells me that he has changed many of his views since coming to college and joining cheerleading. For example, Jeff has undone his homophobia. "I made some homophobic comment when I first joined, and one of the guys pulled me to the side and schooled me on it." A year later, Jeff met his current best friend, Jamie. "Then I met Jamie [who was the only openly gay member on his team]. I'd never call him that. He was a real cool guy, and now I think that gay people are just really cool people."

Jeff has changed his views on other topics, too. Because of his involvement in cheerleading, he now sees women as much more athletic than he had previously given them credit for. Today, he finds it enjoyable to compete with women. "I really think every guy should have the opportunity to compete with women. Not just when they are young, but you know, in high school and college. It totally opened my eyes."

Jeff has learned to open up emotionally to his friends as well. "I used to be so much more macho in high school," he says. "But then, that's football culture isn't it?" When asked about whether he is now glad that he failed to make the college football team, he responds. "I miss it [football] sometimes, yeah. But when I think about it, what I'm missing isn't who I was, or who my friends were, I just miss the fame. I like my friends in cheerleading better than my friends in football." Jeff smiles, "But hey, maybe someday I'll be famous for cheerleading."

Berger and Luckmann on Social Constructionism

Jeff's story highlights an interesting relationship between sport and the construction of masculinity. American football has somehow been socially coded as a terrain in which heterosexual men play, while cheerleading is constructed as a sport for gay men. Because heterosexuality and masculinity are overly valued among male youth in contemporary culture, his father, mother, and even Jeff himself thought that football was the sport to join. Football, he maintained, "Would make me a real man." But this begs the question. Is one's personality, one's gendered mannerisms, even one's sexuality, learned/constructed/influenced by others? Or are these determined by birth instead? Or some combination of both?

Certainly we recognize that we are born with the genetics to either excel in a certain sport or not. I weigh 150 pounds (68 kilograms), and cannot sprint for the life of me. Clearly, I was not born to be a NFL lineman – and no amount of hard work would change this. I simply do not have the body mass or speed for the sport. Perhaps I could eat loads of McDonalds and put on some pounds to protect me in the sport of football? But regardless of my socialization, I just do not have it in me to be an American football player. Conversely, I *was* born to be a decent (not great) long-distance runner – I have a light frame and can run miles without fatiguing. Accordingly, it is fairly obvious that we are mostly born with physical attributes; we cannot for the most part learn or acquire them. These things are largely innate.

But are we born hating a particular group of people? Are we born with a love or disgust for a certain religion, or form of entertainment? The answer is: probably not. Instead, these things are socially constructed.

Social constructionism refers to the development of phenomena relative to social contexts. At some level, we have always recognized this. For example, people born in a Christian country are far more likely to become Christian than Muslim. But the idea of constructionism was greatly expanded in the twentieth century, where it became prominent with the influential work of Berger and Luckmann. Their 1966 book, *The Social Construction of Reality*, argues that all knowledge, including common sense, is derived from and maintained by social interactions. When people interact, they do so with the understanding that their respective perceptions of reality are related, so that when we each look at an elephant we assume that we each see a large animal with a fifth leg more bendy than a garden hose. As we act upon this understanding, our common knowledge of reality becomes reinforced. Thus, our symbols and institutions are part of an objective reality. Collective thoughts gradually crystallize from individual habit into institutions, which are supported by language conventions. Eventually, matters are subjectively internalized through the upbringing and formal education of citizens into a particular culture's identity and belief system. It is in this sense that it can be said that reality is socially constructed.

None of this is to suggest that individuals do not maintain the agency to shape cultures themselves. The building of culture and beliefs is always a dialectic (a struggle), an interaction between individuals and their society. There are always opposing views. Thus, even though we may share one reality (that elephants exist) we may differ in how we view or value elephants.

How this notion of social constructionism relates to sport comes through the work of one of Western cultures' most profound intellectuals. No theorist has been as responsible for helping us understand that the way we think and act is socially constructed than Sigmund Freud.

The Significance of Sigmund Freud

Freud was a medical doctor who specialized in neurosis. In time, he grew to establish the field that we today call psychology. Freud is, undoubtedly, the most influential social thinker of the twentieth century. Freudian thought is everywhere, and we use Freudian ideas daily. He wrote thousands upon thousands of pages of theory, and in many senses, went against the morality of his time. He brought up issues of sexuality, including childhood sexuality, which went against (and still goes against) the pervasive Christian norm of European culture.

Freud's early work coincided with a ferment in the European intelligentsia that produced modernist literature, avant-garde painting and music, radical social ideas, spirited feminist and socialist movements, and even the first gay rights movement. Freud was sufficiently open to this ferment; to question almost everything European culture had taken for granted. Important to the foundation of sport, he was also the first to suggest that all human beings were effectively bisexual – that sexuality ran a continuum and was not polarized. Unfortunately, he (wrongly) linked sexuality to gender expression. He assumed that femininity in men was (always) a sign of homosexuality, something he called inversion.

The concepts "masculine" and "feminine" (and consequently straight and gay), Freud suggested, "are among the most confused that occur in science" (cited in Connell 1995, p. 1). Freud disrupted the apparent naturalness of masculinity and femininity. Until this enlightenment, naturalist beliefs in men's superiority was used to justify keeping women from attending school (it was believed that the blood would go to their brains and away from their reproductive organs, making them infertile), taking jobs, or playing in sport. For example, women were not allowed to run the marathon in America until 1972 and they did not run in the Olympic Marathon until 1984. The notion of women being weaker, more delicate, and in need of men's protection exaggerated the relatively minor biological differences between the male and female. These minor biological differences were then used to justify psychological differences as well. While there is no doubt that *some* sex differences in psychological characteristics do exist, their modest size would hardly register them as important phenomena if we were not already culturally cued into exaggerating them.

Freud made inquiry into this argument both possible and necessary, even though he never wrote a systematic discussion of it. Nonetheless, over thirty years he developed ideas about gender as a continuing theme throughout his various writings. The first step Freud made in his analysis of masculinity came with his theory of the "Oedipus complex." Here, Freud understood that adult sexuality and gender were not fixed by nature, but instead were constructed through a long and conflict-ridden process. He described the Oedipus complex as the emotional tangle of childhood involving sexual and romantic desire for one parent and hatred for the other. In other words, young boys would fall in love with their mothers and hate their fathers. This, however, brought a fear that the young boy's father would seek revenge through threat of castration. Here, Freud identified a formative moment in masculinity and pictured the dynamics of this relationship: if a boy were to develop properly he would have to learn to disassociate himself from his mother and attach his emotional/erotic feelings to other women. If the process went wrong, Freud argued, homosexuality could result. Homosexuality, Freud therefore postulated, was not biological (although we recognize today that it is). Rather, Freud maintained that humans were constitutionally a blank slate; that masculine and feminine currents coexisted in everyone. This implied that adult sexuality had to be a complex construction, just as gender was.

Freud's next step in the development of a theory of masculinity and sexuality came with his account of the structure concept of the superego. The superego, he argued, was the unconscious part of our brain that judges, censors, and presents ideals to the external world. Freud believed that the superego was formed in the aftermath of the Oedipus complex, by internalized prohibitions from the parents. He gradually came to see it as having a gendered character, being crucially a product of the child's relationship with his father. He believed that this was more distinct in the case of boys than girls. In *Civilization and its Discontents* (1929) he began to see sociological dimensions in the superego that he treated as a means by which culture obtains mastery over individual desire, especially aggression – a masculine trait.

While it was not Freud's intentions to develop a complete theory of masculinity (his lines of thought remained speculative and incomplete), his theories nonetheless have profound implications for modern society and sport's role in that society, because of how they were interpreted in society and how this influenced sport as a masculine enterprise.

The progress that Freud made was remarkable, and the tools he used (namely psychoanalysis) gave a map to the unconscious development of masculinity. The point he most insistently made about masculinity was that it never exists in a pure state, rather layers of emotion coexist and contradict each other. And although his theoretical language changed, Freud remained convinced of the empirical complexity of gender and the ways in which femininity is always part of a man's character.

How this all relates to sport is another matter (later discussed), but it is inextricably linked to the Industrial Revolution.

Sport and the Industrial Revolution

Jeff's father would not have so strongly desired for him to play American football if he were born 150 years earlier. This is because the cultural compulsion that boys maintain to play sport is the product of a new way of valuing sport, one that came with the Industrial Revolution.

Although the invention of the machinery and transportation necessary for industrialization began early in the 1700s, the antecedents of most of today's sporting culture can be traced to the years of the second Industrial Revolution – the mid-1800s through early 1900s. During this period, sturdy farmers exchanged their time-honored professions for salaried work. Families replaced their farm's rent for that of a city apartment. The allure of industry, and the better life it promised, influenced such a migration that the percentage of people living in cities rose from just 25 percent in 1800 to around 75 percent in 1900 (Cancian 1987).

However, just as cities attracted people, the increasing difficulty of rural life also compelled them to leave their agrarian ways. This is because the same industrial technologies that brought capitalism also meant that fewer farmers were required to produce the necessary crops to feed a growing population. With production capacity rising, and crop prices falling, families were not only drawn to the cities by the allure of a stable wage and the possibility of class mobility, they were repelled by an increasingly difficult agrarian labor market and an inability to own land.

For all the manifestations of physical horror that was factory life (before labor laws), there were many advantages, too. Families were no longer dependent on the fortune of good weather for their sustenance, and industry provided predictable (if long) working hours. Having a reliable wage meant that a family could count on how much money they would have at the end of the week, and some could use this financial stability to secure loans and purchase property. Also, the regularity of work meant that between blows of the factory whistle, there was time for men to play. The concept of leisure, once reserved for the wealthy, spread to the working class during this period (Rigauer 1981). It is the sociocultural impact of this great migration that is central to the development of men's sport in Western cultures.

Sport maintained little cultural value prior to the Industrial Revolution. Social historian Donald Mrozek (1983: preface) said that, "To Americans at the beginning of the nineteenth century, there was no obvious merit in sport ... certainly no clear social value to it and no sense that it contributed to the improvement of the individual's character or the society's moral or even physical health." However, by the second decade of the next century these sentiments had been reversed (Miracle and Rees 1994). Sport gave boys something to do after school. It helped socialize them into the values necessary to be successful in this new economy, to instill the qualities of discipline and obedience, and to honor the hard work that was necessary in the dangerous occupations of industrial labor and mining (Rigauer 1981). Accordingly, workers needed to sacrifice both their time and their health, for the sake of making the wage they needed to support their dependent families.

In sport, young boys were socialized into this value of sacrifice (for team), so that they would later sacrifice health and well-being for family at work. Most important to the bourgeois ruling class, however, workers needed to be obedient to authority. Sport taught boys this docility. Accordingly, organized competitive teamsport was funded by those who maintained control of the reproduction of material goods. Children's play was forced off the streets (spontaneous street-playing activities were banned) and into parks and playgrounds, where they were supervised and structured in their "play." In the words of one playground advocate (Chase 1909), "We want a play factory; we want it to run at top speed on schedule time, with the best machinery and skilled operatives. We want to turn out the maximum product of happiness." Just as they are today, organized youth sport was financially backed by business, in the form of "sponsors." Today, as part of a compulsory state-run education, they are often backed by the state. This is an economical way of assuring a docile and productive labor force. Sport teaches us to keep to schedule under production-conscious supervisors (Eitzen 2001).

This shift to industry had other gendered effects, too. Although there was a gendered division of labor in agrarian work, there was less gendering of jobs and tasks compared to industrial life; both men and women toiled in demanding labor. Accordingly, in some aspects, heterosexual relationships were more egalitarian before industrialization. Factory work, however, shifted revenue generation from inside the home to outside. Mom's physical labor no longer directly benefited the family as it once did, and much of women's labor therefore became unpaid and unseen. Conversely, men's working spaces were cold, dangerous and hard. Men moved rocks, welded iron, swung pick axes, and operated steam giants.

These environments necessitated that men be tough and unemotional. Men grew more instrumental not only in their labor and purpose, but in their personalities, too. As a result of industrialization, men learned that the way that they showed their love was through their labor. Being a breadwinner, regardless of the working conditions within which one toiled, was a labor of love. Furthermore, because women were mostly (but not entirely) relegated to a domestic sphere, they were reliant upon their husband's ability to generate income. Thus, mostly robbed of economic agency, women learned to show their contribution through emotional expressiveness and domestic efficiency. Cancian (1987) describes these changes as a separation of gendered spheres, saying that expectations of what it meant to be a man or woman bifurcated as a result of industrialization. Accordingly, the antecedents of men's stoicism and women's expressionism were born during this period.

But was sport truly necessary to teach young boys and men the values of industrial life? Before labor laws, children were permitted to enter the workforce well before puberty. Would they not learn these values of toughness, sacrifice, stoicism and courage here anyway? Was sport really necessary to accomplish this? The answer is, no. Not entirely. We learned to value sport for yet another highly influential reason.

Absence of the Father Figure

During the Industrial Revolution, fathers left for work early, often returning home once their sons had gone to bed. Because teaching children was considered "women's work," boys spent much of their days (at school and home) surrounded by women. Here, they were thought to be deprived of the masculine vapors supposedly necessary to masculinize them. Rotundo (1993: 31) writes, "Motherhood was advancing, fatherhood was in retreat ... women were teaching boys how to be men." Messner (1992: 14) adds, "With no frontier to conquer ... and with urban boys being raised and taught by women, it was feared that men were also becoming 'soft,' that society itself was becoming feminized." A by-product of industrialization, it was assumed, was that it was capable of creating a culture of soft, weak, and feminine boys. Boys were structurally and increasingly emotionally segregated from their distant and absent fathers. This set the stage for what Filene (1975) called "a crisis in masculinity."

Simultaneous to this, however, was the first wave of women's political independence (Hargreaves 1986). The city provided a density of women that made activism more accessible. Smith-Rosenberg (1985) suggests that men felt threatened by the political and social advancements of women at the time. They perceived that they were losing their patriarchal power. The antidote to the rise of women's agency largely came through sport.

However, a much under-theorized influence on the development and promotion of sport comes through the changing understanding of sexuality during the second Industrial Revolution, particularly concerning the growing understanding of homosexuality – something attributable to Sigmund Freud.

Agrarian life was lonely for gay men. One can imagine that finding homosexual sex and love in pastoral regions was difficult. Conversely, cities collected such quantities of people that gay social networks and even a gay identity could form. This coincided with a growing body of scholarly work from Westphal, Ulrichs and Krafft-Ebing, early pioneers of the gay liberationist movement. These scholars sought to classify homosexual acts as belonging to a *type* of person; a third sex, an invert, or homosexual (Spencer 1995). From this, they could campaign for legal and social equality. Previously, there were less entrenched heterosexual or homosexual social identities. In other words, a man performed a sexual act, but his sexual identity was not tied into that act. Under this new theorizing, homosexuality was no longer a collection of particular acts, but instead, as Michel Foucault (1984: 43) famously wrote, "The homosexual was now a species." This, of course, means that heterosexuals were now a separate species, too.

Sigmund Freud explained homosexuality's origins in his "Three Essays on the Theory of Sexuality" (1905). Here, Freud theorized that sexuality was not innate. Instead he suggested that childhood experiences constructed men to become heterosexual or homosexual, something he called inversion. Homosexuality, Freud said, was a process of gendered wrongdoing, particularly through the absence of a father figure and an over-domineering mother. In one of his footnotes he wrote, "... the presence of both parents plays an important part. The absence of a strong father in childhood not infrequently favors the occurrence of inversion" (p. 146). Freud even gave child-rearing tips to help parents lead their children to heterosexual adjustment.

Freud's theories are certainly more complex than I present, and my aim is not to paint Freud as homophobic. Freud actually tried to humanize homosexuals by explaining their "condition." Yet in the process of explaining how homosexuals came to be, Freud cemented the notion and value of a nuclear family into popular culture. What is also important about Freud is not what he said, thought or wrote, but what others attribute to him. While Freud was certainly more complex in his thinking, what the populace heard was that an absent father and an over-domineering mother could make kids homosexual. This created a moral panic among Victorian-thinking British and American cultures. It seemed that because industrialization pulled fathers away from their families for large periods of time, it had structurally created a social system designed to make boys gay.

Accordingly, in this zeitgeist, what it meant to be a man began to be predicated in not being like one of those sodomite/invert/homosexuals. Being masculine entailed being the opposite of the softness attributed to homosexual men. Kimmel (1994) shows us that heterosexuality therefore grew further predicated in aversion to anything coded as feminine. Accordingly, what it meant to be a heterosexual man in the twentieth century was to be unlike a woman. What it meant to be heterosexual was not to be homosexual. In this gender-panicked culture, competitive, organized, and violent teamsport was thrust upon boys.

Sport as a Masculine Cure-all

It was in this atmosphere that sport became associated with the political project to reverse the feminizing and homosexualizing trends of boys growing up without father figures. Sport and those who coached it were charged with shaping boys into heterosexual, masculine men. Accordingly, a rapid rise and expansion of organized sport was utilized as a homosocial institution principally aimed to counter men's fears of feminism and homosexuality. But there were other purposes, too. Sport was also useful for maintaining men's power over women.

Another key element in this project was elevating the male body as superior to that of women. Men accomplished this through displays of strength and violence, so sport embedded elements of competition and hierarchy among men. Connell (1995: 54) suggests "men's greater sporting prowess [over women] has become … symbolic proof of superiority and right to rule." But sport could only work in this capacity if women were formally excluded from participation. If women were bashing into each other and thumping their chests like men, men wouldn't be able to lay sole claim to this privilege (Bryson 1987). Without women's presence in sport, men's greater sporting prowess became *uncontested* proof of their superiority and right to masculine domination. Thus, sport not only reproduced the gendered nature of the social world, but sports competitions became a principle site where masculine behaviors were learned and reinforced (Hargreaves 1995).

Social programs and sports teams were created to give (mostly white boys) contact with male role models. The YMCA came to America in 1851, hockey was invented in 1885, basketball was invented in 1891; the first Rose Bowl was played in 1902; and the first World Series was played in 1903. By the 1920s track, boxing, and swimming also grew in popularity, and with much of the nation living in urban areas, America entered "the Golden Age of Sport," and the country was bustling with professional, semiprofessional, and youth leagues.

Unfortunately, when we think of sport today – when we ask why Jeff, his father, and his teammates so valorize extremely masculine sport like American football – few consider its origins and intent. Few recall that Pierre de Coubertin's reinvention of the ancient Olympic Games was because he saw French men becoming soft, not because he wanted to unite the world's nations.

Christianity also concerned itself with the project of masculinizing and hetero-sexualizing men during this period. Muscular Christianity concerned itself with instilling sexual morality, chastity, heterosexuality, religiosity and nationalism in men through competitive and violent sport (Mathisen 1990). This was a project that extended to Native Americans as well. Sport was used to introduce them to Anglican ways of thinking about the individual, opposed to the collective their cultures traditionally valued. This muscular movement aimed to force a rebirth of Western notions of manliness, to shield boys and men from immoral influences by hardening them with stoic coaches and violent games. Ironically, some of those pushing hardest for masculine morality began the Young Men's Christian Association (YMCA), which almost immediately served as a gay pickup joint (something reflected in the Village People's song, "YMCA").

This period of history also saw organized sport being co-opted by adults. Prior to the 1890s sporting matches were controlled by students – they were coached by students, organized and played all by and for students. However, with new reasons for valuing sport, coaches were paid to manage sport (Spring 1974). It was also during this time that recreational sport became enveloped by school systems (in America), a relationship that exists today. This mirrors, and therefore trains youth to cooperate with, the bureaucratic structures that define contemporary America. So while British youth enjoy a bit more flexibility in self-run sporting programs, American youth maintain no control over their organized school sport. This reflects how a once unimportant social institution suddenly found merit and purpose, by those in power.

Few people, outside a select group of sport scholars, think of sport as a social mechanism to demonstrate support for masculine and heterosexual dominance. Most are misled into believing that all is equal in sport because women now have more sporting opportunities. Furthermore, we scarcely think about what types of sport we culturally esteem – those that highlight the differences between the male and female body, such as American football and rugby (Burton-Nelson 1994). We value sport in which bodies clash, jump and sprint, and not those where finesse, extreme endurance or balance determine success. In other words, we value sport that favors whatever biological advantage men as a whole maintain. This is because this sport is thought to imbue its participants with masculinity, and heterosexuality.

Modern sport was therefore born out of the turn of the twentieth century notion that it could help prevent male youth from possessing characteristics associated with femininity. It was designed to compel boys to reject all but a narrow definition of masculinity: one that created good industrial workers, soldiers, Christians and consumers. The construction of sport as a masculine and homophobic enterprise was both deliberate and political, and over a hundred years later, little has changed.

Sport, it would seem, has served well the principle for which it was designed. It has created a social space in which boys are still taught to value and perform a violent, stoic and risky form of masculinity: one based in antifemininity, patriarchy, misogyny and homophobia.

Although parents may not consciously admit that they desire to put their sons into football in America, or soccer in Britain, in order to assure that they grow up heterosexual, glimpses of this thinking often emerge when fathers learn that their kids are gay; where it is common to hear, "I should have put you in football." Extremely masculine sport is valued in our culture for a reason, and this is because they are used to help boys publicly prove to their peers, families, and society that they too are "red blooded" all-American boys; lads' lads. Jeff learned to love football, because he was socially esteemed for doing it. He only learned to love cheerleading once he was able to reconstruct himself not to care what society valued – a lesson most of us could learn from.

Chapter Conclusion

The purpose of this chapter was to introduce you to why we value sport so much, and why we particularly value masculinized sport that requires aggression (football, rugby, soccer, etc). It is not just that these games are popular with the media, they became popular with the media because of the service they were thought to offer boys (and boys only).

There are, however, other reasons we learned to value sport in this particular historical moment. In their excellent book about whether sport delivers on character building or not, *Lessons of the Locker Room*, Andrew Miracle and Roger Rees (1994) point out that psychologist G. Stanley Hall developed and popularized a theory of play that maintained that organized play promoted positive evolutionary traits, and others thought sport was actually useful for building group loyalty in order to stave off the progress of capitalism. I propose that the most salient reason for finding reverence for sport, however, came through a gender-panicked culture that emerged from the structural changes to the family (absence of the father figure) as a result of the Industrial Revolution. With the new-found social constructionist ideals of Freud, and the construction of sexuality and masculinity, we feared that boys would not learn to become proper heterosexual men unless we introduced them to the role-modeling of masculine men. Thus, sport was valued for the first time in Western cultures, because it had an "important" purpose. It was no longer a waste of god's time. It was now an essential ingredient of proper heterosexual adjustment for boys. In the foundation of this ideal, a few important principles were instilled into sport. Namely, sport is the domain of white, able-bodied boys and men. Gay men, those who are lesser-abled, women, and those of color were not welcome.

In the chapters that follow, I highlight that in both the way sport is structured, and the way it is culturally valued, sport remains a bastion for white, heterosexual, able-bodied, boys and men. Others may play, but we are not all playing equally. However, even if we were able to achieve total equality in sport, in the next chapter I question whether we should want kids (and adults) to participate in organized, competitive, sport in the first place. This, I suggest, is because sport teaches us to conform to norms without critically assessing the purpose and effects of those norms. Sport teaches us to be complicit with abuse, and to submit our agency to power structures. These are not the lessons I desire my students to learn. I question why we want children to be so complicit with adult authority.

2 Sport's Use in Teaching Obedience to Authority and thus Complicity with Abuse

Kallella's Story

Kallella loved playing basketball with her older brothers. "We had a basketball hoop in our driveway, and my brothers used to shoot hoops after school." She remembers growing up with a basketball in her hands. "My friends were into other sports," she says, "but I just loved basketball."

Despite her passion for the game, Kallella did not play in organized sport when she was young. "I loved playing with my brothers, and sometimes some of the boys from down the street would join, but I never really wanted to play in a league or anything. Basketball was just something I did at home." In fact, Kallella did not play any organized sport when she was young. "My parents stressed academic work, not athletics," she said. "A lot of my friends played soccer, but I didn't care for that. I think I just really liked playing sport with my brothers." Thus, when Kallella arrived at high school, she immersed herself in her academic pursuits. Her older twin brothers were in their final year of high school, and Kallella recalls this as one of the most enjoyable years of her life. "They used to drive me to school, and then after sixth period they would drive me home with them. It was great," she says, "I had it made."

Things changed for Kallella in her sophomore year. "My brothers went off to college, and all of a sudden, they weren't there for me. I just really missed them." Kallella used to come home from school and see the unused basketball hoop in the front yard. "I remember telling my brother on the phone that I couldn't wait for Christmas break, so that we could play again. He said to me, "Hey, Kallella, remember my friend Dan … he's an assistant coach for the frosh/soph basketball team at your school. Why don't you consider playing for his team?"" Kallella realized that she was growing somewhat depressed with her brothers' absence. "You have to understand, they were my life," so she decided that maybe she should try out for the team.

Kallella looks back upon her years of high school basketball with almost as much lustre as she does the years she played with her brothers. "I made friends with a lot of girls," she says. "But more important, Dan became like another brother to me. I didn't even call him Coach, he was just Dan." Kallella was promoted to the varsity team in her third year of high school, and during her final year she blossomed as a player. Her head coach contacted a division one university's coach about Kallella.

"I couldn't believe it," she says, "I went from just playing basketball for fun with my brothers to having a division one school look to recruit me. I was a scholarship athlete. I never thought I'd play college ball, but I did."

Unfortunately, it was here, at university, that Kallella experienced a darker side of sport. "I went to [names university] because it was a top-notch academic university, that I would not otherwise been able to afford. If I had not gotten a scholarship, I don't think I would have gone." However, since Kallella attended this university on a basketball scholarship, it meant that she could not quit the team. If she did, she would lose her scholarship and not be able to pay the expensive tuition of her university. "I was locked into playing," Kallella says. And the minute one is locked into playing, the nature of the game begins to change.

"My coach wasn't anything like my high school coaches. He was just nasty. Downright mean." Kallella describes a host of experiences that robbed her of her joy of the sport of basketball. "He would yell things at us, telling us we were no good, worthless. He would tell us that we were too fat, that we needed to lose weight." Kallella continues, "He would single a girl out for something and just lay into her. I can't tell you how many girls he made cry … I totally lost my love for the sport." When I ask Kallella why she continued to play, she says that she "had to" otherwise she would have to leave the university. Do the other girls complain about him too, I ask? "Oh, we all hate him." Kallella continues, "One time we lost, and I guess he thought we shouldn't have. Well, he always thought we shouldn't have. There was never a time when he said, 'they were just better than us.' If we won, he was all-over-the-place-happy. But if we lost, you didn't say a word on the bus ride back. We knew that whoever said something first, anything, would be laid into."

This verbal abuse was compounded by physical abuse.

> He made us show up at seven in the morning the next day if we lost. It didn't matter that we needed sleep, or whether we had a paper to write or test to study for. If we lost, we had seven o'clock practice the next morning [in addition to their normal 1:00 pm practise].

I asked Kallella what these workouts consisted of. "Wind sprints," she said. "He would just run us, up and down the court, yelling at us. If your knee hurt, it didn't matter. Nothing mattered except that we do what he told us to do." And what if someone got injured, I asked. "It didn't matter to him. He would either say it was because we were weak, or he'd accuse you of faking it."

Kallella's recounting of her experience clearly highlights mental and physical abuse. Instead of sport being a place where self-esteem and physical health were built, her coach inflicted undue physical punishment for his inability to handle loss. Rather than building up confidence in his players, he tore them down.

In addition to the most obvious question, *so what good did sport on this team do Kallella?* There is another question of importance. *Why didn't these young women do something about it?*

The answer to this letter question is that Kallella and her friends were afraid. They were afraid of losing playing time or starting positions if they questioned the coach. They were afraid of losing their scholarships if they quit. "So why didn't you petition to have the coach fired?" I asked. "If one of us stood up against him, he wouldn't play you. Nobody wanted to risk that." And with extra players on the bench – women who desperately wanted some court time – it's not likely that all of the players would stand by their assertion that the coach was abusive and should be fired.

"I talked to some of the older players," Kallella says. "They say he was like this last year and the year before. I even met a girl who played for this team years ago. She said that he was the same back then. I asked her why nobody does anything about it and she said, 'If you don't like it, leave it.'"

Learning Obedience in Sport

It is this response to the abuse inflicted upon Kallella – this "if you don't like it leave it" mentality – and the utter lack of action that Kallella and her teammates took against an abusive coach that this chapter addresses. Before we begin, however, I would like to suggest two points. First, this is not an atypical example – things like this occur frequently. Second, we permit all types of abuse from coach to athlete (often adult to child) in sport; abuse that we would not permit outside of sport.

For example, if I as a university instructor were to repeatedly yell at my students and tell them that they are stupid; if I were to call them derogatory terms and punish them for not performing well on a test by making them do extra assignments; or if I were to make students show up for extra lectures at 7:00 in the morning, I would be fired for abuse. Most would say that there is a natural consequence for failing an exam, and that consequence is that you fail the exam – no additional punishment is necessary. Yet this same mantra does not apply to sport.

Why can a university coach insult their athletes, belittle them in front of others, and force them to attend extra sessions, while a university lecturer cannot? More important, why do those who are abused, or the parents or friends of those who witness this abuse, fail to do something about it? The answers lie in how sport helps some gain power (usually the coach), and how they use this power to teach obedience to their authority. The answer has to do with who has power and who does not.

Power is the fundamental concept of most social science research (Russell 1938). Power has, of course, multiple definitions, but I prefer to describe power this way: there are only so many goodies in a society, institution, organization, club, family, etc. Whether those goodies are material or social/emotional, they are in limited supply. If one hands out too much money, its value drops – the same is true with praise. In sport, goodies come from winning. Winning brings a coach social capital, respect, promotion, and in the case of Kallella's university coach, a financial bonus. Thus, power is the ability to influence the direction and manner in which those goodies are distributed.

Politics is the arguing over how those goodies are distributed. Those with the most power tend to get most of the goodies. In the case of Kallella's coach, he used his power in order to get his players to do things they otherwise would not.

He used his power to inflict emotional and physical pain, hoping to influence his team to win, so that he might gain more power. As a result, he abused his athletes in order to gain more goodies.

But one must *learn* to take this type of abuse, for much of the violence and risk-taking associated with sport is *unnatural*. I say this because much of what sport requires us to do is to defy our natural instincts that protect us from harm. For example, a batter in softball does not naturally desire to lean into a pitch. She does it just because her coach tells her too – sacrificing her body's health for the sake of taking a base. Similarly, men do not naturally "shake off" injury in order to complete a play, just because their coach shouts at them. That, too, is learned. Whether this obedience is accomplished through submission to parents, teachers or coaches, we learn early that questioning or contesting authority has serious consequences, particularly in sport. In other words, the consequences for disobeying a coach's abuse are often worse than the pain of obeying. Sadly, in time, our sense of self, our agency to stand up for ourselves, withers away. We might just end up learning to obey, even when we don't want to, habitually. Thus, we learn to follow those "in power" without question.

In this chapter, I examine the use of power in terms of teaching athletes to obey authority, limit their agency, and submit to the will of the dominant. I use three famous social psychology experiments to do this, beginning with Philip Zimbardo's (1971) Stanford prison experiment to illuminate the power of conformist thinking. I use Zimbardo to show the ease in which boys and men (I'm sure it applies equally to girls and women) are made docile to authority, and how readily we adapt to culturally determined roles. After explaining his experiment, and its much-discussed implications, I next apply them to the field of sport.

I then look to the social interactions among athletes, showing how easily they are coerced into obeying authority. I do this through discussing the influential social psychological literature of Milgram (1974) and Asch (1951), again relating these findings to sport. Thus, I describe how athletes are trained to be complicit to authority.

Philip Zimbardo and Role Adoption

In 1971, Philip Zimbardo paid 24 men to participate in his prison experiment. Depending on the flip of the coin, the university students were randomly assigned to take the role of either prisoners or prison guards. A Stanford University basement was turned into a makeshift prison to facilitate the experiment. The "prisoners" were first collected by police car, stripped naked, "decontaminated," and placed in gowns with no undergarments. On his website, (www.prisonexp.org) Zimbardo says that this was designed to "effeminize" the men, suggesting that they began "to walk and to sit differently, and to hold themselves differently – more like a woman than like a man." The men's heads were shaved, and shackles placed around their feet. In attempt to begin to wither the men's sense of self (their agency), their names were replaced with identification numbers, dehumanizing them in the process.

The guards were given no instructions, other than to keep order in the prison.

They too were given uniforms, along with whistles and billy clubs (truncheons). At 2:30 am, the first morning, the prisoners were awoken for "count," where the guards forced them to repeatedly recite their ID numbers. The scene was accentuated by jocose behaviors, as neither the prisoners nor the guards took their new role seriously. But the guards' control soon escalated, as the men began to *live* their roles.

The experiment, originally designed to last two weeks, was cancelled after just six days. This was because the guards began to wield abusive power over their "prisoners." Push-ups at first, and then degrading, homophobic and power-laden guard-to-prisoner discourse. Disturbed sleep and humiliating behavior influenced a rebellion among the prisoners, who blocked the door and removed their prisoner hats. The guards then sprayed the prisoners with a fire-extinguisher, stripped the prisoners naked and increased verbal humiliation. Then, borrowing a tactic used to stymie workers from forming unions, the guards gave privileges to some prisoners, and not to others. Prisoners who continued to rebel were starved. The guards soon reversed the "privilege," which further set the groups of prisoners against each other.

When one prisoner broke down, crying and shaking, he was chided by the guards for not being "man enough." He was asked how he would make it in San Quentin (a notoriously rough American prison). When this prisoner said that he wanted to quit the experiment, he was told by the other prisoners to suck it up and not to quit. And, when visiting parents complained about the condition of their sons, the guards chided them. One guard even said to a father, "Why? Isn't your boy tough enough?" The father responded, "Of course he is. He is a real tough kid. A leader." The next day, Zimbardo (who was acting as the prison warden) heard there was to be an escape planned. He began to obsess about how to stop it.

But none of this – the abuse, the pleading parents, or the psychological harm – was enough for Zimbardo to cancel the experiment. What finally caused Zimbardo to cancel is as illuminating about masculinity as his study is about role conformity. On Zimbardo's own website, he writes:

> I was sitting there all alone, waiting anxiously for the intruders to break in, when who should happen along but a colleague and former Yale graduate student roommate, Gordon Bower. Gordon had heard we were doing an experiment, and he came to see what was going on. I briefly described what we were up to, and Gordon asked me a very simple question: "Say, what's the independent variable in this study?" To my surprise, I got really angry at him. Here I had a prison break on my hands. The security of my men and the stability of my prison was at stake, and now, I had to deal with this bleeding-heart, liberal, academic, effete dingdong who was concerned about the independent variable! It wasn't until much later that I realized how far into my prison role I was at that point – that I was thinking like a prison superintendent rather than a research psychologist.

Even after Zimbardo began to realize that he, too, adopted a role (that of prison warden), he did not use his ultimate authority to cancel the experiment. It seems

Zimbardo rather enjoyed the power. Later, several other young men then broke down, crying uncontrollably. One requested medical assistance, and others requested lawyers.

The students internalized their roles so well that when talking to one psychologically disturbed young man, Zimbardo said:

> Listen, you are not #819. You are [his name], and my name is Dr Zimbardo. I am a psychologist, not a prison superintendent, and this is not a real prison. This is just an experiment, and those are students, not prisoners, just like you.

The point, of course, is that the prisoners adopted their roles so well that they ceased to remember that they were involved in an academic experiment. Although, according to their contract, they were free to leave at will (only losing their pay) they seemingly lost their agency to leave. They formulated a form of self-imprisonment. Perhaps most illuminating, on the fifth day, when a new prisoner was brought into the scenario, he rebelled against their treatment. But this was no longer a favored tactic of the older prisoners. Accordingly, they viewed him as an unwanted troublemaker!

Zimbardo eventually did end the study. "I ended the study prematurely for two reasons," he says. "First, we had learned through videotapes that the guards were escalating their abuse of prisoners … Their boredom had driven them to ever more pornographic and degrading abuse of the prisoners." He continues, "Second … [another academic] strongly objected when she saw our prisoners being marched on a toilet run, bags over their heads, legs chained together, hands on each other's shoulders. Filled with outrage, she said, 'It's terrible what you are doing to these boys!' Out of 50 or more outsiders who had seen our prison, she was the only one who ever questioned its morality." Zimbardo adds, "Once she countered the power of the situation, however, it became clear that the study should be ended. And so, after only six days, our planned two-week prison simulation was called off."

Zimbardo's study is well recognized in social psychology literature. The men (prisoners and guards) learned to conform to authority and to act according to their preconceived perceptions of the role they were placed into. Even Zimbardo was swept into overly associating with the role of warden. Thus, as horrific as this study is, there is also illuminating data to emerge from it, much of which relates to sport.

The first lesson comes from role conformity, and the lesson is that if you put a uniform on people, they will enact the role that is signified by that costume. Second, degrading players, even for a short period of time (in this case degrading men with homophobia and misogyny), will erode their will to stand up for themselves. This is where some of the usefulness of "hazing" is found in sport. It permits older team players to wither the agency of new recruits, influencing them to replicate team norms. Highlighting how hazing can erode an individual's sense of self, two months after the experiment, one prisoner said:

> I began to feel that I was losing my identity, that the person that I called "Clay," the person who put me in this place, the person who volunteered to

go into this prison – because it was a prison to me, it still is a prison to me. I don't regard it as an experiment or a simulation because it was a prison run by psychologists instead of run by the state. I began to feel that that identity, the person that I was that had decided to go to prison was distant from me – was remote until finally I wasn't that, I was 416. I was really my number.

Third, those who were given power (the guards) so enjoyed their ability to wield it, that many of the men volunteered to do extra shifts (guarding) without pay. The ability to dominate and control others was their reward. This has implications for coaches who assign students as "captains," anointing them with power over their peers.

There are other striking parallels for sport and masculinity. Boys are culturally compelled to play organized sport. In Britain they are even forced into it through the "educational" state curriculum. And similar to the prisoners being dehumanized through stripping and spraying, sport initiates boys through recruitment rituals, which often include nudity. Just as prisoners are assigned uniforms and numbers, athletes are too. Whereas prisoners are told to follow numerous institutional rules (often designed to diminish their will to resist), athletes are told that part of "team-work" is adhering to a set of often illogical rules, like punishing a whole team because one athlete was not able to keep up on a run.

Just as prisoners are punished for violating the warden's rules, when athletes break the coach's rules, they are corporally punished with push-ups, running, early morning practices or other physical acts that are designed to cause physical pain and social ostracization. Just as homophobic and effeminizing words were used to further compel inmates to comply with the psychologically demeaning behaviors they were subjected to, teammates are normally subject to the same homophobic and misogynistic words.

When an athlete shows fear, cries or hesitates, his masculinity is questioned and the coach or others tell him to "suck it up." If the athlete is lucky enough to find support from his parents, a coach simply dismisses accusations of violation with epithets that punishment or ostracization is "good" for kids, that it "builds charac-ter." If a prisoner/athlete stands to contest the system, he is called a nonconformist, a rebel, and reminded that there is no "I" in team. If he continues to "act up," a coach sets his fellow teammates against him by rewarding the prisoners who do comply with the rules and punishing the athletes who don't. He sets teammates against each other and makes them compete for privileges. This prevents them from focusing their anger at the coach. For the warden, who becomes so consumed with winning, someone might eventually remind him that "it's just a game," but it won't do much good. By this time the warden has one, singular focus – winning. Accordingly, he will cast off the objections by calling the objector, a "… bleeding-heart, liberal, academic, effete ding-dong …"

Is it absurd to say that teamsport is a prison? Yes, it is. But the intertwining of athletic and prison terminology in the above paragraph highlights that is it not at all absurd to suggest that sport and prisons use many of the same mechanisms of social control to erode agency from individuals. The prison analogy is simply that of a total-institution, while sport is a near-total institution. Just as the prisoners and guards played a role (which they soon internalized), so do athletes. Even if we have no personal experience of these roles, they are mapped in our culture for us. All we have to do is don a team uniform or whistle and we begin to act accordingly. I've seen this occur numerous times with young assistant coaches. In fact, I did it myself.

After graduating from high school, I decided to return to my school and coach. Suddenly, I was in charge of the very friends and teammates that I had trained with the previous year. Although I had no coaching experience, I adopted the role of coach as I knew it. I began ordering my athletes around in an authoritarian voice. Of course my athletes (former friends) did not appreciate the style. But *I* was the coach, and just like Zimbardo was the prison warden, I had to keep control.

By the third year, most of my former teammates had graduated. Accordingly, the new runners only knew me as "coach." Consequently, my power and authority grew. One day I found myself in a shouting match with one of my athletes. I was modeling the way my coach had dealt with problems – anger, shouting, and insulting. After a teacher broke it up, I thought, *there has got to be a better way*. The next semester I enrolled in an Educational Psychology course at my university. I began to undo the authority model and adopt a humanist approach to coaching, so my coaching relationships moved to one of friendship and mentorship, not control and power. I sought to increase my referent power, partially by decreasing my coercive power (these types of power are discussed later in the chapter). I began decreasing social distance, and casting off traditional coaching models of authority. I became more democratic in my coaching, and even encouraged my athletes to intellectually challenge the workouts or race strategies I assigned. Occasionally, I would even prescribe preposterous workouts, just to see if they were thinking critically. I would then reward the individual who used his agency to contest me. The point is, most coaches don't do this. Instead, they adopt the Bobby Knight, chair throwing, screaming, "respect my authority" type coaching. Most coaches *like* authority. This is why it is commonly known that once you are a head coach, you can never go back to being an assistant. Most coaches like power.

Today, I teach my students that using power is one of the most problematic ways to get athletes/students to do what you want them to do. I encourage them to increase their referent power with their athletes, so that they can influence them to not only think on their own, but to contribute to the learning environment. Essentially, I stress that *use* of power is *abuse*. There is almost always a better way.

Stanley Milgram and Obedience to Authority

There are other social psychology experiments that help us to understand how athletes learn complicity, complacency, and docility to a coach's authority and team norms. In the wake of World War II, Yale social psychologist Stanley Milgram set out to determine if Adolf Eichmann and other Nazi war criminals were simply following orders, making them accomplices to a crime rather than the assailants themselves. His study was designed to see if a person off the street would obey an authority figure to the point of violating their moral conscience. Accordingly, pretending to have subjects participate in a learning experiment, Milgram set an actor to pretend he was being electrically shocked. The subject asked the confederate (an individual knowingly playing along with the experiment) a question, and when it was wrong, the subject was to administer an electric shock. The actor, who was out of sight, would scream, and the subject would be instructed to continue with the experiment. With each wrong answer, the subject was to systematically escalate the level of electric shock. Milgram summarized the experiment in 1974 in "The Perils of Obedience," writing:

> The legal and philosophic aspects of obedience are of enormous importance, but they say very little about how most people behave in concrete situations. I set up a simple experiment at Yale University to test how much pain an ordinary citizen would inflict on another person simply because he was ordered to by an experimental scientist. Stark authority was pitted against the subjects' strongest moral imperatives against hurting others, and, with the subjects' ears ringing with the screams of the victims, authority won more often than not. The extreme willingness of adults to go to almost any lengths on the command of an authority constitutes the chief finding of the study and the fact most urgently demanding explanation.

As the intensity of administered shocks increased, the actor would pound on the wall, begging for the experiment to stop. They even had the confederate complain about a heart condition. Most of the subjects asked Milgram if they could stop the experiment. But Milgram upped the authority with each plea. First he simply said, "Please continue." The next request to stop was met with, "The experiment requires that you continue." Followed by, "It's absolutely necessary that you continue." Finally, the subject was told, "You have no other choice. You must go on." If the subject again asked to stop the experiment, it was halted. Otherwise, it wasn't halted until the subject had administered an unbelievable 450 volts (enough to kill you) three times in a row!

In the original experiment, none of the participants stopped before administering 300 volts, and 65 percent went on to the final stage of 450 volts, three times each. Many of the subjects continued to administer the shocks even though the confederate had ceased to scream (as if he had died). Since the original experiment, it has been replicated and altered in numerous ways. In one study the wall between the confederate and the subject was removed, so that the shocker could see the (acted) pain the other person was experiencing. Nonetheless, the consistent finding remains that 61–65 percent of people will administer the lethal dose of 450 volts (Blass 2000). And, of those who did cease, none demanded that the experiment stop for others. None bothered to check on the health of the person they thought they were shocking.

Milgram's shocking experiments clearly compliment Zimbardo's study, but instead of studying how people adopt roles, it examines how we submit to authority. His study shows that when people believe they are simply the instrument for carrying out another person's wishes, they no longer see themselves as being responsible for their actions. Once this critical shift of viewpoint has occurred, all of the essential features of obedience follow. Milgram's agency theory holds that when we receive commands from authority figures, we lose our sense of responsibility because it is diffused (diffusion of responsibility) and we lose our capacity to make our own choices. Essentially, we lose our agency. We enter an agentic-free state where we become agents of a higher authority, feeling "responsibility to authority" but "no responsibility for the content of our actions that the authority prescribe" (Milgram 1974: 145–146). Clearly, this is the case with soldiers.

Many individuals who have little power in a group assume that they are supposed to carry out the orders of the authority without questioning these orders (Hamilton and Sanders 1999). They no longer believe they are in control of their own actions, and so become willing cogs in the group machine, carrying out the authority's orders without considering their implications or questioning their effects (Hamilton and Sanders 1999; Kelman and Hamilton 1989). On one website devoted to the experiment (http://home.swbell.net/revscat/perilsOfObedience.html), Milgram is quoted as saying:

> This is, perhaps, the most fundamental lesson of our study: ordinary people, simply doing their jobs, and without any particular hostility on their part, can become agents in a terrible destructive process. Moreover, even when the destructive effects of their work become patently clear, and they are asked to carry out actions incompatible with fundamental standards of morality, relatively few people have the resources needed to resist authority.

Later variations of the experiment show that the closer one is to the damage they inflict the less likely they are to comply with authority. When subjects were told to place the hand of the confederate on the electric shock plate, conformity rates dropped to just 30 percent. Interestingly, although women showed more distress at having to administer electric shocks, they complied equally with men. Also, when other researchers encourage the subject to apply the shocks, compliance increases.

Latane (1981) analyzes these results through social impact theory, explaining that the impact of power on a target from an authority figure is determined by the strength of influence according to three main factors: first, the strength (or importance) of the influencer; second, the number of influencers; and, third, the immediacy (or closeness) of the influencer. As each of these increase, they will cause the power of influence to increase and subsequently will result in increased conformity. Conversely, decreasing these factors will have the opposite effect. Social impact theory can account for a large body of experimental research on conformity, compliance, and obedience (Latane and Bourgeois 2001), all of which offer useful insights into the explanations for the abuse athletes are subjected to by their coaches.

When it comes to sport, one must ask, if 65 percent of people will administer a lethal dose of electricity simply because some researcher in a white coat tells them to, what will athletes do? How easy is it for a coach, who is imbued with social power, to order athletes to perform while injured, to intentionally foul (injure) others, or to comply with the coach against a plethora of otherwise moral objections (including sexual abuse)? Did Kallella and her teammates follow the coach's abusive instructions to show up to run wind sprints at seven in the morning simply because the coach represents a figure of authority?

Collectively, the adoption of roles and the relinquishment of autonomy position athletes into an agentic-less state of mind, permitting horrific acts to be committed by their coaches or teammates, all in the name of obedience. Brackenridge (2000) argues that "authority figures like coaches come to assume dominance and control over athletes, [and] it is clear that these expressions of agency arise from long-term, collective, socio-cultural influences" (p. 5). Crosset (1986) identifies this as a form of a "master-slave" relationship.

For example, Gervis and Dunn (2004) show that of the twelve international-competing youth athletes they studied (aged between 8 and 16), each reported emotionally abusive behaviors from their coaches. They found athletes felt worthless, fearful and humiliated by their coaches, who were shown to belittle, humiliate, shout, scapegoat, reject, isolate, ignore, and threaten their athletes. All reported belittling and shouting, nine reported frequent humiliation, and nine reported threatening behaviors. Seven reported scapegoating, six reported rejection or being ignored, four reported isolation. As a result, the children (now adults) report feeling stupid, worthless, upset, less confident, humiliated, depressed, fearful, and angry.

This occurs because the coach has *too much power*, and because the athletes learn not to contest it. In their study of abused professional athletes, Kelly and Waddington (2006) found that "no matter how abusive or violent the manager's [coach's] behavior may be, his authority was not to be questioned and those who did question it were punished, in this case by being withdrawn from the games" (p. 153). Finally, making the coach's power all the more salient, recall what happened to a prisoner when he contested the guard/coach. He was viewed unfavorably among his prison mates. Accordingly, even when coaches have been abusive, it does not mean their abuse is reported. Brackenridge, Bringer and Bishopp (2005: 261) write:

> Abuses of many kinds have been known about for years, but for a variety of reasons have not been labelled as abuse or not dealt with as misdemeanors. The physical demands of training, emotional toughness and a culture of resilience in sport all acted as masks to the suffering that some athletes faced as part of their sporting experience.

Those who stand against authority are perceived as standing against a norm, and this is something that psychologist Solomon Asch shows us is difficult for people to do.

Solomon Asch and Social Conformity

In his seminal experiment, Solomon Asch (1951) placed a student into a room with other students who were confederates. All of the students were told to say that, of the three lines presented to them, the shorter line was longest. The test was designed to see how one student (the test subject) would answer when he was asked which line was longer. Asch found that although it was clear which line was longer, 32 percent of the time the respondent would answer according to his peers. Asch argues that this is because people do not want to be out of step with other people. People would rather conform, and say something that they do not believe, than be the one to disagree with a group. I suggest that the obedience of athlete to coach is not only influenced by the process men go through in order to be successful in sport, but also by the behaviors of others in the group/team, and their willingness to obey the coach's orders. Deutsch and Gerard (1955) propose social impact theory as a way to suggest that athletes obey coaches, because when faced with an ambiguous situation, they refer to others for social comparison.

Because of the ruthless and hyper-masculine ethos of so much sport, many athletes not only accept the use of intimidation and violence by their coaches, but many see it as an appropriate "character building" way of socializing players (Kelly and Waddington 2006). Even athletes who find the abuse unsettling are unlikely to say anything about it. This is because they see their teammates whole-heartedly accepting the abuse, and even valuing it for making them "real" men and tougher players. This means that they are more likely to accept abuse. In other words, an individual's need for social acceptance and approval can lead them into compliance with the majority, even in the face of abuse and potential injury. In sports teams, where the need for social acceptance is high (and the coach holds such extensive reward and coercive power), athletes will often conform to normative behaviors.

The essential effect of conformist desire plays itself out in sports fields across the world. For example, it is easy for one athlete to be blamed for a team's loss, and then have all the other athletes agree to it. More significant to orthodox masculinity, my research on gay athletes (Anderson 2005a) shows that when a heterosexual team captain, or other team member that retains high masculine capital, says that they have no problem with gay men, the other athletes tend to agree. Conversely, when the individual with the highest masculine capital takes a homophobic stance, others again agree. On one team, the attitudes of the men shifted from homophobic, to gay friendly in one year, and then back to homophobic the next – depending on who the team captain was. This highlights the hierarchical relationship built into sport, and the "follow the leader" nature of sport.

Unfortunately, the desire not to "rock the boat" also gives the coach unyielding power. The initially uncomfortable acceptance of minor abuses by coaches often goes unquestioned, because individuals are influenced not to speak up about them through team complicity. As athletes move through the system the acts of abuse are slowly ratcheted up to be more abusive, coercive, and violent, and they become gradually naturalized as just part of the game (Kelly and Waddington 2006). In the case of sexual abuse, Brackenridge (1995: p. 5) writes that the "process involves gradually building trust and pushing back the boundaries of acceptable behavior, slowly violating more and more personal space through verbal familiarity, emotional blackmail and physical touch."

This is possible because coaches are not only seen as all-powerful, but they have also earned the respect of the players through their previous sporting accomplishments. Coaches encourage the perception of themselves as knowledgeable and infallible by punishing those who question them (Cushion and Jones 2006). Those not directly involved find it difficult to resist a coach because they believe they are doing what they are supposed to. Thus, just as Asch (1951) demonstrated that group members find it difficult to resist because they fear being an outsider to their own group, athletes also find it hard to resist because they are sporting insiders.

Coaching Power

The Zimbardo, Asch, and Milgram studies help us understand how one individual (in this case a coach) can get athletes to comply with their demands, and remain obedient to their authority. But in order to elucidate the full power of the coach, we must also look to other variables. Before we can fully understand the role of the coach in reproducing inequality, we must first understand the system of socialization from which coaches emerge. The development of coaches, who reproduce sport as a socially exclusive and agency-withering environment, is influenced by a number of variables, but the most salient are: 1) the social structure of sport; and 2) the culture of sport.

The *social structure* of sport refers to the manner in which the game is physically structured and played, the manner in which athletes are promoted, divided, and rewarded. For example, one structure (of almost all sport) is that it is performed in order to determine a sole winning individual or winning team over other losing individuals or teams. Yet this is not the only structure upon which one can play sport. One could, for example, follow the historical tradition of many Native American tribes and begin a sporting competition with two teams of unequal ability but equal number, adding or subtracting players until all teams achieve parity in skill but not quantity (Anderson 2006; Oxendine 1988).

This is the way kids naturally play games. That is to say, before adults socialize them into what adults maintain to be "fair" rules, and how one "properly" plays sport from an adult perspective. Before an adult socialization into sport, kids tend to balance teams out to equal ability, even if it means one side has considerably more players than the other. Kids seem to believe that equal ability is what is "fair," not equal team size. Also, kids seem to feel that a close competition is what is fun and fair about sport, and they create structures to assure this. Thus kids of lesser ability might be given more tries, or allowed more room for error. Alternatively, one could play a sporting game without keeping score at all. One *can* enjoy sport for the sake of movement alone. Competition is not necessary to enjoy sport.

A final example of the influence of structure upon sport comes from the near-total segregation that occurs in sport. Sport is unique in that it near totally segregates women from men – something more akin to orthodox religions than state-sponsored social welfare programmes.

The *culture of sport* simply refers to the values and norms associated with any given sport. The collective value of all sport can also be generalized into that of a sporting ethos for our society as a whole. You have heard the mantras before; sport is supposed to teach the value of "hard work" and sport certainly esteems "giving it one's all." But there are other creeds within our sporting culture. We value a hyper-masculine disposition in sport. There is after all "no crying in baseball"; there is no room "for a sore loser"; and "there is no "I" in team." Dropping out of sport is frowned upon, as is "throwing like a girl," challenging a coach's intelligence or authority, or giving less than a hundred percent.

Finally, and of primary concern here, the socially exclusive nature of sport is influenced by the coach who came up through this system, and may therefore utilize his or her individual agency to reproduce a system he/she believes worked for them. The coach maintains a great deal of power in socializing individuals into a particular belief system and, to a lesser extent, the coach also maintains the ability to alter certain sport structures. Thus, as gatekeepers, coaches maintain a great deal of sway in determining the social outcomes of sport.

There are several reasons why coaches maintain such power in shaping the norms of their teams. First, social psychologists frequently refer to five basic categorical types of power (French and Raven 1959), of which coaches often possess all five. And while it is not absolutely necessary to understand exactly what and how each of these powers operates, it is important to understand that few other occupations/ professions offer individuals the ability to associate with all five types of power (Jones, Armour and Potrac 2004). These powers are described as: 1) *legitimate*, defined as power given by one's elected or appointed status; 2) *coercive*, defined as power because of one's ability to take something away; 3) *reward*, defined as power derived from the ability to give something desired; 4) *expert*, defined as power accorded individuals who have undergone formal training; and 5) *referent*, defined as power given because of the respect the coach might have as an inspiration or mentor. For more on these types of power read the section "Revise How Coaches are Recruited, Trained and Evaluated" in Chapter 8).

Clearly coaches use reward power by offering players social promotions, more playing time, or public praise, and they use coercive power in punishing athletes with the opposite. Coaches establish their legitimacy in the eyes of their athletes primarily through having "come up" through the system, often as a successful player first and then by producing quality athletes. This legitimacy, coupled with the title "coach," is then thought (often erroneously) to make one an expert, as coaches are assumed to possess technical knowledge beneficial to advancing an athlete's career. Finally, coaches sometimes gain the respect of their athletes through referent power because athletes desire to accomplish the same feats, times, or levels of play as their coach, or because they look to the coach as a mentor or parental figure.

With these five types of power in mind, I challenge you to think of another occupation or social position (other than a parent) that maintains all five types of power.

The closest my students can come up with is that of a teacher. A police officer, for example, is high in coercive power but maintains no reward power. A doctor is high in referent power, but cannot punish you. Occupation after occupation, you will determine that some have multiple types of power, but only a coach maintains all five types. Well, there is one other – one's commanding officer in the military. Perhaps that should tell us something about the nature of sport.

Chapter Conclusion

Chapter 1 helped explain why we value sport so much in contemporary Western cultures. It helped us understand why we value highly competitive, masculinized, invasion teamsport, and the importance of the coach in dispensing masculine ether to the young boys he was in charge of heterosexualizing and masculinizing. This chapter picked up on the power of the coach and helped explain how sport teaches athletes to undo their naturally protective instincts, obey authority, and accept and inflict emotional and physical pain in the name of sport.

In sport, we learn early that questioning or contesting authority has serious consequences. Should we fail to adhere to a coach's request we can lose playing time, or be socially ostracized and mocked in front of our friends/teammates. Failing to conform gets one stigmatized as not being a "team player."

Because we attribute so much social good to sport, we assume that virtually any means of delivery of sport is good. Sport has obtained near religious fervor in many countries, so those leading us down the path of sporting enlightenment are given undue power (particularly for their level of training). Thus, coaches maintain a great deal of cultural power, too.

In this chapter, I used three famous social psychology experiments to illustrate that human beings all too easily follow authority anyway. I began with Philip Zimbardo's (1971) Stanford prison experiment, highlighting the power of conformist thinking. I also used Zimbardo to show the ease in which we are made docile to authority, and how readily we adapt to culturally determined roles. After explaining his experiment, and its much-discussed implications, I applied them to the field of sport, describing how athletes are victimized by hazing and abusive coaching practices.

I next looked to the social interactions between athletes and coaches to show how easily players are coerced into obeying authority. I did this through discussing the influential social psychological literature of Milgram (1974) and Asch (1951), first detailing the experiments and then relating the findings to sport. Thus, I describe how individuals are not only trained to be complicit to authority (and the abuse that comes with it), but how sport teaches athletes to accept and inflict physical damage onto others as well.

Finally, I complemented these social psychological studies with the work of French and Raven (1959) who identified five basic types of power (legitimate, coercive, reward, expert, and referent). I suggest that coaches and military commanders are unique in that they are imbued with all five types of power.

When one considers these factors woven together, you see that we overly value sport and that we therefore give coaches undue power in helping us achieve sporting goals. This, combined with the decreasing opportunity structure that sport is built upon (next chapter), sets a stage for coaches to abuse their power.

But the problems associated with coach-to-athlete abuse do not end there. Sport is also a field in which coaches are relatively untrained (there is no bachelor's degree required to be a coach), and they are relatively free of supervision and/or evaluation by other professionals. So whereas I am both peer and student evaluated as a lecturer, the same is not the case as a coach. Without these systems, abuse of all sorts is ripe.

Do not come away from this chapter with the idea that I critique or dislike all coaches. My point is that coaches have (for various reasons) *a lot* of power. They can use this power to do wonderful things, like Kallella's coach did in high school. Or, they can use this power to do destructive things, like Kallella's university coach did. I'm just not so sure that one who maintains so much power should have no formal education required to dispense it. It strikes me as odd that coaches, who have so much power, are so relatively unsupervised in their use of it. Finally, it strikes me as odd that coaches should escape formal evaluation by peers and their athletes, when educators do not.

However, this chapter is not just about critiquing the power that coaches have. It is also about asking critical questions about whether we, as a society, desire people to learn such over-obedience to authority in the first place. Because almost all kids are socialized into formal, competitive, institutionalized teamsport, it means that almost all kids learn to obey authority, to do as one is told without question, and to accept violations against one's body and mind. Perhaps such complicity remains a valuable state of mind for an employer who seeks obedient and complacent workers. Perhaps capitalists continue to sponsor sport for this purpose. Perhaps the indoctrination of our (particularly) male youth into warrior sport helps prepare a community of soldiers, and develops a tolerance to war. After all, the US and the UK are both war-fighting countries and this requires a steady state of young men (and now women) who are willing to obey, obey, obey, regardless of the absurdity of the "call to duty."

But whether the obedience one learns from sport is intentional or not, the outcomes are the same. It means that youth who partake in organized sport are trained to obey, so that they are less likely to stand up and protest when an injustice occurs. They are, as with Kallella and her teammates, more likely to put up with the violations without overthrowing their abuser. It means that soldiers continue to fight, viewing it as their job, when their moral conscious tells them that their country has no business fighting. You see, sport teaches the opposite of democracy, sport teaches conformity. This might have benefit for capitalists, career-minded coaches, and military leaders – but I certainly would not want my kids to be so obedient to authority. I do not think this is good for them intellectually or emotionally. And as we will learn in the next chapter, it certainly is not good for them physically.

3 Learning to Accept, Inflict, and Enjoy Violence and Injury

Ben's Story

Ben loves rugby. If there is anything clear about Ben's life, it is that he loves playing the sport of rugby. It is not just the thrill of the game that Ben enjoys; it's the brotherhood, the bonding with other men, and the sense of camaraderie that he experiences when out drinking with his teammates. In fact, Ben goes drinking with his teammates quite often. It is something known in England as "going on the lash." In Britain, the drinking age is 18, so unlike most university athletes in the US, athletes in the UK normally begin drinking publicly, and legally, before they enter university. Drinking large amounts of alcohol is normal in British culture, well before one turns 18, and nowhere is this more true than in rugby culture.

Often after training, and always after a match, Ben's university rugby team heads to a pub in order to have several pints of beer – a rugby tradition. "Certainly I drink more with my rugby mates than I do with my classmates," Ben says. "In rugby, you play it up a bit. You know, to be one of the boys," he says.

I ask Ben how much he drinks after a match, to give me a minimum and maximum number of pints (not bottles) that he consumes on a night out with his rugby friends. "I don't really know, mate," he says. "It all depends, really." However, a bit more conversation reveals that it is not uncommon for Ben to consume 12 to 15 pints of beer in a single evening. In addition to this costing a great deal of money, 15 pints of beer is the same amount as drinking 2.2 US gallons of beer, and this is not the only type of alcohol that is consumed. Furthermore, the latest a pub remains open until is 2:00 am in Ben's town, many close around 11:00 pm. Accordingly, all of this alcohol is consumed during just a few hours of drinking. Adding to this, Ben is not a large person. He weighs a mere 170 pounds (77 kilograms); hardly a behemoth on the rugby pitch.

Ben was socialized into this drinking culture long before coming to university. "I was in the pub drinking at 16," he tells me. But upon arriving at the university, he was formally introduced to binge drinking. Each year the rugby team holds an initiation ceremony. Hazing is not as much a part of British culture as it is among American sportsmen. Instead, the British formalize their hazing into one night of drunken debauchery – something they call initiation. During the university's rugby initiation, Ben's freshman year, he and the other new players were required to consume three liters of 7.5 percent alcoholic cider simply on the walk into town to *begin* their initiation. The initiation itself involved the consumption of numerous pints of beer through funnels. They also consumed numerous shots of whisky and vodka. Worse, many of these drinks were mixed with milk or tabasco sauce. The object of the ceremony was to get the initiates to repeatedly vomit. It worked, too. I remember being on campus that night; everywhere you went it reeked of vomit.

When one consumes alcohol in the massive quantity that Ben does with his teammates, it has an effect on drinking for other purposes, too. Drinking massive amounts of alcohol for initiations, or even post-match celebrations, raises one's tolerance to alcohol and this means increasingly larger amounts of alcohol are needed to get the buzz that most social drinkers enjoy. If one drinks 15 pints on a Wednesday night after a match, drinking four pints the following night does not seem to be such a big deal. Thus, when Ben goes drinking with his non-rugby classmates, he drinks more than twice as much as they do.

Throughout the three years of his university degree, Ben has steadily consumed more and more alcohol. In fact, as his professor, this is something many of his classmates have come to speak with me about, hoping I might be able to influence him to reconsider his behavior. I tried, but Ben does not feel that he has a problem. Why should he? He is valorized within rugby culture for excessive drinking and it is normal social interaction to consume two or three pints of beer a day (nearly half a gallon) with friends. Ben laughs when I ask him about the potential damage he might be causing to his body, "I'll ask for a liver transplant as a graduation gift," he jokes.

But it's not just liver damage that's at risk here. With about 200 calories per pint of beer, and 3,500 calories per pound of body fat, Ben can drink nearly a pound of body fat after a match. Thus, the damage that he is causing to his liver, kidneys, nerves and a multitude of other bodily parts and systems is complicated by the increased risk of weight gain and heart disease. Of course this is just the damage that rugby drinking *culture* causes. Ben has paid for the game itself in other ways, too.

On the same night that Ben and his fellow rugby initiates were drinking noxious concoctions of vodka and tabasco sauce (in order to aromatize the university with eau de vomit), they took part in physical assault too. One of the many humiliating and dangerous initiation ceremonies that Ben and his fellow rugby players went through was a paddling on the head. Ben and his mates were systematically smashed with wooden pallets – hospitalizing two men with gashes to their skulls. Ben was fortunate that the guy beating upon his head used less force; he managed to escape being knocked unconscious, or having his skull split open. But Ben has not managed to escape the other forms of violence that rugby has to offer.

"The first time I tore my ACL [anterior cruciate ligament] was during my first year at uni," Ben tells me. "I had to rest it a few weeks before the surgery, and then after the surgery it was four months before I was even allowed to jog on it. It took nearly nine months before I could play rugby again." Ben continues, telling me that although the surgery is free (because England has socialized medicine) he has paid a lot of money in physiotherapy in order to aid his recovery.

Ben tore his ACL during his second year of rugby, too. "I couldn't believe it. I lost my first year of play to an injury, and now my second," he says. After a simi-larly long recovery period, Ben is now back hoping to play in his third and final year of university rugby (university degrees are just three years in the UK). So, "Is this all worth it?" I ask him. "It seems you've really put your body on the line for rugby, and you are only 20 years old." Ben answers, "I really love the sport. It's all I know. You can't blame me for pursuing my passion, can you?"

One might take a libertarian stand and support Ben for his decisions. After all, he is an adult, and as such, he is free to make decisions that will affect him for decades to come. It hardly seems fair to berate one for choosing to play a violent game. But I wonder just how free Ben was in making his decisions, or whether he has simply adopted a role – like Zimbardo's prisoners. I ask, is Ben making a free choice, or simply acting out a role that is culturally scripted to him by a sports obsessed culture? After all, rugby is highly esteemed in English culture. So did Ben choose to be a rugby player, or was he socialized into it less consciously?

This raises interesting questions. When we talk about what "sport" does, we normally frame our analysis according to what occurs on the pitch. But being an athlete is more than simply playing a game for a designated period of time on a patch of grass. Sport is also about adopting a role that is mapped out in youth cul-ture. What one learns in sport spills over into other arenas of their social life, too. After all, it is this belief that what we learn on the pitch helps us improve our lives off the pitch that is upheld in justifying exposing kids to competitive teamsport. I therefore question not only if Ben is making free choices, but also whether or not Ben's socialization into sport is at least partially responsible for an incident that horrified his classmates.

One night, Ben grew frustrated with a young lady who he had been having sex with. Witnesses say that she was telling him that he needed to make up his mind as to whether they were going to be romantically together or not. In frustration over the question, or the persistence in which she asked, Ben shoved her backward. The woman fell over, and hit her head on the concrete.

One will never be able to say whether this would have happened if Ben had not been socialized into a violent sport, or if he had not been drinking. It is difficult, of course, to confirm that the physical abuse Ben puts his body through, the copious amounts of alcohol that he poisons himself with, and the manner in which he chose to handle his frustration with a potential girlfriend is related to his rugby socializa-tion, but this chapter will help explain how these variables might be influenced by Ben's socialization into rugby culture, and his desire to over-conform to its norms.

Erving Goffman and Sport as a Near "Total Institution'

At the beginning of each year, I ask my new freshman students (who are also ath-letes) to tell me something about themselves. They are instructed to each stand and introduce themselves to the class. Without prompting, the men and women alike almost exclusively begin by telling the class what their name is, and then what sport they play. "I'm Kim, and I play netball." After this, they tell the class what city they came from, and what other hobbies they may have.

These students have been successful enough at sport that they have developed their master identity as that of an athlete. They do not list their race, sexuality, or even their religious orientation first. Instead, most have come to recognize themselves first and foremost as athletes. They do this because they have been successful at sport, and they have therefore chosen to pursue it as their university degree. But are there problems with identifying so heavily as a sportsperson? Developing the identity of an athlete is not as simple as saying, "I love movies."

Strongly identifying as an athlete is a proclamation that one not only loves the sport they "play" but it is also an indication that they adhere to a set of shared "values" that athletes aspire to, and are encouraged to achieve. Some call this positive deviance. For example, part of being an athlete is valuing winning, and that means that playing in pain is normally seen as courageous. Pathogenic weight-control practices are also accepted in the quest for victory, as is the sacrificing of other aspects of one's life (school, family, lovers, travel, other sport, etc.). In fact, most of this is expected. This is not to say that all athletes follow each of these expectations, but being an athlete indicates that one generally ascribes to these principles. This is the difference between going outside to play some basketball with friends, and being a basketball player.

This is very much the same as saying, "I am Christian." Saying that one is Christian, Jewish, Muslim or Catholic means much more than they believe that a particular deity is responsible for creating humanity. Normally, it also means that the person identifies with "a prescribed set of values," a framework of beliefs and practices that are determined by an institution with specific political purposes. Saying, "I am Christian," is to say that you believe – perhaps not every point of a particular religious dogma – but that you generally ascribe to it.

Similarly, individuals who emulate the institutional creed of being an athlete are proclaiming that they largely ascribe to the tenets, the beliefs and practices of organized sport. Now, this may certainly be different for one who says, "I'm a runner," compared to one who says, "I'm a center in volleyball." The runner can be someone who laces up a pair of shoes and runs down the road with her dog in trail. To be a center in volleyball, however, requires you to partake in an organized sporting team, with official and unofficial (overt and covert) rules of behavior. So being an athlete often (not always) means that one adheres to the norms set out in that particular sport. Sadly, it often means that they overly adhere to them as well.

Ewald and Jiobu (1985), for example, show that some athletes so overly adhere to the norms of sporting culture that they disrupt family relationships, work responsibilities, and even their physical health – all guided by a masculine creed of "giving it all" for the sake of sport and team. In my research, I have previously shown that many gay athletes largely remain closeted for these same reasons, fearing that coming out will thwart their athletic matriculation (Anderson 2002, 2005a).

Hughes and Coakley (1991) describe this type of adherence to sporting ethic as a form of social deviance. But over-conformity is a form of social deviance that is also rewarded. Hughes and Coakley say, "the likelihood of being chosen or sponsored for continued participation is increased if athletes over conform to the norms of sport" (p. 311). Of course, athletes do not see over-conformity as problematic, rather "... they see it as confirming and reconfirming their identity as athletes ..." (p. 311). Building upon Hughes and Coakley's over-conformity theory, I examine the structural and cultural mechanisms that help reproduce organized sport as closely approximating what the great (deceased) sociologist, Erving Goffman, describes as a "total institution."

Goffman, my favorite sociologist, observed people in everyday situations, deriving his theories from his observations. Rather than coming up with a theory, and then looking for data to support it, he generated his theory from the ground up. His theories explained the behaviors he observed in humans, but more important than this, Goffman wrote about his theories in a highly accessible manner. Not only is Goffman easy to read and comprehend (which is much more than we can say about many sociologists) but he is absolutely entertaining in the way he explains his ideas. Goffman maintained that sociology was something one did, and he generated simple but useful theories for explaining everyday life.

Some critique Goffman, suggesting that he was more a generator of concepts and insightful interactional principles, rather than what most today consider to be a "social theorist." For example, some scholars suggest that his powers of observation merely gave him a sociological common sense. However, some do not agree.

Throughout his works, Goffman provides insight into ways in which social order is determined through the interactions of individuals. He helps us understand the use of language in shaping cultural ideas and norms and, important to this chapter, he helps us understand hierarchy, stigma, and power. For example, Goffman called the individual an actor, because he observed that people are always putting on an act. When we act (behave) in a pattern repeatedly, it becomes part of the way we present ourselves not only to others (front stage), but to ourselves as well (backstage). Accordingly, one's self is socially constructed, and as individuals we cannot be understood as separate from the social milieux in which we reside. Others are taken in by these performances, so that they appear to be reality when it all began with simple acting. Our social interactions (performances before observers) deliver impressions to others according to the actor's goals, though the actor may have no intent to do this. He or she may be unaware or uncertain of their performance.

Goffman therefore suggests that all interactions, no matter how seemingly meaningless, are important toward the establishment of social order. That, for the most part, people honor rules and work together in order to promote order. To do this, we often "act" out certain roles. This is very much reminiscent of the Zimbardo research I described in the previous chapter, where normal college students were told to act as prison guards, and that, in just a few days, they internalized the role so well that they began torturing their classmates.

All of this relates to sport, because sport is one social arena that is designed to use peer culture in order to achieve a certain order. But it is not just peer culture that influences athletes; they are also influenced by strong institutional guidelines, rules and procedures, with certain paths to glory.

Goffman (1961) describes a total institution as an enclosed social system in which the primary purpose is to control all aspects of someone's life. The military serves a useful example of what Goffman discusses. Through intense regimentation and implementation of a standard ideal of behavior, the military is capable of transforming peasants into soldiers. Men and women become more docile to the system because their growing identity as a soldier is essentially one of subordination from agency. This means that just as the prisoners in Zimbardo's experiment seemed to lose their ability to protect themselves by simply saying, "I quit this experiment," or the way those administering electronic shocks in Milgram's experiment failed to enact their agency and say, "No. I will not shock him," soldiers lose the ability to stand up for themselves. They are trained to do only as they are told to do, regardless of the consequences. This is packaged and delivered as courage and honor.

French Philosopher Michel Foucault (1975) suggested that the longer a soldier remains in the military the less agency he has to contest it. This is, after all, the purpose of the military. If some sergeant is going to get young men to run up a hill where people are shooting at them, just so they can "take" some piece of dirt for no particular reason important to them, then these soldiers must be trained from the time they are young to follow orders. The purpose of military training is to break down one's agency, so that they begin to lose their sense of self. Individual names are replaced with numbers; phone calls to home (where soldiers are reminded that they have a life outside the institution of the military) are therefore limited. Soldiers in boot camp are essentially dehumanized, in order that they lose their human values, instincts, and self-protection mechanisms. Only then can some sergeant tell young men (and now women) to run up a hill, with guns blazing, firing at an enemy that they have never met.

Goffman described the loss of agency as occurring in prisons, too. Goffman (1961: 4) maintained that prisons are "total institutions," defining this as something that is, "symbolized by the barrier to social intercourse with the outside [world] and to departure [freedom to leave] that is often built right into the physical plant [building] …" He described four conditions of total institutions, but suggested that not all total institutions had to share these. In reading his definition below, you will begin to see its application to sport (p. 6):

> First, all aspects of life are conducted in the same place and under the same single authority. Second, each phase of the member's daily activity is carried on in the immediate company of a large batch of others, all of whom are treated alike and required to do the same thing together. Third, all phases of the day's activities are tightly scheduled, with one activity leading at a prearranged time into the next, the whole sequence of activities being imposed from above by a system of explicit formal rulings and a body of officials. Finally, the various enforced activities are brought together into a single rational plan purportedly designed to fulfil the official aims of the institution.

Though I do not maintain that competitive, institutionalized teamsport *is* a total institution (athletes do have the legal freedom to quit sport), I borrow Goffman's concept, and argue that sport approximates a "near-total" institution. This is because, much like the military, sport uses myths of glory, patriotism, and masculine idolatry, along with corporeal discipline and structures of rank, division, uniform, rules, and punishment in order to suppress individual agency and construct a fortified ethos of masculine cooperation (Britton and Williams 1995; Woodward 2000).

When individual athletes' thoughts are aligned with those of their teammates, they are given social prestige and are publicly lauded. Athletes who toe the line are honored by their institutions and celebrated by fans and their community (Bissinger 1990). Hughes and Coakley (1991: 311) say, "Athletes find the action and their experiences in sport so exhilarating and thrilling that they want to continue participating as long as possible." Coakley (1998: 155) adds, "… they love their sports and will do almost anything to stay involved." Thus, it is understandable that from the perspective of an athlete, particularly a good athlete, sport is a socially positive vessel. And while I think that the reasons athletes will do almost anything to remain within teamsport are more complicated than just the thrill one receives from playing them, the point remains that athletes who withstand the selection process do so because of both their outstanding athletic ability *and* their willingness to conform to the role of "an athlete."

In conforming to the norms and excelling in sport, athletes limit whom they befriend. They shut out other cultural influences that might open their consciousness to new ways of thinking, and they are therefore less exposed to those who do not fit orthodox sporting requisites (Robidoux 2001). This is particularly true the further athletes progress in their sporting careers. For example, men who spend their formative years in competitive teamsport are much less likely to meet gay men, feminized men, and other types of men who do not fit the jock model. Similarly, men who spend their formative years in competitive teamsport are sheltered from understanding women's athleticism and leadership capabilities. They are sometimes even challenged to get to know women as friends; instead, women remain on the sidelines, sexually objectified and socially demonized for their femininity.

Women who spend their formative years in competitive sport learn a similar masculine ethos. They learn to do what they are told. Is this not why Kallella and her teammates failed to stand up to their abusive coach? Conversely, athletes who do not adhere to the sporting ethic are sanctioned by verbal insults and are less likely to be given valued playing positions within sport. "Failing" to meet the formal and informal norms of sport generally results in one being told that she is not a team player. This is a mark of shame that is likely to drive nonconformists away from the sporting terrain.

In Goffman's studies of mental hospitals, he celebrated accounts of inmate resistance. I concur. I appreciate students who fake an illness to be removed from physical education, for example. I am proud of these students because they are finding creative ways to utilize their agency to defy a system of tightly structured rules. They are using their agency to escape an oppressive environment. This is why I think learning to rebel is important in children. It is important for kids to learn to say "no" to their parents, teachers and coaches. We must learn to enact our agency if we are to ward off damage that can be caused by oppressive social environments – like sport. One wonders if Ben and his friends had not grown up playing sport, whether they might not have stood up to the team's older players, refusing to allow them to hit their heads with wooden paddles. The reason they permitted this is complicated, but it has to do with desiring to be one of the boys.

From an early age, athletes befriend each other, on and off the field. Their social lives are routinely dictated by a rigid schedule of athletic practices, competitions, and other team functions. Teamsport athletes report that the further they move up through the ranks, the less freedom exists to inhabit any social space outside this network, and the more their identity narrows in order to be competitive with other men (Nixon 1994; Robidoux 2001). By the time most athletes get to university, their social lives normally revolve around their team membership. Athletes train together, play together, live together, party together, and travel together. Thus, the collective policing of their lives inside of sport is reflected in athletes' social lives, too.

The near-total institutional aspects of sport are nicely complimented by the governor of most sporting programs (particularly in America) – schools. One can see why school administrators like sport. Schools are faced with a difficult challenge: they must hold captive and attempt to teach a large population, often comprised of students who do not wish to be there. Accordingly, schools must socialize students to become somewhat obedient and submissive to authority. Schools seem to partially mirror the operations of a prison. In order to function efficiently, they exercise control and regimentation over their students. Sometimes this means that they control what might seem to be inconsequential behaviors, like what students are permitted to wear to school, how they fashion their hair, or whether they are allowed to have piercings or visible tattoos. Just as with sport and the military, this is done with the intent of minimizing individual differences and promoting reliance on the authority structure of the school (Miracle and Rees 1994).

Applying all of this to sport, I suggest that having a master identity of "athlete" makes it all the more difficult for athletes to break from the gendered ideology embedded in the athletic institutions that they earned their identities from (Messner 1987). And centering one's identity on athleticism carries risks. This is because sport is a volatile field, where careers end on poor plays. Athletes can, at a moment's notice, be cut from a team. In fact, as an athlete, the only thing that one can be assured of is that one's career *will* end. And, relative to other occupations, it will do so very early. Thus, whether an athlete suddenly loses their association with their athletic identity, or their body ages out of competitive form, all athletes must disengage with competitive sport. And when this happens, they are generally no longer valued in the sport setting (Messner 1987).

The Role of the Coach in Reproducing Sport as a Near-Total Institution

Not all men and women wishing to join a sports team will put up with such abuse. However, those who see things differently, those who are less likely to crave the peer recognition and social promotion that sport provides, and those who are less likely to put team expectations before their individual health, are not likely to be chosen for a team. Conversely, those who sacrifice their individual agency and contribute to the reproduction of a rigid sporting culture are more likely to be chosen for the next level of play. Of particular concern here is that this virtually necessitates that those who aspire to the next level of sport must publicly disengage with any notion that is inconsistent with the athletic mantra.

Those who drop out, are forced out, or otherwise do not make the next level of sport often find themselves detached from the prestige they once enjoyed – something sport psychologists call the disengagement effect (Greendorfer 1992). Athletes who rode atop the social hierarchy feel the greatest loss upon disengaging from that elite status. So, for those with no further opportunity to play competitive sport, coaching becomes one of the few alternative venues for returning to the game. This coaching recruitment model means that sport almost always draws coaches, managers and other leaders from those who over-conformed to the previous cohort's ideals, something perceived to give them expertise as coaches (Anderson 2007).

These individuals have had almost entirely positive sporting experiences and therefore hold unqualified acceptance of, and an unquestioned commitment to, its value systems (Hughes and Coakley 1991). As a result, the authoritarian method of coaching is viewed as a necessary part of sport, "to get the best out of athletes" (Kelly and Waddington 2006). As coaches, these ex-athletes rely upon narratives that promote their individual experience in order to inspire a new generation of youth into a similar ethos.

Playing a specific sport before coaching certainly authenticates a coach. The more successful one's abilities as an athlete, the more competent he or she is assumed to be as a coach (Lyle 2002). In other words, athletes tend to think that a world champion athlete would make a better coach than a second-string athlete. This is because it is assumed that the journey one takes to become the world's greatest necessitates having as much intellectual mastery over the sport as physical. For example, one of my students told me that he truly liked his coach, until learning that his coach did not actually play football (soccer). "I mean I really liked the guy, he had studied the sport and knew what he was doing; but once we [the team] found out he had not played, he got no respect ... It's like if you haven't bled for the sport, you can't know it."

This, "I did it, so you can too" narrative serves several functions. First, it prevents those not weaned on a particular sport from coaching it, and it also influences the system to forgo a more rigorous manner for judging the abilities of a coach. This system limits the awareness, observations, or formally learned ways of thinking that others might bring to the field. Furthermore, if a coach learns to coach via how he or she was coached, does this not make the system ripe for reproducing errors? Finally, this system limits the agency of athletes, because coaches can negate their players protest with, "I played professional and you have not."

Making the transmission of poor coaching practices easier, coaching positions (public or private), at almost all levels, require no university degree in coaching pedagogy, sport psychology, or physical education. Certainly, one needs a bachelor's degree in physical education in order to teach physical education courses, but one does not need a bachelor's in physical education in order to coach. While many organizations and institutions may require coaching certification courses, they are generally not substantive of good coaching practices. Most of these workshops are concerned with litigation – teaching coaches how to avoid getting their institutions sued. Programs that talk about coaching at a more practical level tend to be focused on the basic motor skills and tactics of the sport. I cannot speak for all of these, but my experience, in talking to my students who earn coaching certificates in a variety of sports in England, suggests that they are vastly insufficient programs. They do not address sport as a complex field where identities, as well as bodies, are in peril. They do not address tactics and strategies for developing human beings; instead the focus remains on how to train and compete for victory while avoiding lawsuit.

The fact that individuals are merited for overly conforming to the sporting ethos; that they develop their identities as "athletes" first (which then influences them to further pursue their athletic careers); that these athletes will, sooner as opposed to later, be forced out of their sport, means that they look to find sporting value – to align their personal identity with their occupation – by looking for occupation in the sporting industry. In doing this, they reproduce the ethos of sport, including the various forms of violence, that goes along with sport. Sadly, coaches who abuse their athletes excel in this. Let me explain.

I once had one of the nation's top 3,000 meter runners compete for my high school team. This runner earned himself a scholarship to run for one of the best cross-country programs in the United States. Here, we soon realized just why the coach had such a successful team. He yearly hired (through the mechanism of scholarships) four of the fastest graduating high school runners in the country. Considering that university athletes compete for four years, this means that at any given point he had 16 top-notch athletes on his team. He then runs these athletes into the ground, doubling their training load. When athletes protest, he showers them with narratives of "not being a quitter" and of "sacrificing for one's team." Inevitably, his approach suckers 16 (or more) young athletes into risking their health, and this inevitably leaves a trail of broken and battered bodies behind.

Out of this malady, however, five of his 16 athletes survive and positively respond to the training. Because only five athletes score in a race, he consistently has a winning program. In other words, he willingly risks all of his athletes' health in order to produce five runners that help him win national championship titles. The system continues for several reasons. First, everybody sees the victories and few see the carnage in their wake. Second, athletes who figure the system out and decide to quit become brandished as quitters or losers. This adds pressure for them to remain within the abusive system. Third, all athletes on the team (injured or not) get a sense of the glory that his winning five players receive (as the "team" wins), and they are therefore influenced to take the chance on his training in order to achieve the same personal glory, and to reproduce the collective team glory.

In short, this abusive system works. Proving this, the coach is widely known as being one of the greatest in the country. He is routinely promoted to higher paying salaries for his "efforts." Thus, this coach has learned to secure personal gain through the abuse of others. He is permitted to do so because the ethos of sport encourages this type of violence. The athletes fail to stand up for themselves because they have been trained to follow the coach's orders, and to sacrifice at all costs in order to win. Sadly, when this coach someday retires, a coach who thinks in more humanistic terms will not be hired. Instead, he will recommend that his assistant coach take over, so that the program can "continue with the tradition of success."

Of concern here is that socializing youth into a violent ethos of sporting culture may have serious implications for the symbolic and physical violence that people commit against not only themselves, but against others. Concerning harm against one's self (overtraining, playing with injuries, accepting a coach's emotional or physical abuse, or harming one's body through diet or drugs in order to achieve better performance), I problematize the argument that athletes willingly accept these risks when they agree to play. Playing is often socially forced upon youth through physical education, and kids are nearly compelled culturally to play sport in order to fit in with their peers. This socialization may also, however, lead athletes to learn to accept transferring that violence onto others, inside and/or outside of sport. I begin this discussion with the point at which many players become members of their team, hazing/initiation rituals.

The Role of Peers and Hazing in the Near-Total Institution

Dominant expectations of sporting character maintain that athletes should be tough, strong, aggressive, courageous, and able to withstand pain (Allan and De Angelis 2004; Connell 1995; Kivel 1999). To this extent, the very definition of "athlete" is predicated upon these characteristics. As previously stated, Hughes and Coakley (1991) suggest that strict conformity to the sport ethic is both learned and idolized in competitive teamsport. Here, athletes are expected to pay the price thought necessary for victory – playing with pain, taking risks, challenging limits, over-conforming to rigid and sometimes exploitative team norms, sacrificing other social and academic endeavors, and doing as one is told – are all behaviors that are thought to be socio-positive markers of appropriate sacrifice.

Hazing initiations may have several purposes for teamsport players (purposes that are likely to differ slightly from hazing among fraternity and military men), but above all, they mirror – in one event – the sacrifice and subordination that existing team members expect of new members throughout a season of play. Hazing initiations serve as a test of an individual's willingness to adapt to a near agentic-less state, according to power structures of team leadership (Kirby and Wintrup 2002). Hazing corporally structures some as leaders (with coercive and reward power), and others as docile followers in thought and action.

Historically, sport represents a hierarchy where deference to authority and sacrifice of self is commonplace. Here, power and status is earned through seniority, athletic ability, social prominence, and affiliation with the team. This creates a superior-inferior dichotomy in which those with years of experience possess the greatest power and privilege, and recruits (new members) hold the least (Allan and

De Angelis 2004; Messner 1992). The endorsement of hazing within the institution of sport serves to emphasize this power (Trota and Johnson 2004). As Allan and De Angelis (2004) write, "Players who are in power have risen to that status by proving themselves the most masculine" (p. 73). This matriculation process starts with proving oneself in hazing initiations.

Hazing occurs in multiple sporting institutions – from recreational levels of youth sport, through university levels of play – for a variety of social control purposes (Kirby and Wintrup 2002). For example, Donnelly and Young (1988) elucidate how initiations serve as a socialization process to shape the identities of recruits into a form that suits the team's subculture by galvanizing their identities around a common experience (Bryshun 1997). Kirby and Wintrup (2002) support this, suggesting that the main purpose of hazing initiations is to "grow the team" with only those that are like-minded; those who are willing to share team norms, values, attitudes and behaviors.

Accordingly, the process of initiation rituals presents the opportunity for recruits to prove their commitment to the team, and for veteran members to gauge how successfully recruits have been socialized into adopting the behaviors and attitudes of the team's subculture (Bryshun 1997). The extent to which athletes are accepted on a team is often determined by their compliance with and adoption of the team ethic (Young 1983). If recruits are able to demonstrate appropriate roles and behaviors, they are more likely to be accepted and welcomed as a worthy member of the team (Donnelly and Young 1988).

The consequence of an unsuccessful initiation, or a resistance to the tasks being asked of recruits, often results in veteran members coercing and punishing recruits by socially isolating or excluding them, ostracizing them, or even physically abusing them (Robinson 1998). This humiliation and isolation is usually more intense and enduring than the humiliation experienced in the initiation itself (Holman 2004). Thus, this creates the perception that recruits freely choose to be initiated (Holman 2004). Considering the two options, the hazing experience is normally regarded as the lesser of two evils, culturally compelling recruits to submit their agency and undergo initiation. Furthermore, by deferring to veterans in the hazing process, recruits reaffirm veterans as the holders of power (Holman 2004).

The diminishment of recruits acts as a form of intimidation that coerces others to accept the autocracy and inequality of the team's structure. Hazing initiations therefore become an avenue through which this power structure is maintained and seasonally reproduced. Recruits who have been hazed are less likely to pose a threat to the power structure because they have (in seasons past) conformed to the group by obeying orders and placing themselves in compromising positions, for the perceived good of the group (Allan and De Angelis 2004).

The most common rationale for athletic hazing initiations, however, is that they are a key means of creating team cohesion, which is believed to be an element critical to team success (Bryshun and Young 1999); although the literature is inconsistent concerning the relationship between team cohesion and performance (Hardy, Eys, and Carron 2005). Literature on hazing also varies on whether hazing promotes group unity (Allan and Madden 2008). Nonetheless, athletes are largely convinced that initiations succeed in promoting legitimate bonds among team members.

Recruits often describe the experience of hazing initiations as a positive bonding experience between friends (Bryshun 1997; Feist *et al.* 2004). And, because hazing initiations are believed to create team cohesion, it is thereby assumed that the more extreme a hazing initiation is, the greater the level of commitment and interdependency that is established. In other words, by completing the extreme tasks asked of them, recruits are demonstrating just how far they are prepared to go for the team (Holman 2004).

So just how far are athletes willing to go? Violent acts of physical risk are particularly common in highly masculinized sport. This is designed to test recruits' willingness and ability to tolerate pain and take bodily risks for the sake of team and victory. The severity of these acts sometimes escalates to cause hospitalization, and on occasion, fatalities.

Deviant behaviors are also common in initiations. These serve to test recruits' willingness to take risks, obey those higher in the power hierarchy, and compel athletes to conform to team norms. For example, Hoover (1999) identifies how many of the National Collegiate Athletic Association (NCAA) athletes interviewed in his study were "forced to commit crimes – destroying property, making prank phone calls and harassing others" (p. 1). Highlighting this, in 2009 hockey recruits at Cardiff University in Wales were given a list of items that they were to steal from throughout the city in order to demonstrate unqualified acceptance of, and unquestioned commitment to, a value system framed by the sport ethic.

An excessive consumption of alcohol occurs in about half of US hazing incidents (Nuwer 2004). In one national study of US university hazing incidents, 23 percent of recruits drank to the point of being sick or passing out (Allan and Madden 2008). Alcohol acts as a dis-inhibitor (for both hazers and recruits), permitting an escalation of activities to occur (Robinson 1998).

But in the UK, recruits are regularly urged to consume vast quantities of alcohol, or suffer social punishment for not doing so. This is easier in the UK because public alcohol consumption is legal at 18. And, just as in the US, heavy drinking is also considered indicative of masculine accomplishment (Gough and Edwards 1998; Graham and Wells 2003). Here, the body's ability to endure and withstand the effects of heavy alcohol is considered a masculinizing "achievement" (Peralta 2007). Of course, this is a recipe for bodily injury, and occasionally death (Salkeld 2008; Sutton 2008). Interestingly, in Britain, women in my classes now report drinking as much as the men.

Finally, same-sex sexual behaviors serve the purpose of humiliating, feminizing, and homosexualizing male recruits, in order to establish and reaffirm their position at the bottom of the team's heteromasculine hierarchy. At the most extreme, several episodes of anal rape (usually with objects) have been reported in hazing episodes. For example, in 1998 the recruits of an American high school wrestling team were anally raped with a mop handle by senior wrestlers on the team (Finkel 2002). And in 2003, three varsity American football players were arrested after sodomizing recruits with broom sticks, golf balls, and pine cones.

One wonders how young players learn to enjoy such sadistic acts. One also wonders why, when a group of men begins gang rape, none try to stop the sexual violence? I'm sure these are much more complex problems than I can address here. However, I do wonder if we do not learn to accept acts of violence in sport. I question whether violent teamsport does not desensitize us to violence, and perhaps even teach us to use it.

Learning Violence

It is not easy to "prove" that the aggression taught in certain sports is directly related to violence "off the field." It is possible, for example, that violent people are attracted to sport, meaning that sport has not taught them such violence. But the way I personally measure the evidence, sport seems to have a key role in socializing youth (particularly males) into solving problems, getting their way, or earning respect through violence.

One way of measuring the outcome of a socialization into teamsport and violence comes with the research of Shields *et al.* (1995). These researchers presented fictional accounts of moral dilemmas, including violence in sport, to high school and college students (athletes and non-athletes). These dilemmas included questions as to whether, for example, Tom should follow his football coach's instructions to intentionally injure another player in order to promote the team's chances of winning. Most athletes felt that some violence was part of the game, and few expressed empathy for the recipient of the violence. Overall, results suggest that athletes tend to justify aggressive behaviors, especially when compared to the approach of non-athletes. Again, it is difficult to attribute this to sport. But one thing is for certain, sport does not teach youth to abhor violence. Instead, it teaches them to accept violence as "just part of the game."

Supporting the role of competitive teamsport in promoting violence, in a four-year study on US military academy students, Krause and Priest (1993) measured students with pen and paper survey tests on moral reasoning and moral behavior. At the end of the students' four years, they surveyed them again. The results found a decrease in ethical value choices over the four-year period. Of particular interest, intercollegiate team athletes scored lower than athletes of individual sports, or athletes who played on intramural sports. This highlights that teamsport reduced ethical climates among these participants. Similarly, Rudd and Stoll (2004) compared college athletes to non-athletes at all US divisions of collegiate sport play (595 participants). Here, non-athlete women scored best, followed by non-athlete men, followed by individual sport athletes (women then men) and at the bottom were male teamsport athletes. More recently, in 2007 the Josephson Institute in Los Angeles surveyed 5,275 high school athletes on ethical issues. Forty-seven percent of the boys believed it was okay to illegally push others in basketball and 42 percent thought it was okay to trash talk an opposing player. Girls, meanwhile, are about half as likely to boo, taunt, or jeer opponents (Hyman 2009).

In a more telling experiment concerning sport and altruism, Kleiber and Roberts (1981) conducted an experiment with 54 ten- and eleven-year-old kids. In order to test them on sport's supposed character-building properties, the children were randomly assigned to one of two groups. One group played a game of soccer for two weeks, and the other group (a control group) did not. In order to mimic proper teamsport, the kids in the soccer-playing group were divided into two teams, scores were kept, and at the end of the two-week trial one team was announced the winner. Because the children of both groups were measured on a social behaviorial scale, both before and after the two-week exercise, the study effectively examined for the influence of organized sport on character building. The results? There was no substantial change for girls. However, boys who played in sport scored lower on a measure of altruism. In other words, the boys became more rivalrous after playing sport. Furthermore, quarrelling occurred frequently, as did crying due to perceived failure in front of one's peers, and one fight broke out between two of the boys over a sport-related matter.

Finally, let us not forget the violence that athletes inflict upon themselves. In one three-year study (1989) of high school football, basketball, and wrestling conducted by the National Athletic Trainers Association in America (including 3,200 high schools) it was found that 1.3 million injuries per year were found to occur in the US (cited in Miracle and Rees 1994). Twenty-two percent of the boys and 23 percent of the girls who played basketball (for example) were injured each year. Now, most of these injuries were minor, but a quarter of them resulted in athletes not participating for more than a week. These statistics also show that the chances of needing surgery (per year) is 1 in 90 for girls basketball, 1 in 128 for boys basketball, and that American football results in 24 fatalities a year. Sport, it would seem, is a violent place.

Violence as "Part of the Game"

When sport sociologists discuss violence in sport, we normally draw distinctions between legitimate and illegitimate violence. Legitimate violence, for example, is the violence that is necessary to collide with a catcher in baseball, so that a runner might score a run. Illegitimate violence occurs in purposeful fouls against an opponent: committing an act prohibited by the rules of the sport. What is odd, however, is that both types of violence are supported in sport. Sport naturalizes these types of violence as being a natural outcome of the game. Thus, physical assaults are played out on sporting pitches and fields across nations.

Here, athletes are taught that it is better to foul an opponent than permit him to score a goal. In American baseball, for example, pitchers are sometimes encouraged to throw a brush-back pitch, one that comes dangerously close to the batter in order to back him away from the plate. At other times, pitchers are actually encouraged to hit the batter, sacrificing a base, rather than letting the hitter score a run. In this manner, the structure of the sport (the need for one's team to win) creates the culture of the sport (acceptable violence). It essentially institutionalizes, sanctions, and normalizes violence. This is something that is quite visible in the employment of goons in American hockey (large players with the specific job of beating up players from other teams). This violence is accepted because we are socialized into it as "just part of the game." Accordingly, Messner (2002) suggests that the aggression in sport is naturalized, ubiquitous, and all-inclusive. Is this what we mean when we say that sport builds character?

Bredemeier and Shields (1995) define four dimensions of character that sport allegedly generates among players: compassion, fairness, sportsmanship and integrity. You could probably think of a host of other describing words to compliment good character: civility, courage, honesty, responsibility, respect, etc. But when it comes to assessing how good a job coaches do in teaching these qualities through the medium of sport, we fail – and we fail miserably. Athletes are not interviewed about these factors at the end of a season of play; nor are they generally asked to rate their coaches on such matters. Even if a team is fortunate enough to rate their coach, these ratings are not used in a formal system for hiring and firing coaches between institutions. Employers do not look at the performance of a coach's athletes on university attendance, or measures of their self-esteem, or other indicators of the "character" coaches are supposed to have inculcated in their players in the coaching process. Instead, all evaluation comes from "success." Winning remains not just the benchmark for judging the "quality" of a coach, but the only category of importance. Accordingly, some famously violent coaches are fired for violence, only to be rehired elsewhere because of their winning record.

Worse, when coaches win, they are permitted more freedom to exploit their athletes' fears of social rejection, of being denied playing time, or not making the team the following season, which in turn helps the coach win further matches. "Sacrifice" (defined here as violence against the self for the sake of the team) becomes part of the game, as athletes (particularly those with low self-esteem or poor social support networks) are willing to risk their health because they are overly eager to be accepted by their coach and peers. Thus, coaches frequently push athletes too far and often knowingly have them play with injuries. In fact, research shows that over 80 percent of the men and women in top-level intercollegiate sport in the US sustain at least one serious injury while playing their sport, and nearly 70 percent are disabled for two or more weeks (Edwards 2006).

Accepted Acts of Grievous Bodily Injury

Sometimes, illegitimate violence breaks the structure of sport itself. Players of all ages and levels often attack one another with fists and sporting equipment. Sometimes even parents attack each other while watching their eight-year-old kids play. But while these types of violence are ostensibly looked down upon with a slow head-shaking of disgust, most of this violence is nonetheless condoned, and sometimes encouraged, by the ethos of sport.

There is no shortage of team brawls. Simply type "soccer brawl" or "sports brawl" into YouTube.com and you can watch hours of (mostly men) battering the hell out of each other. In fact, just last night I saw a clip of a (staggering) ten-minute team brawl in a college game of lacrosse in the US. The news reported that a total of 173 minutes of penalty time was handed out to the various players (no jail time, nobody kicked off a team, no coach fired). This prompts me to ask, why is it that when two groups of men fight on the street it's called a gang fight (and men are arrested), but when two groups of men fight on the field, it's called a team brawl and the only punishment is 173 minutes of penalties?

Just as we accept assaulting another player with a weapon (striking a batter, or an illegal check in ice hockey), we mostly condone team fights, too. We permit grievous bodily injury to occur in sport, because (as some of my students say) it *is* sport. This attitude perplexes me. Why can one get away with committing acts of grievous bodily injury in one context, but not another? For example, I taught high school health in California years ago. I also coached a bit of soccer at the same school. Here, I was amazed that if one student punched another in my class, he would be suspended from school for a week or expelled from the school outright. However, on the soccer field, if this same student punched another student, he would only be given a "red card," meaning that he had to sit out a game. Are these fair and adequate punishments? Does it matter whether little Johnny got his nose broken because he said something to a kid on the soccer pitch as opposed to the school's hallways? And is there not a message of support that we send to kids when we permit athletes to behave so violently, without consequence?

If we were serious about eliminating such violence, players would be treated the same on the field as off. If I were to punch a colleague of mine at work, I would be fired – and arrested. If coaches, managers, and those who own professional teams were serious about athletes ceasing to be violent (at youth or professional levels), they would exercise their power to kick players off their teams when they commit violence – and we would call the police and have them arrested for their illegitimate violence as well.

However, I figured out, long ago, that those who own and control professional sport rather enjoy the violence. It likely helps them fill seats in their arenas. When I was eight, my father took me to my first (and last) professional hockey match. I was rooting for one of the Los Angeles Kings players, until he proceeded to punch another guy out. I was horrified at the violence of it all. I told my father that he should be kicked off the team. I asked my dad why they permit fighting and he responded, "They don't, he was given a penalty." But even at eight, I knew that if the National Hockey League really wanted to stop fighting in the sport, the rules would be one hit and you're out, for life. Athletes certainly wouldn't batter each other if they were going to lose their multimillion dollar contracts for doing such. And, if professional athletes stopped their battering, perhaps younger athletes might stop modeling their behavior on professional athletes as well (something known as the trickle down hypothesis). It is hard to expect kids not to fight in sport, when their heroes do.

Violence outside of Sports Parameters

Research on sport and violence outside the sporting parameters goes back several decades. For example, in research on youth hockey in Canada, it was found that the longer a kid played hockey, the more they accepted cheating, and the more they felt that the expression of violent behavior was both legitimate and expected by the coach (Vaz 1972). Accordingly, they were more likely to use illegal tactics in their play. This research was later replicated by using adult hockey players (Bloom and Smith 1996). Here, older players in highly competitive select leagues were more likely to approve of violence and to act violently in other social settings than were younger select-league players, house-league players, and non-players of all ages.

In another study of ice hockey players, young athletes expressed that it was important to fight, and that fighting was only problematic when it resulted in excessive penalties for the team (Smith 1975). Supporting this research, sport psychologist John Silva (1983) used slides of athletes committing violence against each other to measure the acceptance of this violence between athletes and non-athletes. Perhaps unsurprisingly, of the 203 university students he studied, boys rated the violence as acceptable more than girls, but also, those with more involvement in sport rated the violence as less problematic than those with less involvement in organized sport. He concluded that involvement in sport (again, particularly for men) encourages athletes to see dangerous acts of physical violence as legitimate in sport.

The hypothesis that sport violence carries over into violence away from sport is hard to prove or disprove. To date, there have simply not been enough studies on this. Some studies, like that of Wacquant (1995) on boxers, suggest that sport can teach men to control their violence. Other studies (Bloom and Smith 1996), however, suggest that when male athletes have years of experience in competitive sport they are more likely than recreational athletes to approve of off-the-field violence, and to use violence when they play sport that is not their primary sport.

The best evidence comes from Kreager (2007) who uses the American National Longitudinal Study of Adolescent Health on over 90,000 youth. Because the study also asks for other information (such as sport affiliation) Kreager is able to select men who play football, basketball, baseball, wrestling, and tennis to examine for violence. He finds that football and wrestling (the only contact sports in the study) are positively associated with male serious fighting, compared to those who play individual sports. This effect is mediated by peer football participation, such that embeddedness in all-football networks (near-total institution) substantially increases the risk for serious fighting.

In talking with Ben from the opening vignette, he tells me that he has been in a few fights on the rugby pitch as well. I therefore return to the question as to whether Ben learned to solve his problems with violence in rugby; wondering if that is why he pushed the girl? Does sport not only teach men to take their sporting violence outside of sport, but can it teach them to use that violence against women, too?

Men's Violence against Women

It is not just violence against men that I discuss here. Carry-over is not just germane to same-sex violence. Male teamsport participation may also be *at least partially* responsible for the promotion of violence against women. When examining violence of men against women, it is theorized that the anti-feminine, sexist and misogynistic attitudes that are socialized into male athletes (Muir and Seitz 2004), might spill over into actual violence against women.

Indeed, male teamsport athletes have been shown to objectify women – often viewing them as sexual objects to be conquered (Schacht 1996). Kreager (2007) suggests that this socialization of men into teamsport might also influence symbolic, domestic, and public violence against women. Explicating this, in Jill Neimark's *Out of Bounds: The Truth About Athletes and Rape*, teamsport athletes from highly masculinized teams (football, basketball, and lacrosse) were responsible for gang rape in second highest number, behind fraternities. Furthermore, Crosset and his colleagues (1995) show that while student athletes make up only 3.7 percent of the men at Division 1 universities, they are responsible for 19 percent of sexual assault reports to campus Judicial Affairs offices. Crosset (2000) has also shown that football, basketball and hockey players are responsible for 67 percent of the sexual assaults reported by student athletes, although they only comprise 30 percent of the student athlete populace.

These findings are complicated by a number of variables, and do not in and of themselves prove that competitive teamsport athletes commit more violence against women. It is also hard to put a finger on teamsport participation, because most youths play teamsport at some time. Of course, one undocumented concern I maintain is that even if teamsport athletes are not responsible for elevated rates of violence against women, their propensity to inflict harm when they are violent is raised through their muscularity, and ability to block pain – something sport does teach.

Violence against One's Own Body

We seldom look at injuries in sport as the result of receiving "violence." However, there certainly is a tremendous amount of injury that is promoted, albeit not intentionally, in sport. This is not just in teamsport either. Certainly, the physical pounding required in American football, rugby, or even baseball can be hazardous to one's health. But in my own sport, that of distance running, going too far, too soon (particularly on concrete) leads to short-term injuries. Running excessive miles (say more than 40 per week) can even lead to life-long knee and hip injures. Overuse injuries in sport are so common that they have become an accepted part of playing sport. Since 2007, the American Academy of Paediatrics has been so worried about the issue that they have issued three policy statements on overuse injuries in children.

Much of this is the fault of parents, and the pressures they place on children. Hyman (2009: 66) quotes the chief of sports medicine at the University of California, Los Angeles as saying, "Little League shoulder, tennis elbow, you don't see it unless kids are in organized sport." This is not just boys' sport either. In her (1996) book *Little Girls in Pretty Boxes*, Joan Ryan discusses the influence of parental and adult pressures on girls in gymnastics and figure skating: stress fractures, torn ACL ligaments, tendonitis, etc. The point is that thirteen-year-old kids should not be popping ibuprofen along with their chewable vitamins.

However, the most under-scrutinized aspect of competitive sport comes in our absolute and total failure (as a society) to critically examine and prevent trauma to the head. When we think of life-long, debilitating and deadly head trauma, we tend to think of the sport of boxing. We falsely assume that the helmets worn in American football protect one from head trauma – they do not. I once heard it put that helmets do a good job of holding the head together in an accident, but they do not prevent the brain from slamming against the skull, which scrambles the inside of the brain. Perhaps you have heard car accidents described similarly. A car accident is really three crashes; your car hitting another car, your body hitting the car, and then your organs hitting your body. It is the last crash that kills you. This is the case with sport that requires using the head (and this includes heading the ball in soccer).

Chronic traumatic encephalopathy is a progressive neurological disorder found in people who have suffered brain trauma. It has many of the same symptoms as Alzheimer's, in that it begins with behavioral and personality changes, is followed by disinhibition and irritability, before the individual moves into dementia. It takes a long time for the initial trauma to give rise to nerve-cell breakdown and death, but chronic traumatic encephalopathy is not the result of an endogenous disease. It is the result of injury.

At first, we believed that this type of damage was caused by concussions, and there are plenty of concussions in sport – in the US alone there are over 60,000 reported concussions in high school sport – but research in the Clinical Journal of Sport Medicine (McCrea *et al.* 2004) shows that less than half of football players who receive a concussion report it. And because most university athletes who receive concussions see the team's physician, there is often pressure on this physician to clear an athlete to play before it is medically sound. Colvin and colleagues (2009) report that because only about 20 percent of those who receive concussions are aware of it, there are in total between 1 and 4 million concussions per year in America. And it's not just American football or boxing that causes them. In one study of British soccer players aged 12 to 17 it was found that 47.8 percent of the athletes experienced a concussion in that year of study alone. On average, this means that a player is likely to experience a concussion every other year (Delaney *et al.* 2008). But the study also found that of those who experienced a concussion that year, 69 percent had experienced more than one that same year, indicating that certain players are more prone to use their heads in dangerous ways than others. Women were even more prone to concussion in soccer.

In recent research carried out on soccer players (Colvin *et al.* 2009) it was found that, among youth aged 8 to 24, those with at least one concussion perform worse on neurocognitive testing than those without. More so, women who report the same amount of concussion as men, do even worse than men on these tests. Thus, gender may account for significant differences in post-concussive neurocognitive test scores in soccer players and may play a role in determining recovery. These differences do not appear to reflect differences in mass between genders and may be related to other gender-specific factors that deserve further study.

Concussions are a dangerous norm in many sports. Football, ice hockey, lacrosse, and rugby all report similar rates of concussion (Delaney *et al.* 2008). I must point out that while much literature points out that many youth suffer from deficits in verbal and visual memory as a result of concussions, and certainly athletes die from them as well, others find no relation between concussions and ill-effects (Collie *et al.* 2006). The problem with these studies is that they test for short-term effects – not long-term ones.

In terms of long-term effects, it is no longer just concussions that we fear in causing serious trauma, but much smaller jars that go unnoticed – hits that are simply part of the game – that may also cause long-term problems. It is, of course, difficult to sort out what the affect of smaller hits is, because most athletes will have also suffered larger hits. When discussing NFL players, neuropathologist Bennet Omalu says, "There is something wrong with this group as a cohort" (Gladwell 2009: 3). This is a new "understanding" in the sport of American football, and hard evidence from deceased football players has only been documented since 2002. However, in one player (just 18 years old), a researcher found that his brain resembled that of a person older than 50. This same researcher says that this type of damage occurs in every single deceased American football player's brain that he sees. Kevin Guskiewicz, at the University of North Carolina, uses sensory pads in players' helmets in order to measure how much impact the brain of a football lineman takes. He shows that in one season of play, it can take well over 1,000 impacts, suggesting that this causes permanent brain damage (Gladwell 2009).

Sport that requires full contact, like American football and rugby, may be to blame for a host of other problems as well. Anecdotal evidence about professional American football players (who suffer from unimaginable diseases and die decades earlier than non-football players) exists. To this extent, I recommend you read a November 23, 2008 article in the *Winnipeg Free Press*, by Randy Turner, "The Killing Field: Pro football offers fame and glory, but the price is terrible," accessible at www.winnipegfreepress.com/life/The_Killing_Field.html. The first time I read it, I arrived at my lecture (aged 40) stood on top of a desk, jumped off the desk, landed and bounced back up into the air. "I'm 40," I told my students, "but I can shake my hips on the dance floor and I can still outrun any of you from the mile to the marathon. You see, that is what exercise (in my case running) *can* do for you – if you do the right exercise in the right amounts. Sport that requires us to collide our bodies, however; well, that's an entirely different matter, isn't it?" I then read to them a selection from the article:

> … But it was the final year of his [46 year old] life that was the hardest. Benjamin was in kidney failure, taking dialysis treatments four times a week. The soft-spoken giant who played [American football] with the [Canadian Teams] Bombers and Ottawa Rough Riders from 1985 to 1993 was deteriorating in front of his family's eyes. And only his family's eyes. After all, the fans don't see what happens after the final whistle blows and they turn off the lights. "They just watch the game" [his wife said]. But when you live with somebody, you see it … "Near the end, it killed me," Debbie Benjamin said, "He was absolutely depressed. To see somebody that was a big, burly football

player crawling on his hands and knees up the stairs, or getting up to go to the bathroom in the middle of the night and falling down and crawling to the toilet, it was heart-wrenching ..." Last August, at age 46, Nick Benjamin died of kidney failure. But Debbie ruefully believes it was an occupational homicide, and points her finger directly at football.

Although the author is careful to discuss the difficulty of acquiring statistics, he gives evidence to the figure that professional football players themselves understand, that they will die on average at age 55, from football-related problems. Turner says:

> After all, professional football is the perfect storm of occupational hazards. Think about it: what other occupation involves prolonged and repeated head trauma; the need to carry up to 150 extra pounds for several years; coping with a post-career in the civilized world and aging with the battle wounds that turn joints into sworn enemies and body organs into weakened hosts of disease?

This is ironic – sport (and exercise framed as sport) is supposed to be healthy for us! I recently paid for a sport massage – good money to help undo the damage that my running too hard (much harder than I need for health) has caused. While massaging me, the therapist asked what my book concerned. I responded, "It highlights all of the damage that's caused by sport." She disagreed, expressing that in a society where most people work behind computers, sport was good because it combated sedentary lifestyles. I asked, "Is it sport that we need, or is it simply exercise that we need?" Ironically, she stuck by "sport" as her answer. I do not think that the fact that her profession is repairing broken bodies is what influenced her to this, either. Instead, she views broken bodies as a necessary by-product in the promotion of healthy bodies. It is a hegemonic logic that I do not understand.

Still, all agree that because post-industrial Western culture has removed labor from most occupations – combined with the ease of processed and fast foods that industry has brought – we have seen a steady increase of "disease of lifestyle" in Western cultures. Cardiovascular disease is the top killer in the US, and disease of lifestyle might also contribute to the second leading cause of death, cancer.

Ostensibly, sport certainly is one solution to the ever-broadening cultural waistline. However, one of America's most esteemed sports instead encourages obesity – over half of NFL players are technically obese (as reported in Hyman 2009), and in one *Journal of the American Medical Association* study (Laurson and Eisenmann 2007) 45 percent of high school football linemen in Iowa are shown to be overweight, and another 28 percent are in danger of it and 9 percent are obese. This means that 82 percent of the students in this study are putting on too much weight. Sadly, this behavior is learned early in life. In a 2007 study of football players aged just 9 to 14, 45 percent are either overweight or obese. In other words, kids are being rewarded for being big and overweight in the sport of football, so they will receive the approval of their coaches, parents and peers. This is socially condoned violence.

This violence is only perpetuated because those who play such violent sport are young to begin with. Youth believe they are immune from the affects of the sport, or do not care about the affects because they can't very well imagine themselves being "old" in the first place. They do, however, pay for using their bodies as a weapon. Sadly, when they are in pain, like forgotten war veterans, nobody is there to cheer for them anymore. The allure of sporting glory, the masculine idolatry it brings (mostly men), and the sense of belonging and self-importance that esteemed, competitive teamsport brings to youth, all too often means that two decades later they will sit, in pain, as they watch their kids put through the same glory-making system. At 41, I'd still rather skip watching kids pound their heads together, and instead head out on a ten-mile run. So, I ask, is Ben (from the opening vignette) healthy? Is this why our government invests money into compulsory sport for kids? And wouldn't we all be better off just walking or jogging for fitness instead?

Body Image Disorders

More so (and this is not the case for Ben), what about all those contact sport athletes who are desperately trying to bulk up, or all the female runners who are trying to drop weight? There has been much concern about eating disorders, particularly for women, but increasingly for men as well as a result of the necessity to have a particular body morphology in sport.

Body image refers to a person's individual perception of his or her own body (Grogan 2007). While liking one's body has been linked to positive self-esteem, negative body image has been related to a host of biopsychosocial negatives, including eating disorders (Thompson *et al.* 1999). Poor body image has become endemic within Westernized cultures. In general, women desire a body considerably thinner than their own physique; this drive for thinness is so pervasive as to have been coined the "normative discontent" (Grogan 2007). By contrast, men typically desire additional muscle mass (Thompson and Cafri 2007), a trend described as "The Adonis Complex" (Pope *et al.* 2000). Thus, irrespective of gender, many individuals within contemporary society wish to alter their physiques to achieve a culturally idealized body type.

Due to their ability to generate considerable calorific expenditure, and potentially encourage muscular hypertrophy, exercise and sport provide a means by which a person who is dissatisfied with their body image can work to achieve an idealized body. Indeed, for many people, body image dissatisfaction provides an influential attitudinal antecedent to begin an exercise program. For example, Grogan (2007) found a desire to change body shape was a primary motivation for straight women and gay men to take up a gym membership. Likewise, interviews with (presumably heterosexual) adolescent boys and young men demonstrate that a fear of fat and a desire for hypertrophy is a primary motivation for exercise initiation (Grogan and Richards 2002). Given these trends, it could be concluded that many people partake in competitive (or excessive) physical activity not out of enjoyment or desire for enhanced health but, rather, out of a desire to improve their body image.

This trend is troubling, since those motivated to exercise out of concerns for body image are also those most likely to quit exercise, and are also more likely to exhibit signs of psychopathology, when compared to individuals who commence exercise for health enhancement or for enjoyment (Drummond 2001, 2002; Lindeman 1999; Miller and Jacob 2001). Additionally, individuals who exercise to enhance body image also experience enhanced risk of the development of exercise addiction – a profound psychological dependence and compulsion for exercise, which is similar in phenomenology to a chemical addition (Cockerill 1996).

Despite that general relationship between physical activity and body image, some evidence suggests that competitive sport may enhance body image, or mitigate the importance of body image to some individuals. For example, in a qualitative study of elite gay athletes, Filiault (2009) found these men expressed little concern for body image. That finding is counter to the considerable literature about non-athletic gay men, who generally experience heightened levels of body image dissatisfaction (e.g. Yelland and Tiggemann 2003). Likewise, participation in sport may attenuate the severity of eating disorders symptoms in adolescents (Madison and Ruma 2003). Thus, sporting participation seems to be of benefit for some individuals who are already at risk of eating disorders or body image disturbance.

Although sporting participation may improve (or mitigate the importance of) body image in some athletes, that trend does not hold true for all sporting participants. Indeed, a widespread study of Division I NCAA athletes showed a relatively high rate of disordered eating patterns, with 2.85 percent of female athletes exhibiting subclinical signs of anorexia, and 9.2 percent showing some signs of bulimia. The male athletes demonstrated considerably fewer signs of eating disorders (Johnson *et al.* 1999). These results are corroborated by other studies demonstrating a greater prevalence of eating disorders in elite athletes compared to the general population (Sundgot-Borgen and Torstveit 2004).

Findings such as these demonstrate the potential for some female athletes to develop what has been called the "Female Athletic Triad," which consists of eating disorders, amenorrhea (cessation of menstruation), and osteoporosis (Yeager *et al.* 1993). Due to the constant focus on either achieving or maintaining a prescribed weight goal as a result of sporting participation, compounded by the social pressure to be thin, female athletes are at considerably higher risk of developing the conditions in the Triad than are non-sporting women (Byrne and McLean 2001). Likewise, some groups of male athletes may also be at enhanced risk for eating disorders and dangerous behaviors in the pursuit of an idealized weight, particularly those in sport that utilize weight divisions (Baum 2006). For instance, some of the weight control techniques used by wrestlers are similar to bulimic symptomology, such as laxative use and purging behaviors (Kininham and Gorenflo 2001). Similarly, competitive body builders may engage in disordered eating and use dangerous substances, such as anabolic steroids, in pursuit of an ideal physique (Monaghan 2001).

Thus, although exercise and sport can provide health-related benefits for participants, those benefits very rarely serve as a motivation for non-athletes to initiate an exercise program. Instead, body image often serves as the primary motivator for exercise, which is a dangerous trend given that such a motivation can serve as the antecedent to disordered eating, psychopathology, and exercise addiction. Although for some athletes sport may serve as a psychoprotective factor, in general, athletes – especially female athletes – are at greater risk for eating disorders than are non-athletes. This trend may be reflective of the intense focus athletes must keep on maintaining an ideal body for their athletic pursuits.

Chapter Conclusion

This chapter examined how sport helps socialize us into accepting violence, risk of injury and pain. Using Erving Goffman's notion of a total institution, I explained that kids are socialized into sport from early youth, and that they are taught the socio-positive myths about sport in the process. This helps produce such a strong notion that sport is good, that it prevents us from critically examining the negatives of sport. Even when the negatives are made obvious (like a team fight), we nonetheless manage to defend sport, characterizing those who quit or contest it as not living up to the sport ethos.

If we are to excel at it, the authoritarian lead-decreasing opportunity structure of sport compels us to over-conform to its norms. This leads to a host of socio-negative problems that are directly attributable to sport, like injuries and violence, but it may also influence athletes to spill this violence into arenas outside of sport. Sport might influence men to fight one another outside of sport, and it might also contribute to men's violence against women. It certainly contributes to a variety of eating disorders and multiple other forms of bodily harm in many individuals.

This chapter also discussed the structural mechanisms that help reproduce the socio-negative aspects of sport. This is largely because those athletes who best emulate the sporting creed, over-conforming to taxing norms, are those that are likely to be selected for the next round of competition. Eventually, it is these men and women, those who have spent their youth in sport and developed a master identity around it, that go on to coach. Here, they use their personal narrative to justify the coaching system, reproducing the damage. These coaches teach us to accept injury, because they believe that injury is an inevitable, character-building aspect of sport. They break down our sense of self, withering our agency, realigning our thoughts and actions according to the athlete's creed. Therefore, instead of sport teaching health and fitness, it instead reorients our values to include acceptance of extreme pain, physical and personal sacrifice, and all sorts of violence.

Sport essentially institutionalizes, sanctions, and normalizes violence against others, something that is perhaps made more visible in the employment of so-called goons in hockey, or the brush-back pitch in baseball. Each is acceptable in the sport as it is naturalized as "just part of the game," even though one is tantamount to hiring a thug to commit a violent crime for you, and the other amounts to an intentional assault with a deadly object. Put into these contexts, we are more able to see the absurdity of the acceptance of brush-back pitches, and our revelry for "goons" and team fights.

Institutional sanctioning of violence can be seen at all organized levels of sport.

It is visible when two high school kids fight during a high school soccer match and are penalized with a red card, but when the same kids perform the same actions in the school's hallway they are suspended for five days or expelled from school. Similarly, legal sanctioning of violence in sport is made obvious when one considers that while two men who willingly agree to fight in a public place are subject to arrest, two baseball players who slug it out in front of tens of thousands of fans (including thousands of kids) are not. In this, and many more ways, boys and men are socialized into thinking that violence against other men is not only permissible, but expected. And because violence is naturalized as unproblematic as the way we do sport, boys and men are also taught to be receptive victims of violence. Alarmingly, this expectation does not seem to raise doubts about the value of sport to ourselves or society. We are obsessed with sex and sexuality but not violence. For example, we were thrown into an uproar when Janet Jackson exposed part of her breast at the Super Bowl half-time show in 2004, but we do not critique the violence of the game itself. Parents were upset that children were exposed to a partial breast but unconcerned with the violence they willingly exposed their children to.

Just because we have naturalized violence as an outcome of sport, it does not, however, mean that people enjoy being splayed out by a linebacker twice their size, taking a pitch in the shoulder for the sake of a "free" base, or running through shin splints. Kids must be socialized into such sadistic acts. They are forced to ignore the warning system of the human nervous system that inflicts one with pain in order to deter potentially injurious behaviors. It is against their own stopgaps and bodily urges to cease an activity that boys (particularly) must learn to repress their reflexes, suppress their fears, and oppress their peers. Even when the denial of protective instincts and physical damage manifests in the form of immediate and overuse injuries, boys and girls, men and women are not allowed to criticize the system. A fear of being stigmatized as a quitter or being labeled "not man enough to take it" discourages them from withdrawing. Instead, they are encouraged to "get back on the horse," walk it off, or do whatever is necessary in order to get back in the game. In such manner, athletes are conditioned to view aggression toward themselves and others as not only part of the game, but (for males) as a necessary component of masculinity – the athlete's mentality.

Furthermore, coaches exploit their athletes' over-dedication to the system and fears of emasculation by pushing them too far and by knowingly having them play with injuries. Sacrifice becomes part of the game and athletes, particularly those with low self-esteem or poor social support networks are willing to risk their health because they are so eager to be accepted by the team and their peers. In fact, research shows that over 80 percent of the men and women in top-level intercollegiate sport in the US sustain at least one serious injury while playing their sport, and nearly 70 percent are disabled for two or more weeks. The rate of disabling injuries in the NFL is over three times higher than the rate of men who work in construction. Professional contact sport is the nation's most violent workplace.

In addition to the physical violence that sport both produces and naturalizes as part of masculinity, sport also provides a psychological violence against the self and others because it is a public activity. Along with verbal hazing, and the dehumanizing initiation rituals of many sporting programs, we also need to consider the way sport elicits schadenfreude, an engrained concept in sport because sport is played out publicly, and is predicated upon the advancement of one player at the expense of another.

Sport is more than just a zero-sum social arena, it is a public zero-sum social arena. While this may have a boastful effect on the self-esteem of the winners, the nature of losing in public carries with it problematic circumstances. If a sixth-grade boy fails a test in his math class, the only other person to know his score (unless he elects to tell others) is his teacher. The teacher does not post the students' scores on the board for the class to take delight in the fact that they scored a higher grade. However, when a student fails to catch a football in physical education, his failure is visible for all to see (the fishbowl affect I discussed in the Introduction), and his failure may upset his teammates, who were depending on his performance for their needs. Thus, egos are built off the public humiliation of another. More so, William Pollack (1998) argues that boys (and assumingly girls) are simply not cognitively capable of dealing with such public failure. It is for all of these reasons that we need to recognize that much of what we consider "character building" for kids is instead child abuse. In the words of Joan Ryan (1996: 3), from her book about women's gymnastics, *Little Girls in Pretty Boxes*, "What I found was a story about legal, even celebrated, child abuse. In the dark troughs along the road to the Olympics lay the bodies of the girls who stumbled on the way, broken by the work, pressure and humiliation."

I find it sad that a child is not permitted to work a few hours in a shop in order to learn the values "necessary" for success in life; but they are permitted to bang their heads into each other in sport. Whereas a parent would be arrested for putting their kid to work stacking shelves in a store, they are praised for putting their kids into often violent sport. If we want to teach children the value of work, and how to get along with one's workmates, then it seems small doses of working is more appropriate than teamsport.

4 Sport's Use in the Maintenance of Class

Nathan's Story

It's Friday night, three hours before tip-off. Basketball fans have been lined outside the gymnasium for several hours to see a highly anticipated match between two men's basketball teams. As the gymnasium swells with spectators, conversations can be heard in multiple languages. Although the arena holds thousands, the seats fill to capacity, and hundreds of disappointed fans are turned away.

When the competing teams are introduced, the fans stand and cheer with an energy reminiscent of the opening of an NCAA championship match. Yet, this is not a collegiate or professional match. These fans come from a rather remote region of the American Southwest in order to watch two high school teams compete. While they compete team to team, they also compete nation to nation. This is a match between two cultures, each using basketball as a tool to achieve cultural objectives. This is basketball in Navajo country.

The infertile red soil of Navajo country in the American Southwest is occasionally broken by the splattering of striking red-rock formations and small towns that are usually separated by more than fifty miles. These towns are not marked by tall buildings, impressive bridges or highways. They are more rural than any American town I have seen before. Many homes are without the luxuries of modern capitalist societies, like telephones, electricity, or plumbing.

On my first day of research, at one of the Navajo Nation's high schools, I met Nathan. His bright eyes and large smile make me feel welcome. Nathan is finishing his third year of high school, where he is a star member of the men's basketball team. This surprises me, initially. Nathan is shorter than I, and I'm not even six feet tall. Still, "He is good," his coach tells me.

Later that day, I examine *The Navajo Nation* newspaper. Here, I am in awe of the lack of arts and entertainment. I am struck, however, by the reverence for which the paper discusses sport. But not sport the way the *Los Angeles Times* or *New York Times* would cover sport. This paper's sport section does not carry news of the major leagues; the ink in this paper is devoted solely to high school sport. "Sports are really it," one of the teachers tells me. "They are all we have around here. I mean we have our annual pow-wow … but in terms of regular stuff, it's *all* about sports." I ask, "All sports? I mean do they get a ton of people to say a cross-country meet?" "No. Not really," he responds, "It's mostly basketball and football.

I mean they will talk about other sport, and the newspaper talks about them, but it's basketball that everyone goes to watch out here."

One of the most notable differences between this and other American towns is that there are no mega shopping complexes, no music halls, museums, or concert halls on the Navajo reservation, so there are few places for the community to gather. There is a weekend swap meet, but there seems to be little other draw for residents to drive from the outskirts of their town (often 35 to 50 miles out) than perhaps the Walmart 50 miles outside of town (and off the reservation). It is clear that sport serves as a reason for the community to gather.

However, when driving through the reservation, one notices that almost every house, hogan, or mobile home has a makeshift basketball hoop. Few of the hoops are of regulation height, and few stand with concrete beneath them (kids bounce the ball on dirt). However, the sheer number of basketball hoops on the reservation signifies the importance of this sport in Navajo society. One might wonder why a sport like basketball has become so immensely popular when other sport, like running, have historically maintained deep spiritual meaning and cultural significance to the Navajo? A track coach told me, "Nobody wants to run anymore. Everybody wants to be a big basketball or football star." It seems that the Navajo have shifted their emphasis away from certain sport (or cultural activities) and centered them primarily on basketball and football. For the Navajo, who are reported to be conservative in retaining their culture, devaluing sport such as running and instead emphasizing colonial sport (white sport), must certainly mean that they derive something valuable from them. In Nathan's case, that value comes from the possibility of earning a college scholarship, so that he can afford to leave the Navajo Nation. "I want to go to one of those big universities, like ASU or UCLA," Nathan says, "but then I want to come back and help my people."

I spent a considerable portion of my ethnographic fieldwork hanging out with Nathan, meeting his mom and aunt. Nathan maintains a great deal of freedom, he can sleep at whoever's house he feels like, and nobody pressures him to excel at basketball, or his school work. But Nathan is highly self-motivated, so this is not necessary. "I want to make it out of here," he repeatedly stresses to me. Thus, Nathan spends hours making shots on his basket – which is not hung at regulation height. His efforts have paid off – compared to his Navajo teammates, he is outstanding at basketball.

However, Nathan's excellence is limited to the reservation. He is slower, less accurate in his shots, and doesn't have the same mass to block other players I've seen in Los Angeles or Orange County. "What are your chances of getting that scholarship?" I ask Nathan. "Pretty good," he says. "My coach says that if I work hard enough, I can get one." I ask Nathan, "Have you had any offers yet? Have you been in contact with any coaches?" He answers, "No. Not yet."

Not a lot of university coaches drive out to the Navajo Nation to scout for talent. So I find myself in a precarious position as a researcher and sport sociologist. Do I challenge his dream, telling him that he really doesn't have a chance at earning a UCLA scholarship? Or do I simply watch from the sidelines? When I ask the school's athletic director about the possibility of him earning a scholarship, he says,

"We're certainly hoping he can." But when I ask him if anyone has been given a basketball scholarship last year, the answer is no. "They year before?" I ask. Again, the answer is "No." In fact, the athletic director can only name one athlete who earned a college scholarship in his twenty odd years at this high school, "And she failed out the first year," he tells me.

As a researcher, it is not my job to change the cultures I visit. Some might consider that to be a breach of what research is about; and in this case, it is likely that some could view my actions as colonialism. Certainly, the problem of believing that sport is "the way out" of the reservation is much larger than I can handle alone, but in this case, I decided to intervene. I decided to make a difference to this one kid. After I returned from my ethnographic research, I spent some time searching college scholarships for Navajo students and I even found information about reduced fees for Native American students at several of the universities he was interested in. I helped Nathan fill out the forms and worked with him for several months in applying for scholarships. In the end, Nathan had earned enough small, yearly scholarships, to be able to afford a university education without basketball. It was a good thing, too. No basketball coach ever came knocking on his door.

Karl Marx

> The history of all hitherto existing society is the history of class struggles. Freeman and slave, patrician and plebeian, lord and serf, guild-master and journeyman, in a word, oppressor and oppressed, stood in constant opposition to one another, carried on an uninterrupted, now hidden, now open fight, a fight that each time ended, either in a revolutionary reconstitution of society at large, or in the common ruin of the contending classes.
>
> – Karl Marx and Friedrich Engels in *The Communist Manifesto*

Although it had little impact on revolutionary movements of mid-nineteenth century Europe at first, this thin book soon became one of the most widely read and discussed documents of the twentieth century. Marx and Engels wrote *The Communist Manifesto* in an attempt to differentiate their brand of socialism from others, insisting that it was based in a science of the study of history. These giants of social theory maintained that, just as feudalism had naturally evolved into capitalism, so capitalism would inevitably give way to its logical successor, socialism. Eventually this would give way into communism. Although strongly capitalist-identified countries, such as the US, have resisted, stigmatized and even (under McCarthyism in the 1950s) sanctioned/arrested those who identified or were suspect as communist, the bank failures of 2008–2009 highlight that perhaps they were right – with the government owning the banks (or at least a large portion of them) today, we are moving into socialism. Could communism be next?

The events of the 1950s, the House Committee on Un-American Activities, and the Hollywood Blacklist were not the only political actions influenced by the writings of Marx and Engels. Their ideas, simply known as Marxism, have been more than just a profoundly important social theory for sociologists, economists, historians, and political theorists to utilize in their academic work; their theory has also enabled revolutionaries like Vladimir Lenin to put Marxist ideas into action. Although I personally identify as a Marxist, I must also highlight that the ruthless-ness in which some (such as Joseph Stalin) sought to achieve communist ideals has lead to the death of millions. However, the political/military resistance against communism has equally caused millions of deaths (the US-led invasion of Korea and Vietnam is responsible for around 2 million deaths). This of course, is not a book about war, but it is necessary to highlight that Marxism is much more than just a social theory – it has influenced political theory that millions have died for, either in trying to achieve or resist.

The utility of Marxism in sociology is also paramount. Marxism has inspired countless similar theories – and, at some level, it's likely fair to say that almost all sociologists use Marxist thinking in their examination and analysis of sport.

The last category of the class struggle that Marx discussed, those who own the capital and the means of production (a class that Marx calls the bourgeoisie) and those who work for them (which Marx calls the proletariat) came with the Industrial Revolution. I spoke at length about how the Industrial Revolution changed society in the first chapter, and I continue with this here.

The same new technologies that permitted us to mass-produce sporting goods, to transmit sport scores through the medium of print, radio, television, and (later) the internet, also brought people geographically together so that we could have enough people, and fans, to make sport a profitable business. All of this, of course, came with the plight of people moving from the country to the cities in search of wage labor (see Chapter 4).

Wage labor (money given per hour of work) offered many advantages. People did not have to rely on the weather for the maintenance of their crops (fewer farm-ers were required because machines could do many times the work of people). Wage labor also brought an end to the variable hours of farming. Men (and some women, too) could now literally set their watches to the factory whistle. When it blew, they went to work. When it blew again, they got out of work. As described in Chapter 1, this shaped the work sphere as belonging to men, and the domestic sphere as belonging to women.

Marx and Engels observed this change, and saw it as a move from a time in which one had some mastery over, or connection to, their labor, to that of labor-ing for a factory owner instead. He (I will just refer to Marx and Engels as Marx, henceforth) noted, however, that capitalism requires unemployment. The reason for this is that when the only choice for putting food on the table comes through purchasing, rather than growing food, one needs money (currency) to do it. The advantage of unemployment to a factory owner (boss) is that, if you have unem-ployment, you can offer increasingly less pay for those jobs.

To illustrate this, I ask my students to imagine that they are married (gay or straight), with two children, and that they have been forced off the farm where they lived because the owner of that land has recently purchased modern, indus-trial, farming machinery. This means that the work of many hands can now be accomplished through one machine. In need of a living, "you" (each member of the class) is now forced to leave the farm, and head to the city in search of employment. Here, you find that there is massive unemployment. Yet, there is one factory hiring that makes sports drinks. They have a job advertised for screwing tops onto the filled bottles.

There are 50 students in class who need this job (to put food on their family's table) and there are no other jobs available. I ask the class, "Who would take this job for fifteen dollars/pounds an hour?" at which point all of the students raise their hands. But if I'm the employer, and I have 50 people lining up for this one job, why not keep some of my profits by instead offering the job to this group of 50 at ten dollars an hour; then nine, and then eight ...

Somewhere around what is currently minimum wage, my students will stop putting their hands up. I then say to them, "Wait, your family is starving, there are no other jobs, and yeah, five dollars an hour might not be much, but it will keep your two kids alive. You can at least buy bread to eat and a paper box to live in. Are you sure you're willing to let your kids starve because you think your labor is worth more than five dollars an hour?" Without exception, they put their hands back up.

The point of the exercise, of course, is that I can drive down the "minimum" wage only if there is unemployment. This is precisely the same decreasing opportunity structure upon which sport operates (Chapters 2 and 3). As long as there are multiple athletes competing for one position, they must adhere to the criteria of the coach. Marx calls this "a reserve army of Prolympian labor." If, on the other hand, there is more work to be done than there are workers to do the job (or more positions available in sport than can be filled), the workers (players) now have the power – they can bargain for more money, to be treated better, etc. This is why Kallella (in Chapter 2) was unable to organize her teammates.

Thus, capitalism (and sport) depends on unemployment (decreasing opportunity structure in sport), and unemployment drives wages down. In both these cases, the structure of the system removes one's fellow workers/players from shared humanity. Marx calls this *alienation*. Capitalism, as a form of work, or competitive sport, as a form of play (that increasingly turns into work the higher one advances), is designed to strip away our connections to the joy of creating (as work) or playing (as an athlete). When one loses control over the ability to make and create what one wants, charge what one wants (such as a craftsman), or to play what and when one wants according to democratic rules that make sport fun, they enter a state of alienation from what it is they used to love. Essentially, they become drones in a capitalist system aimed solely at making money for the owner. This is particularly true of professional teamsport athletes.

However, employees learned that their protection from the driving of wages downward was to join together. As Marx said, "workers of the world unite." If employees formed unions and walked off the job when their demands were not met, then the employer would lose massive amounts of money because their production lines would stop. Yes, they could hire others to fill the vacancies, but the time that it would take to train these new employees would come at great cost to the factory's owner. Furthermore, if you had a contract with one factory to deliver sports drinks to your shops, and a strike caused them to break that contract you would simply hire another sports drink manufacturer to deliver their brand instead. Thus, a strike that lasts too long can cost the factory owner permanent losses, because chances are they are not the only factory producing those particular goods.

Unions are a very effective strategy for workers in helping them secure higher wages, better job security, and (in modern times) better health insurance. Accordingly, factory owners found it in their interest to prohibit workers from unionizing. In years past, they hired "goons" to secretly police the social lives and social networks of the factory workers, and then report the "trouble makers" to the "union-busters." In other words, the employer would pay a small extra wage to one particularly needy employee, in order to secretly snitch to the boss about the unionizing activities of the employees. When one was identified, the factory owner might pay a small wage to a thug to physically beat the potential unionizer(s) in a dark alley. This would prevent others from taking up the union charge.

In modern times, owners try to discourage unions in other ways. For example, Walmart is America's largest private company, with around 1.5 million employees. Human Rights Watch, an advocacy group based in New York, released a report in 2007 detailing what it called "excessively aggressive tactics" by Walmart in stopping the organization of unions. The report highlights that while much of Walmart's actions are legal, they are nonetheless heavy-handed. This includes a rapid-response team to prevent organization, a hotline for store managers, and tips for store managers on staying union free. In addition, the report cites more than a dozen rulings against Walmart by the National Labor Relations Board, finding Walmart illegally confiscated union literature, prohibited discussions of unions, and retaliated against union supporters.

When capitalists (the bourgeoisie) fail in preventing unions from forming, they nonetheless succeed at controlling their profits in other ways. One way of doing this is to hire line managers. These are workers (usually men) who police the rest of the workers. If, for example, one factory has 100 employees, each paid 5 dollars an hour (500 dollar output per hour), the factory owner might divide the workforce into two, and pay two managers 7 dollars an hour (thus 514 dollar output per hour) in order to police the workers into squeezing 5 percent more productivity out of them. The 5 percent increase would far offset the 7 dollar an hour manager cost; and, hour on hour, this adds up to serious profit for the employer. So paying a middle manager to squeeze those unionized employees might yield much more profit.

The manager serves another other vital function under Marxist thinking. This manager provides employees the illusion that if one works hard enough, they too can be promoted to manager (the myth of meritocracy). Just as with sport, for every hundred workers/players on the factory floor/pitch, only one or two will move up to middle management. Nonetheless, the system keeps the illusion that one will be promoted, and this prevents people from striking. Rather than contest their boss for more money, they simply put their heads down, listen to authority (Chapter 3), and hope to be selected for promotion. If one were to strike, they would jeopardize their chances of being promoted.

Another way to keep employees from striking is to divide similar jobs into departments, and create an in-group/out-group mentality between them (Chapter 7). By giving one group a small pay rise, those in that group feel that their rise is justified. After all, who doesn't feel they deserve more money? This has the effect of aggravating members of the other department (or team). Interestingly, the anger of the team who does not get a pay rise tends to come out against the other group, not the boss. Essentially, by dividing all of the workers into departments and giving them stratified pay, the owner prevents employees from working together to unionize or contest them. This is a divide and conquer strategy. From the capitalist (coach's) perspective the notion is, don't let your employees gang up on you, instead set them against each other.

All of this has the additional effect of withering away at the agency of workers. Workers simply get beat down by the system. It also teaches them to follow orders; not to rock the boat. It teaches them "to be a team player." Those who do follow the orders of the coach (capitalist owners) are likely to be selected to rise through management. Those who do not follow the orders of the coach/manager are seen as "not being a team player," and are thought to "get what they deserve."

Marx also implicates Christianity into this formula as well, suggesting that the notion of "the meek shall inherit the earth" uses religion to suppress people into not challenging their bosses for better wages, or a part of the company. For Marx, religion is a distraction that focuses attention on the supernatural, providing people with a spiritual lift, but this has the deleterious effect of emphasizing improvement through an individual's changing to fit the system, rather than challenging the system. Eitzen (2001: 29) says, "Religion destroys awareness of material reality and promotes the maintenance of the status quo by giving priority to the goal of spiritual salvation." Marx summarized this by saying that "religion is the opiate of the masses," meaning that, just as an opiate (heroin, morphine, codeine) dulls the mind, and leaves one useless, so does religion – it removes one's critical thinking from the mix, because one is told what to think by his/her religious leader. The danger of religion, Marx argues, is that while it dulls your critical mind, it simultaneously makes you feel overjoyed with good feelings.

Now, I challenge you to think about how Marxism might apply to the army for a moment. Is the army not also made of ranks and divisions? Does a squad not also have a line manager? Do those at the bottom not suck it up and take one for the team so that they might be promoted? Does the army (or all military forces) not use god and country as a way of keeping soldiers (mercenaries) from uniting and striking for more pay?

Next, think about how Marxism applies to sport. Where the roles of "owners" and "workers" were established through the industrialization of society, in today's sport-dominated world these roles are easily substituted for those of "coach" and "athlete." The structure of modern sport is modeled on capitalist thinking and the maintenance of hierarchies. In fact, as I pointed out in Chapter 1, sport was designed to socialize youth into the capitalist models; it was designed to make good (heterosexual and masculine) workers, soldiers, and followers.

Coaches (the factory owners), pit players against each other by selecting certain players for certain positions, giving them more playing time, or promoting them to the next level. Athletes are afraid to rock the boat because they fear not being selected to play, and because dissent gets one labeled as a "loose cannon." Coaches thus pit players against each other with a "it's just him and you, and only one of you is going to get the spot" mentality. In sport, coaches have power because athletes are pitted against each other in a promotion/demotion system (i.e. do it the coach's way or lose your spot on the team ... "there will always be other people to play in your position if you do not obey my rules.") Sport therefore teaches athletes to obey the coach. Coaches use their "power" to abuse athletes and maintain themselves at the top of a social hierarchy in the same way that the bourgeoisie exploit the proletariat workers in order to keep themselves in positions of privilege.

Finally, just as Marx says that religion is an opiate of the masses, I argue that sport is an equally strong opiate. Hoch (1972) suggests that sport perpetuates problems by providing people with a temporary high; one that takes their mind off the problem. For example, as I write this book (in England), the country is gearing up for the 2012 Olympic Games. People are certainly "buzzing" about these forthcoming games, but the buzz makes one forget about the great financial cost. Similarly, the high of winning a game helps a young linebacker forget about the price he will pay (with his health) for that victory in later years. Sport, like a narcotic, draws your attention to the here and now. It fails to display upfront what the price of that here and now will ultimately be.

Democracy at Play

I argue for a more democratic and even socialist approach to sport. One that is opposed to the ownership/exploitation system of capitalism, one that suggests that everyone can have a "piece of the pie."

Marx believed that "from each according to his abilities, to each according to his needs." He envisioned a society where all worked to their capacities, taking their innate talents and training into account, and distributing an equal amount of wealth and power to all. According to the communist ideal, the upper and lower classes would be squashed, so that all lived a middle-class life. I desire to see something similar occur in sport.

Marx, however, believed that we needed to move through capitalism in order to get to communism. Thus the progress he thought would happen would be a shift from capitalism to socialism and then another shift to communism. Marx maintained that communism would not be achieved by shooting straight out for it. Instead, he thought that the way to do this was for the trade unions to break the system of capitalism.

Unions serve to destroy power by allowing workers to stand up for themselves against owners without fear of being fired. By forming unions, workers could use the power of the owners against them, using the tools of the master to destroy him. Without workers there are no profits for the bourgeoisie. I desire teamsport athletes (at all levels) to do the same. I hope for them to unionize, so that they can make their demands of the coach, and not the other way around.

The problem, however, is that one only plays sport for so long. And, if one's sport career is short, there is little desire to invest time into unionizing, contesting coaches, and developing a group of athletes to change the nature of sport. This was the problem with the players on Kallella's team (from Chapter 2).

For years, I heard from women on this particular university team about how abusive, mean, and uncaring their coach was. Yet, every time I tried to get one of the players to contest their coach by unionizing the players against him, they said something similar to, "But I'm only going to be here four years. If I do that, he won't select me to play." Year after year passed before one player was finally strong enough (and tuned to Marxist ideology) to finally stand up and do something about the abuse. In doing so, she changed the way her coach operated. With her teammates behind her, she said, "As of now, Coach, we all quit. You can tell the athletic director and the press why you have no team for the game tomorrow. Unless," she said, "you give in to our demands."

Her actions benefited not only her and her present team, but the players on this coach's team for years to come. The players passed down the message of the collective power they held. They made demands about how the coach was to treat them. They stood up against injustice. In doing this, they made the team more socialist. They made it their team, and not the coach's.

Capitalism, False Consciousness, and the Myth of Meritocracy

The "American dream" is that anyone (if they work hard enough) can be rich. Among more critical thinkers, this is known as the myth of meritocracy. It is a myth because it is (generally) not hard work that makes one rich, rather it is contacts, education, and other resources. Just as it is talent, not hard work, that makes one good at sport. However, the reality of a few sportsmen/women from the lower classes working hard to make millions sends a message to the entire lower class that "it can be done"; that if you work hard, you too can be a rich and successful athlete. Alas, belief that sport is the way out of poverty is a myth that keeps whole communities from focusing on the factor that can actually make a difference in their lives – education. The danger of the myth is that it focuses many of the underprivileged to look to sport as their way out, and not education.

Consider this. Of the top four men's sports in the US (basketball, baseball, American football, and ice hockey) there are only about 3,500 professional team-sport positions. With 150 million men in America, one can see that the odds of making it to the professional ranks are extraordinarily low. Even if the professional leagues did not hire workers from overseas (and they hire lots of them) figuring out the odds of making it from youth sport to the professional class is illuminating. Jay Coakley (2004) shows that the chances of making it from a high school varsity team (the highest ranking team in a high school) to the professional level of baseball is about 1 in 1,000. The odds for making it in men's football are worse, about 1 in 1,300. Men's basketball is around 1 in 2,500. Women's professional basketball is the worst, with odds around 1 in 4,500. Those who fail are led to believe that they just did not work hard enough.

Sadly, these odds have a disproportional effect on kids from underprivileged backgrounds. Eitzen (2001: 258) reports on a study by the Center for the Study of Sport in Society, in which two thirds of African American males between the ages of 13 and 18 believe that they can earn a living playing professional sport. This is more than double the percentage of white males who believe this. Contributing to the problem, black parents are four times more likely to believe that their sons are destined to professional sport compared to white parents. Part of this disparity may come from the fact that 1 in 3,500 black youths makes it professional, compared to 1 in 10,000 whites. But these are still incredibly long odds.

For women (of any color) the statistics are far worse. If a woman does make it professional, the money and fame are also far less. Still, these unreasonable statistics are supported (in all communities) because of the myth that hard work will necessarily yield success, and that we all have equal chance of athletic success. This encourages us to look up to those who are successful as "paragons of virtue" (Eitzen 2001: 30), and to look down upon those who fail as lacking in quality of character. Nowhere was the improbability of making it in sport more salient to me than when I visited Nathan on the reservation.

I argue that this overemphasis on sport helps reproduce the existing class structure in Navajo country and in America, and I argue that it helps reproduce Navajo poverty as well. In neo-Marxist theory, sport, like capitalism, gives the illusion that all is fair, that the playing field is the great leveler – a true meritocracy. However, not all is equal in sport, and sport is the farthest thing from a meritocracy. Sport discriminates against biological groups, and there is much institutional racism in sport. But for the impoverished, sport often *seems* to be one of the few vehicles out of poverty. And for those who are not as academically inclined, or for those who have never applied the same rigor of sport to their academics, athletics can seem the *only* way out.

The myth that sport is a meritocracy, that one can readily earn an athletic scholarship if he/she works hard enough, appeals to the young Navajo athletes I studied. In fact, almost every high school athlete I talked with shared with me that he or she thought a college scholarship was obtainable, much worse statistics than are provided for African Americans. The illusion of success is made by the fact that some athletes have succeeded in obtaining a college scholarship. Coaches, teachers, and parents further this widespread belief. For example, I was talking with a freshman basketball player, and I asked him what he planned on doing after high school. He said, "I'd like to play ball for a big university if I can earn a scholarship. You know, I'd like to play for Duke or North Carolina, or somewhere like that." He, just as Nathan did, then turned to his coach and said, "If I'm good enough to make it?" His coach responded, "Just keep working hard." Although the coach is certainly correct in asserting that hard work is part of the equation to the type of performance that will be necessary to earn a college scholarship, height is another. The kid in question was 5'5.

I argue that this is one case where sport presents a false front – it appears to do good for the Navajo (building national pride when they beat white teams) but it actually reproduces their inequality. Earning a scholarship is taken as a sign of great pride, and it is seen as a vessel to escape the poverty of reservation life. However, this strategy appears to be highly ineffectual. High school athletes face the same overwhelming odds that inner-city youths face in obtaining an athletic college scholarship, yet the Navajo have several other disadvantages as well. They do not have the same height as members of other communities and there is an over-abundance of hoops on the reservation, which diffuses competition for play. Finally, the inaccessibility, and the great distance that the Navajo high schools tend to be from metropolitan areas, airports, etc. makes it much more difficult for college recruiters to travel to see them perform. This cultural location places Navajo athletes into a difficult situation, ultimately, trapping young Navajo athletes into a false consciousness in which they believe sport to be the ticket off the reservation.

Institutional Discrimination against Inner-City Black Youths in the US

Native Americans are not the only people to suffer at the hands of a white ownership society. A short history of the treatment of African Americans might read like this: America's founding fathers adopted a constitution that legalized slavery in 1776 (although slavery was part of American culture since 1625). Over these centuries, Americans made the "land of the free," a very rich nation, off the backs of slave labor. When Abraham Lincoln finally administered the emancipation proclamation in 1863, it came three years into the Civil War, casting doubt on American folklore of the Civil War being fought over slavery. And unlike other survivors of government-induced atrocities, no reparations were given to the living survivors of slavery or to their descendents. None received the promised forty acres and a mule. The Emancipation Proclamation did not end slavery, the 13th Amendment did.

Without a means of production, without owning capital (land, factories, or resources) newly freed black slaves survived by hiring their hourly labor to the owners of industry. Here, under capitalism, they were more free, but Jim Crow laws still discriminated against African Americans, and covert racism made life very difficult for them. They were institutionally discriminated against through their lack of resources. Thus, African Americans became ghettoized, living in squalor, paying rent on buildings owned by white people, and working in white people's homes, farms and factories.

In the US today, African Americans finally have full legal equality with whites, but there still exists a great deal of cultural and economic inequality. Much of this can be traced to the fact that white America made its wealth off black labor, and that they have passed this wealth down, often tax free, through generations. President George W. Bush's repeal of "death tax" helps maintain this historically driven economic disparity.

Poverty has left much of the African American community with no inherited capital. Without capital, and facing various forms of cultural discrimination, many young people try to make it out of poverty through sport. Here, athletes who do make it out help reproduce the image that "you, too, can achieve in sport (or rap music) and make it out of poverty." But this is far from reality. The myth, of course, is held in place by the very few who do.

When most fail, and without inherited privilege, education, or other forms of social capital, the selling of drugs becomes alluring. Despite the fact that blacks only make up 10 percent of the US population, they account for 70 percent of US prisoners, mostly because of drug-related crimes. Here, they are sentenced to federally mandated prison terms that came into existence as part of Reagan's "war on drugs." Judges have no discretion in reducing these sentences, so drug offenders often remain in prison longer than murderers. Here, they provide cheap labor and call center employees for white-run companies: a new form of slavery.

Sport is certainly not responsible for the reproduction of neo-slavery, the ghettoization of a disenfranchised people, or the violence that plagues inner-city communities. But one must wonder if sport does not greatly contribute to the reproduction of this poverty through two central mechanisms. First, by serving as a central distractor from academic excellence that might get more inner-city youths to top-quality universities. At university, black youths would not only benefit from the education, but they might make social contacts that would help them achieve a rewarding career (networking).

Finally, inner cities represent areas with significantly elevated rates of violence, particularly concerning gangs. One cannot help but wonder whether the in-group/out-group mentality (Chapter 7) and illegitimate violence that organized competitive teamsport teach youth do not help escalate this violence. As outlandish as it might sound to a sport-loving nation, one must wonder if there would be as much violence among youth if our culture was obsessed with theater or dance, and not violently pushing one's self through other men in order to score against them.

Applying Marxism to a College Scholarship

I coached high school distance-runners for 12 years in Southern California. Although many of my athletes dreamed of earning a college scholarship, only two did. One of them, Jess Strutzel, always dreamed of attending the University of California (UCLA). As one of the fastest 800-meter runners in the nation while in high school, he earned a scholarship to run for UCLA. This was fortunate, as without his athletic scholarship (something I call athletic affirmative action) he would not have had the grades to be accepted.

Ironically, half way through his university education, he emailed me to say, "I'm a UCLA prostitute. I sell my body to them. They pay me to perform for them." He added, "When my teammates and I perform well, the school makes lots of money [gate receipts, merchandise, and endorsements]. Regardless of how much money the school makes, we get the same, just our scholarship." Many high school athletes dream of receiving a full college athletic scholarship to a NCAA Division 1 program. But could it be that many of these athletic scholarship recipients are in a state of what Marx calls false consciousness? Is it possible that these athletes are actually being duped by the system?

At face value it appears not. Athletes on full scholarship have their tuition paid for, their books are free, and they also get room and board. To most, this sounds like a rather good deal. However, in return for this package, the athletes give up their freedom of economic production. I suggest that because of these limitations, Division 1 scholarship athletes are exploited by the system. They are exploited for their labor in the same Marxist manner that the factory owners exploit their workers' labor.

Of course, in order for it to be shown that the NCAA exploits their scholarship athletes, it must be shown that the athletes produce some goods – goods that the administration (bourgeoisie) make a profit from. In this case, I argue that athletes are entertainers who perform for the school's income. In return, they are housed, fed, and, arguably, educated. The athlete's "scholarship" is their meager salary; it pays many of their expenses, but it gives them no pay check, and puts no actual cash into their pockets. They own no stock in the company and one's scholarship does not even cover the cost of living. One cannot, for example, pay auto or health insurance, or other necessities with what one is given as a student athlete. Meanwhile, the administration might bring in millions of dollars from gate receipts, advertising, contracts, merchandise sales, and alumni contributions. Thus, the university's administration, who owns the means of production, acts like a capitalist corporation, despite the fact that UCLA is a public institution. The institution gets richer, while the athletes sacrifice their study time, personal lives, and their bodies (particularly if they are football players), all for a financial reward that is below the subsistence level.

Ironically, this scholarship is considered "a free ride."

The athletic department fails to publicly recognize the huge profit-making system that they own. Rather, they point to departmental losses, claiming that athletics cost more to run than they bring in. In fact, of almost 500 Division 1 college programs in America, they will argue that only about 20 athletic departments show a profit. This is the same argument that athletic departments used to justify the lack of women's sport and scholarships before the passage of Title IX. But does this argument make sense? Why would schools offer six-digit salaries to coaches with winning records if athletic departments are in debt?

College athletic departments are notorious for extremely creative bookkeeping. Most athletic departments are run as businesses, with financial affairs that are somewhat separate from the rest of the school. They have their own budgets, contracts, and businesses. When they report their gains vs losses they usually show gate receipts vs expenses, conveniently leaving out their merchandising contracts, donations, and grants from alumni. They are like insurance firms who show how much money they charged vs how much they paid out; claiming to have a net loss while forgetting to show their capital gains through investment.

College sport at the NCAA Division 1 level are pure business. They exist for commercial entertainment and athletes are recruited for athletic, not academic purposes. Highlighting this, athletes *often* receive admission to colleges with GPAs (Grade Point Averages) and SATs (Scholastic Aptitude Tests) that their non-athletic counterparts would deny admission to (athlete affirmative action).

Still, one might argue that sporting teams exist for more than just profit-making. One might argue that college sport improves student cohesion and sense of belonging, thus preventing detachment from one's university. All of this is true. However, it is also true that many universities own a means of entertainment production, and that they exploit young athletes who maintain a false consciousness of what it means to be an athlete.

Tragically, these same athletes are also prohibited from profiting from their labor. In fact, NCAA regulations stipulate that Division 1 athletes are prohibited from using their name, or their image, in advertising, or even the promotion of their own business. Division 1 athletes are not permitted to advertise anything through any means, for anybody.

Now, let's compare Jess with my (then) boyfriend (now husband) who was on a full academic scholarship at the same university. Both were theater majors, and both desired to pursue careers in film. The difference was that my husband was able to shoot commercials, or be paid to perform in professional theater, while going to college. In one car commercial (ten hours of work) he made more than ten thousand dollars. Jess, on the other hand, could not do any of this. Jess was prohibited from making money using his face or image. Sadly, this also thwarted his development in the world of acting.

My boyfriend had the security of knowing that his school was paid for via an academic scholarship. Because academic scholarships do not make the same types of demands as athletic scholarships, he was free to pursue economic liberties in professional theater/commercial and film. Meanwhile, Jess was not allowed to shoot commercials, pursue professional theater, start a business with his name in it, or in any way profit from the fame he had as an athlete. Of course commercials are not a steady income, so Jess chose not to give up his scholarship. Thus it was his "choice" to sign the athletic scholarship contract, but the choice was affected by economic and structural determinants that limited the "choice" he really maintained.

Not allowing athletes to advertise or work is a ploy to keep the merchandizing contracts that the university makes with other companies solid. In other words, if Nike signs a contract with UCLA, it wants to make sure that the star member of the basketball team is not making millions of dollars advertising for Adidas. So in order to attract and maintain multimillion dollar deals with capitalistic industries, university systems prohibit its employees from advertising any product at all. And, by setting an income cap, the administration helps ensure that the athlete will be dependent upon the system for the financial means necessary to attend school. If athletes were permitted to make big bucks, as pro athletes can, by advertising, or working, they would no longer need the system's scholarship, and would not be chained to working for the school as an athletic entertainer.

Highlighting this, I spent around twenty dollars to purchase the UCLA athletic calendar, because Jess was featured as one of the month's athletes. I asked Jess what his portion of the cut was. "None. It is just an honor to be on it," he answered sarcastically. Now, I don't know how many of these calendars were sold, but with the athletic reputation of UCLA, one can imagine it to be in the tens of thousands. This means that the university's athletic department potentially made hundreds of thousands of dollars, but the athletes who worked hard to succeed at their sport made nothing. The balance of power is such that if one complains, the athletic department can easily say, "If you don't like this, there is always someone else willing to take your scholarship." And this is true. There are more workers (players) than jobs (scholarships) available; without unionization it is unlikely the system will change.

Chapter Conclusion

This chapter applied Marxist thinking to sport. Marxism is one of the oldest, and perhaps most powerful, theoretical tools used to analyze sport. What is important to highlight about this chapter is that sport is built upon a competitive, capitalistic, exclusionary model. It is a model that was developed in response to the Industrial Revolution (see Chapter 1) and it gives some people (the bosses and coaches) overwhelming power compared to others (the workers and players). This power imbalance, however, is maintained through multiple exploitative tactics. Ultimately it permits the bosses/coaches to distribute the goods (power, wages, playing positions, and promotions) as they see fit.

I intentionally chose to discuss the Navajo in this chapter, because I wanted to stress that it is not just poor inner-city black youths that are lured into the false consciousness of sport as a way out of poverty (although this is an endemic problem among poor youth). Intentionally or not, sport is used by white, middle- and ownership-class society to keep the disenfranchised down.

Sport does this through the Marxist notion of exploitation. By dividing a workforce and offering managers a financial benefit to squeeze productivity from the laborers, the owners of a factory/sports team create a tool to control workers/players to increase efficiency and to reduce direct confrontation with their workers/players. Essentially, owners/coaches hold the carrot of occupational promotion to an under-salaried workforce, thereby reducing the chances of rebellion or unionization. Industry managers (assistant coaches) are therefore selected from a pool associated with an even higher degree of obedience than the workers/players they supervise.

This, "I did it so you can, too" ethos is embedded in much of the managerial leadership styles even today. It is therefore no surprise that it appears in sport. Here, players are promoted for adhering to the coaches' directives, and inspired by the opportunity of local fame, or even making it professional. Because sport is also (falsely) considered to be meritocratic, we maintain the belief that the harder one works the better they will perform in sport. While this may be true of an individual's performance, working the hardest does not guarantee one victory – talent is more important in this equation.

In this capacity, sport reminds me of a skilled magician. The job of the magician is to get you to focus your eyes in the wrong place. By distracting you, the magician is able to do something without your knowledge. This is how I see sport's use in keeping the lower classes down. Sport, in all its shimmering glory, says "look over here, you too can be a sports star" when the real solution to class mobility lies in education. By emphasizing sport to a racialized lower-class citizenry, there are fewer students to compete with kids from white, middle- and upper-class areas for college entrance and other career opportunities. Even when high school athletes earn a college scholarship, they are not free from the exploitation. Here, they continue to make money for the owners, sacrificing their own labor power.

5 Sport's Use in Stratifying Men

Blake's Story

The wooden floor of the high school gym squeaks as Blake shuffles his 6'4, 190-pound body up and down the court. Only a sophomore, Blake is already one of the best players in Indiana, drawing coverage from local media and praise from his community. Despite the fact that the rest of the team has gone home, Blake remains late into the evening, shooting basket after basket in order to better himself as an athlete.

Blake had no dreams of superstardom when he began playing basketball, but today he hopes that putting a ball through a hoop will not only provide him with the image of being heterosexual, but that it will also provide him with a college scholarship. "Basketball is my ticket out of here," he tells me. Blake hopes to escape the homophobia of his Midwestern community by relocating to a metropolitan area for college.

Blake grudgingly picked up basketball in the fourth grade because he perceived that popularity among boys was based primarily on athleticism, and he desired to raise his social standing among his peers. "I was actually more interested in reading," Blake tells me, "But that's not really cool. I mean I really hated basketball; I'd much rather read a book; but other boys didn't do that. Everybody played basketball, and I wanted to fit in, so I did too." Blake learned long ago that male athletes are commonly perceived as incapable of being gay – a façade that he strategically takes advantage of as a basketball player.

It was during sixth grade that Blake began to worry about a sexuality he increasingly recognized as "gay," and by the eighth grade Blake knew with certainty that he was what he feared. "It's not easy to be the thing that all the boys use as a put-down. It's what you call someone when you're trying to dis them, and I certainly did not want to be that!" So Blake learned to play both the game of basketball, and the game of heterosexual passing. On the court he was "straight," off the court, he was able to shed the heterosexual façade via the internet. "I met one gay friend online, and then another, and then I discovered XY.com, where there are like thousands of gay teens online." Near the end of his eighth-grade year, he even ventured out to meet other gay boys and eventually found a boyfriend during his freshman year.

His boyfriend helped Blake realize that he was not alone, and that loving another boy was nothing to feel guilty about. "We dated for a few months, which at 14 seemed like forever, and then one day he just stopped calling. I couldn't figure out why he wasn't returning my calls or my e-mails." Blake began dealing with the taxing emotion of being rejected. Being closeted, however, Blake had no adult to express his anguish to. So he returned to venting online. "I was talking to a friend, asking him if he had heard from Chris." His friend responded, "Didn't you hear? Chris was killed in a car accident." "I started to cry. So I ran to the bathroom and turned the radio up as loud as it went so nobody could hear me."

Alone, Blake had nobody to turn to, nobody to hug him and hold him. He would have to mourn this devastating loss in secret. But while the blaring music cloaked his tears, it couldn't change his loneliness.

> I tried to tell myself that it didn't matter. But it did. I loved Chris. He was my first love, and I was young, and it hit me twice as hard. I only wished I could have told others; but I didn't have anyone I could talk to about it. I made a reference to him in a paper my freshmen year but I couldn't tell my teacher or my parents why he died, or who he was, or why I was upset. Hell, I couldn't even tell them that someone had died at all.

Blake's story highlights some of the hardships of concealing one's sexual identity. Blake repeated to me, "I just wish I could have talked to someone." His voice began to crack, and through muffled tears he angrily said, "If it had been a girlfriend it would have been easy, but no, it was my boyfriend, and nobody wants to know about that. I was all alone."

Today, Blake walks the hallways of his rural high school publicly popular, but emotionally alienated. He describes his high school as "a typical jock high school." Ironically, where others think that Blake has it all, from where he stands, towering above the others figuratively and physically, he feels alienated. There are no openly gay students at his school, and Blake isn't even sure if there are any in his community. "If there are, I certainly don't know of them," he says with sadness.

Blake is also daunted by the insistent fear of being discovered as gay.

> I fear all the time that others will find out. That people's opinions of me will change if they find out that I'm gay. Like my teachers, they won't think the same of me; they make gay comments and say them in a derogatory manner. Even my own bro will say stuff about gay people. It makes it hard, I'm always thinking in the back of my mind, *would you feel this way about me if you knew I was gay?*

He adds, "My friends, it's the same thing with them. I have a lot of good friends, but a lot of them are religious, which strikes quite a bit of fear with me."

Compounding matters, Blake fears that his parents may have an inclination that he is gay. "They don't want to think about it. Mom says, 'Blake you need to get a girlfriend.' 'Mom I don't want to,' I tell her. 'I don't have time. I'm too busy. I have to get my workout in.'" Thus, basketball becomes the all-purpose excuse for

Blake. It not only provides him with a veneer of heterosexuality, but it gives him something to do other than date women.

Coming out is certainly something Blake ponders – daily – but he just has not been able to bring himself to do it yet. I asked him how he thought he would be treated if he were to come out to everyone in his town today. "In all honesty, there will be some people who are not okay with it. But, at the same time, I think it might open a lot of people's eyes. Like the people at my school, they don't have any gay friends. They don't know any gay people at all. They might just look at me and say 'Blake has been my best friend since I was little, and he's gay, and he's cool.' I just hope they see me as the same goofy Blake." His response is pleasantly absent of fears of being victimized by homophobic violence, partially because he embodies the ability to commit violence himself – he is tall and muscular. "Nobody would mess with me," he says. "I'm bigger and stronger than all the other guys at my school."

Blake's decision to postpone his coming out is complicated. Gay or straight, out-of-state tuition is expensive, and a scholarship for playing ball would help; Blake fears that coming out would hurt his chances of getting that scholarship, something hard to refute. "I definitely plan on coming out when I'm in college; there is no question about that. The question is, will I come out during my junior or senior year of high school?" Bravery is not so easily bought. Coming out in a small, homophobic town, with homophobic parents, teachers, and teammates, is more pressure than any million-dollar athlete would have to handle. It is, without doubt, as tough a decision as any 16-year-old should have to make.

Antonio Gramsci and Hegemony Theory

There is a reason Blake felt unable to come out in his high school. This is because heterosexuality maintains cultural power and privilege in most societies. Heterosexuality is esteemed, while homosexuality is (at best) tolerated. Thus, from the time Blake was young, he was taught the "virtue" of heterosexuality and the "vice" of homosexuality. This message was touted to him from every major institution: the church, the family, school, and sport. The message (that heterosexuality is the esteemed sexuality) is so powerful, that it has become hegemonic. However, before we can understand how the notion of hegemony applies to masculinities (and thus sexualities) it is important to understand where this theory emerged from, and what it means.

Hegemony, a concept created by Antonio Gramsci (1971), refers to a particular form of dominance in which a ruling class legitimates its position and secures the acceptance – if not outright support – of the classes or archetypes below. While a feature of Gramsci's hegemony theory is that there is often the threat of force structuring the belief, the key element is that force cannot be the causative factor that elicits complicity. This is what separates hegemony from overt rule.

Gramsci was a Marxist who believed that Italy should become communist. Under the tyranny of fascist dictator Benito Mussolini, he was arrested for his philosophy and sentenced to five years of confinement on a remote island. Recognizing his political might, the prosecutor said, "For twenty years we must stop this brain from functioning" (p. 127). The following year Gramsci received a sentence of an additional 20 years. Poor prison conditions withered his health, and so although he gained freedom in 1934, he died that same year, aged 46. Isolated in prison, Gramsci was, however, able to write his political theories.

Gramsci was not the first to write about hegemony; that came from another Marxist, Vladimir Ilyich Lenin. But Gramsci developed the idea into a focused analysis in order to explain why the "inevitable" socialist revolution that Marx predicted had not yet occurred. Instead, it seemed to Gramsci that capitalism was more entrenched than ever. Capitalism, Gramsci suggested, maintained control not just through political and economic coercion and violence, but also ideologically, through a hegemonic culture in which the values of the bourgeoisie became the common-sense values of all. Thus, a culture of consensus develops in which people in the working class identify their own good with the good of the bourgeoisie. In doing so, they actually help maintain the *status quo* rather than revolting against it.

Gramsci's theory is difficult to pinpoint, various people attribute different things to him, because the notes he made in his prison notebook can be difficult to decipher. However, the basic premise of hegemony theory centers on controlling people by getting them to think that the ruling ideas are their own ideas, and that it is in their own best interest to act this way. Gramsci suggested that, in order to compel people to empathize with the ruling class or identity, those who do not fit within the dominant ideal must believe that their subordinated place is both *right* and *natural*.

Hegemony is a serious theoretical tool that I use to help explain the dominance of all types of cultural beliefs. First, it is necessary to understand that the basis for all of this belief persuasion and coercion business is that all of our ideas and beliefs, all of what we code as good or bad in society, is socially constructed, and therefore relative. For example, we don't emerge from the womb believing that urinating on the sidewalk is bad, and that monogamy, heterosexuality, Christianity, honesty, or sport are good. Instead, these things are taught to us by our culture. Had we grown up in a different society, we might very well have learned to see things differently. We might have been socialized to believe that men should have multiple sexual partners, perhaps multiple wives. In other cultures (in previous times), homosexual relationships were esteemed over heterosexual ones. Still, in other cultures, Christianity is looked upon as an evil religion. In other words, in one culture the cow is a meal, and in another it is a deity. The point, quite clearly, is that our beliefs and values are learned.

Consequently, the way we see ourselves as affected by these things is also socially constructed. Thus, you can imagine that a culture might so socially value self-sacrifice that those who commit suicide do so gladly because of the amazing honor it will bestow upon themselves and their family (think Japanese kamikaze fighters). Today, some use the constructed belief in religion (and the promise of 72 virgins) to motivate men to even commit martyrdom, while other soldiers are taught to believe that they are bringing "democracy" to people with no real history of it. Others are taught to value body multilation in the form of circumcision. But, just as these things once maintained their value, one thing you can be sure about is that things change. Thus, I doubt Japanese culture today would value a kamikaze,

Muslim culture is at odds with martyrdom, and boys who are circumcised are increasingly thought to have been abused by their parents.

Our culture not only teaches us what to value, but it teaches us to view ourselves as victims or heroes of that culture. The best example of the power of culture to create pride or shame in one's self comes with sexuality. As a young man I was amazingly depressed (even attempted suicide) over the shame, disgust, guilt, and fear that I maintained as a closeted gay boy in the early 1980s. But none of this came from simply being gay; my manifestation of horror, my suicidal desires, were produced by a culture that demonized me. Now, 25 years later, our culture has turned, and gay kids do not internalize shame as much as I did. In fact, for many, they are damn proud of who they are. Similarly, in 1993, when the athlete you read about in the introductory chapter beat up my athlete, he was made a hero among his players, and he probably felt good about himself for having done that. But I very much doubt that this would be the case today. Although I've not talked to this individual, I would not be surprised if, according to today's culture, he is highly disappointed in himself. Thus, culture determines victors, victims, and even emotional pain.

This notion of constructionism is easily applied to sport. If your teacher turned to you in class, and called you "a worthless piece of shit" or yelled at you, "you're a fucking pansy," that teacher would be in very serious trouble. But, if the same individual were to go to the sport field at the same university, and say one of these same things to an athlete in the course of "coaching," this individual would (supposedly) suffer no harm. Nobody would report it, and nobody would care. So why is this?

The lesson to be extrapolated about sport, and the social construction of abuse, victimization, pain, guilt and shame, is again obvious: while I might view sport and coaching as being abusive because coaches produce physical and long-lasting injuries – coaches berate, sport discriminates and ostracizes those who fail at it – and because it produces a whole lot of unnecessary pain and grief, none of this matters. None of this matters because society tells boys (and increasingly girls) that they are worthy, special and wonderful if they play sport. Our culture determines that if one ends up elevated above the shoulders of others, for putting up with all this mental and physical pain, then clearly they will view their pain as a worthy sacrifice. They will be proud to have given it all and will not feel victimized for failure. Thus, I might suggest that our nation's psychology clinics are full of patients who feel abused by their parents, neglected, unloved, berated, and often those who are physically beaten. But it is rare for a counselor to come across a patient that says, "My coach ostracized or caused me great emotional distress." Instead, the power of our culture maintains that the only victim in sport is one who is sexually abused by their coach. But why is this the only form of abuse that ends up putting athletes in the counselor's chair? The answer: hegemonic notions of victimhood (in the home, school, church, or just about any other locale) do not apply to sport.

I might add to this notion of hegemonic victimization/valor model a comparison of being sexually molested to sport particpation. We arrest adults for this because kids are too young to consent. I agree that this is a correct and logical understanding of such a relationship. However, I am baffled as to why we do not extend this same principle to that of organized, competitive teamsport? Particularly when that sport requires kids to engage in physically dangerous or emotionally abusive situations. Are kids not also too young to make a choice to consent to playing a violent game? One where their performance is put into a fish bowl for all to see; where they are criticized and shamed for failure? Aren't kids too young to consent to being yelled at, ostracized, and even physically punished for their sporting failures? Aren't kids too young to consent to donning a football helmet and bashing their puerile skulls into another kid, punching one in a boxing ring, or being told to repeatedly smash his or her brains against their craniums while undertaking heading "practice" in sport?

Similarly, why do parents force their kids into a conservative and shame-producing religious doctrine when they are young, instead of waiting for them to find god (or not) as adults, where they can make up their own minds about what they believe? These are the types of questions you need to explore in order to think sociologically. The larger issue at play in this discussion is really one of power and the ability of groups with power to control the way we think about "others."

Hegemony theory works very well when applied to marginalized people (whether it be by race, sexuality, or ability). Here, each falls at the bottom of a continuum of power and privilege (white people, men, heterosexuals, and the able-bodied). Thus black people are praised for speaking "normal" (white), gays are praised for "acting straight," and those with a disability are praised for approximating able-bodiedness (i.e. playing basketball from a wheelchair). Together these groups share a very common plight in terms of how they are treated by society and how they respond. These are examples of a dominant cultural group maintaining their power by requiring others to assimilate to them – this is hegemony in action. And when a disabled athlete finishes a race, a gay man acts so straight to be indistinguishable from a heterosexual, or a black woman learns to speak in a posh white accent, they are praised. You can therefore see the power (and beauty) of hegemony theory, because even the oppressed desire to be associated with the group in power, even though they will never gain full and equal membership.

The final caveat to hegemony theory is that whatever is in current hegemonic favor tends to escape critical (even academic) scrutiny. For example, monogamy is the favored relationship ideal in contemporary culture. Never mind that it rarely works, or that the rates of cheating are astronomical (Anderson 2010), it nonetheless remains the cultural ideal. The opposite of monogamy, open relationships, polyamorous relationships, those who choose to remain single, or those who choose celibacy, are critically scrutinized for their "failure" to live up to the ideal. Similarly, we don't critically evaluate sport (culturally, or hardly even academically) because sport is hegemonically seen as a "good." So, sport goes uncritically examined and those who speak negatively of sport are critically examined for their "wrongheadedness."

Because hegemony is a culture of consensus of whatever class of people, ruling party, social ideal, or institution is currently in favor, undermining hegemony is never easy: you are up against *a lot* if you try. However, no hegemonic system is seamless; there are always cracks, fissures, and pockets of resistance to any dominating social message.

Accordingly, hegemony is actually a process of struggle, a permanent striving, a ceaseless endeavor to maintain control over the "hearts and minds" of subordinate classes (Ransome 1992: 132). The work of hegemony is never done; one voice is a radical; a handful of voices is a cult; but more than that and it is a rightful social movement. We all have agency (individual power) to contest or reify sport (or any other dominating cultural message). So the question is, what do you do with your agency? Do you choose to use it to patronize sport? Do you pay for it, glamorize and help glorify it? Does sport occupy your thoughts, conversations and time? Or do you use your agency to contest the system, and highlight the socio-negative role that sport plays in our society?

For most readers, the answer is the former. This is because hegemony theory is complimented by cognitive dissonance theory (discussed in the Introduction). When most people see, feel, or express two simultaneous but competing and contrasting attitudes – and therefore feel cognitive dissonance – the way they rectify this feeling of disharmony is normally to choose to align their beliefs with their emotions. And, one's emotions toward a topic (monogamy or sport) are determined by one's culture. Thus, if you read my examples above, saw logic in them, but "felt" differently about them (saw a glimpse of the other side), chances are you will leave this section saying to yourself, "Boy the author sure was on a rant, there" and you will use that key word, "rant" as a way to discredit the arguments I make, and excuse yourself from thinking more seriously about sport.

If you permit yourself to see, think, or feel differently to the masses, it could evoke guilt, shame, or anxiety. Thus, we tend to ignore or repress contrarian ideas, so that we might again feel normal, and consistent with the dominant cultural belief. This is why religious doubters (throughout the ages) have felt guilt for questioning god; why women have felt ashamed to admit that they think women deserve better; and why gays and lesbians, until only a few years ago, have felt that they don't deserve marriage. We are all victimized by hegemony.

R.W. Connell and Hegemonic Masculinity Theory

Sociologists recognize that there are various forms of masculinities found among differing cultures, and that there is no one way of being masculine within any given culture. We recognize that the definitions of what it means to be masculine shift within the same culture over time in response to social forces, and that not all masculinities are treated equally. In her book, *Masculinities* (1995), R.W. Connell gives an excellent discussion of the various and often competing forms of masculinities in Western cultures, especially in regard to understanding the operation of hegemony as it relates to masculinity.

Much of the study of masculinities centers on how men construct hierarchies that yield decreasing benefits the further removed one is from the flagship version, something known as hegemonic masculinity. This form of masculinity is privileged in social structures, particularly in the institution of sport. While it is difficult (perhaps impossible) to come up with an archetype of what *exactly* hegemonic masculinity is, psychologist Robert Brannon (1976) has came up with four rules that have influenced but not limited the definition most people use when referring to hegemonic masculinity. Brannon's rules are (1) no sissy stuff; (2) be a big wheel; (3) be a sturdy oak; and (4) give 'em hell.

While Brannon's definition foremost includes not acting in ways associated with femininity, lots of research into masculinities (e.g. Messner 1992) suggests that the primary element toward being a man in the hegemonic form in contemporary culture is, not to *be*, *act*, or *behave* in ways attributed to gay men. This means that Western notions of masculinity are based on gender-exclusive heterosexual behavior – a homophobic ascription similar to the "one drop" rule of race in which a person of mixed racial background is described as being black even if having one distant black ancestor. When applied to masculine sexualities, the one time rule asserts that one homosexual act necessarily defines one as a homosexual. This homophobic ascription conflates behaviors with identity. In other words, homosexual *acts* in Western culture, whether active or passive, have been uniquely, and publicly, equated with a homosexual *identity*, despite the fact that self-identified heterosexual men frequently engage in same-sex behavior, while publicly and privately maintaining the identity of heterosexuality (Anderson 2008).

Hegemonic masculinity not only requires that a male maintain 100 percent heterosexual desires and behaviors, but that he must continually prove that he is heterosexual. In a homophobic culture this is best accomplished through the sexual objectification of women and the public discussing of heterosexual "conquests," something exemplified in "locker-room talk" (Curry 1991). But this is also accomplished through the use of homophobic discourse. Frequent use of the words "fag" and "faggot" as well as the expression "that's so gay" are used to disassociate oneself from homosexuality even though only about half the men who use it mean it in a derisive manner (McGuigan 1995). Sociologist Tim Curry (1991) maintains that it is often not enough for heterosexuals to simply say that they are not gay; he posits that they must also behave in *vehemently* homophobic ways if they desire to cast off homosexual suspicion. In this way, homophobia can be used as a vessel toward the continual maintenance of a defensive heterosexual identity in an attempt to prove that the speaker is not gay.

Furthermore, Brannon and other gender scholars assign primary importance to durable sociological understanding that contemporary masculinity is strongly based on patriarchal opposition to femininity (Messner 2002). Feminist gender scholars such as psychologist William Pollack (1998) and sociologist David Plummer (1999) have suggested that men avoid effeminacy because it is associated with homosexuality; maintaining that this rigid contention carries with it a measurable cost that begins as early as the first grade. Pollack maintains that fear of homosexual stigmatization limits males from engaging with anything that is designated feminine. Sociologist Michael Messner (1992) says that men must, therefore, avoid at all cost emotion, compassion, and the appearance of vulnerability, weakness, and fear. If one becomes too emotionally open, he risks being labeled a "sissy" or a "fag."

In this aspect, homophobia and misogyny work together in the construction of men as "masculine." However, in order to ascend the masculine hierarchy toward the most esteemed version of hegemonic masculinity, one must also maintain a host of ascribed variables (things that one is born with such as skin color), and one must behave in accordance with a number of achieved variables, too. One of the achieved variables that Brannon points out with "be a big wheel" is that men must be better than and/or be in charge of other men. This is also described as being the "top dog." Sport, of course, provides a perfect venue for the establishment of this sort of hierarchy. Sport is an arena in which men can literally battle for supremacy.

Brannon's other attributes – "be sturdy as an oak" and "give 'em hell" are also reflected in sporting culture. This is reflected in the phrase "game face," and the expression, "never let them see you sweat." Perhaps, "give 'em hell" is the *essence* of almost any pre-game pep talk, half-time speech or motivational word from coaches and fathers. "Give them the whole nine yards"; "Show them who's boss"; and "Go for the throat," epitomize these attitudes.

Together, these aspects are embedded in the scripts of men, and the more a man adheres to them, the more worth he is said to have in masculine peer culture. Similar to the ways sociologists describe human capital (Becker 1964) as the worth one has because of his skills or education, I describe this as *masculine capital*. The more a male adheres to these traits the more he raises his masculine capital – his worth among other boys and men.

However, while (1) not associating with homosexuality, (2) not associating with femininity, (3) being a big wheel, (4) being a sturdy oak, and (5) giving them hell will raise the masculine worth of an individual, they alone do not qualify one as *hegemonically* masculine. As mentioned earlier, in order to gain this status, certain ascribed variables must also be possessed. These variables are out of the locus of an individual's agency because they are primarily ascribed traits that fall in line with dominant power positions in current culture. For example, white Americans are privileged over blacks, youth is valued over the elderly, abled over disabled, and so on.

Therefore, I use the term *orthodox masculinity* as a way to describe someone who fits all of Brannon's aforementioned tenets (including not being gay), but who does not necessarily maintain the ascribed traits to be considered hegemonically masculine. Hegemonic masculinity describes men who have not only achieved all of these tenets, but who also possess the ascribed variables of the dominant form of masculinity, in whichever status or context it currently exists. That is to say, men who possess hegemonic masculinity are white, able-bodied, heterosexual, athletic, attractive, *and* their masculine behaviors meet Brannon's tenets. Most men tend to (or at least have tended to) desire to achieve this position. Any male who fails to qualify in any one of these ways is likely to view himself as somehow a bit unworthy, incomplete, or at least, inferior.

Maintaining Masculinity: Homophobia at Work

Primarily fearing gay stigma, boys (gay and straight) rigidly police their gendered behaviors to best approximate orthodox masculinity, something Pollack (1998) describes as attempting to be "a real boy." He suggests that, in an attempt to dis-place homosexual suspicion, boys learn at a very young age not to ask for help, to hide weakness, and disguise fear or intimidation. They learn that they must fight when challenged and that they must sacrifice their bodies for the sake of the team. Pollack calls these mechanisms a "boy code," which he maintains puts boys and men into a gender straitjacket that constrains not only themselves but everyone else. He argues that this reduces us all as human beings, and eventually makes us strangers to ourselves and to one another.

McGuffey and Rich (1999) show that those who cross the boundary (especially boys who move into female space) risk being ostracized and accused of being like a girl, or being (directly) accused of homosexuality. Thus, transgression is met with the violent language of homophobic and misogynistic discourse. Terms like "fag" are employed to police and pressure the individual to devalue their behavior and return to conventional masculinized space and/or behaviors, thereby securing men's privilege over women as a whole.

Athleticism is the primary axis of masculine stratification among school-aged boys, even though athleticism has little practical value in modern society outside the athletic arena. The most athletic boys occupy the top positions within the masculine hierarchy, and the least athletic the bottom. Every elementary or high school male knows that the more athletic they are, the more popular they will be. High-status boys stand to gain considerably from the hierarchy as they earn social prestige and secure resources for themselves. This hierarchy is maintained in high school and university cultures.

Boys with the most masculine capital are provided with many social privileges, including near immunity from homosexual suspicion. This effect is largely a product of the association between athleticism and masculinity. Because masculine capital is achieved through athleticism, and because masculinity is thought to be incompatible with homosexuality, it follows that athletes must not be homosexual. Another way to examine this is to say that the better the athlete is – and the more masculine the sport he plays – the less homosexual suspicion there is about him. Consequently, American football players are provided near-immunity from homosexual suspicion, while band members are inundated with it. From the top of the hill, the male is able to marginalize others by using homonegative discourse, and his derision is legitimated because he has earned the respect of his peers.

Surprisingly, boys at the top of the masculine hierarchy are actually provided more leeway to transgress the rigid gender boundaries, because few other boys would be willing to challenge their sexuality for fear of social or physical reprisal. This phenomenon is also found when it comes to homoerotic activities between heterosexual men. The more masculine capital one maintains, the more homoerotic activity they seem able to engage in without having their sexuality questioned. For example, Michael Robidoux's ethnographic research on professional hockey players (2001) shows that they are permitted homosocial play that many would code as homoerotic. Both in Robidoux's and my research (2005a, 2008, 2009), this homoerotic play is expressed at a number of levels. For example, it is found in towel-snapping and wrestling, but it is also found in more homoerotic activities. Robidoux found that hockey players often grabbed each other's testicles, and I found this among water polo players as well (2005a). Additionally, in my own experience as a collegiate coach, I found a great deal of mock intercourse between heterosexual men.

This phenomenon illustrates why when a popular and well-muscled volleyball player came to one of my classes (of 450 students at UC Irvine a few years ago) dressed in drag, he was met with positive laughter and commendations of his bravery, but when an unknown 115-pound non-athletic male came to the same course in drag (a different semester), he was received with cold stares and indifference. It is precisely in this ironic juxtaposition that football players are theorized to be able to slap each other on the butt and be thought straight despite it.

Although athleticism has little practical value for men once they disengage from the sporting arena (particularly as masculinity becomes more scripted in professional occupations in later stages of life), the jock identity may be maintained, or the individual may publicly recall his youthful sporting accomplishments, in order to influence his level of masculine capital. In other words, masculine glory in one's youth can sometimes be tapped to influence one's perception among peers in the future.

While the masculine hierarchy is mainly built via athleticism, consistent association with femininity or with things considered to be associated with gay males are important determinants in the downgrading of one's masculine capital, whether the association is real or perceived. Sociologist David Plummer (1999) points out that an accusation of homosexuality is the primary manner in which to verbally marginalize another male. He maintains that homophobic terms come into currency in elementary school, even though the words may not yet have sexual connotations. Still, he posits that these terms are far from indiscriminate, as they tap a complex array of meanings that he says are precisely mapped in peer cultures.

Young boys who slip out of their bounded zones may be able to recoup some of their masculinity and be reabsorbed back into the masculine arena by deflecting the suspicion of homosexuality onto another boy. A higher-status boy, for example, who transgresses gender boundaries, might call a lower-status boy a "fag" in an attempt to displace suspicion (Pascoe 2005). By negatively talking about and excluding members who are presumed gay, boys are delineating their public heterosexuality, while collectively endorsing hegemonic masculinity. In such a manner, the marginalized attempt to gain power and control by marginalizing another, almost as if it were a game of "tag, you're it" with the "it" being the label of homosexuality. More so, in certain highly masculinized social locations, demonstrating one's heterosexuality is not sufficient to maintain an unambiguous heterosexual masculinity. In these locations, such as within football culture, it is also important to show opposition and intolerance toward homosexuality (Anderson 2005a).

Because homosexuality is equated with femininity, in order to avoid accusations of homosexuality, boys must vigilantly adhere to behaviors coded as the opposite of feminine at all times, something described as "femphobia." Should boys transgress these boundaries, they are quickly reminded of their transgression through a litany of homophobic and misogynistic scripts. Sociologists McGuffey and Rich (1999: 116) show, for example, a case in which older boys observed a seven-year-old crying and said that he will "probably be gay when he grows up." To these young boys, being soft and/or emotional is a quality associated with females, and a boy possessing such characteristics must subsequently be gay. In this manner, a homosexual accusation marginalizes boys, and their status as a marginalized boy is then naturalized through their association with other marginalized people.

Highlighting the vicious nature of homophobic discourse and the use of stigma in the policing of masculine behavior, once a boy is labeled as gay, few other boys will associate with him. The stigma of homosexuality brings with it a guilt-by-association fear that the stigma will rub off onto those not already marginalized. In this aspect, homosexuality is looked upon as a contaminant, similar to the childhood notion of "cooties." Thus, after I came out of the closet as an openly gay high school coach, my athletes were frequently perceived as gay because they had a gay coach. Also illustrating the contaminant effect, McGuffey and Rich (1999: 116) quote a nine-year-old boy yelling, "I don't care if I have to sit out the whole summer 'cause I'm not going to let that faggot touch me!" Making boys contaminated in this way sends a strong warning to the other boys not to act like a girl, or they will be isolated and ostracized by their male peers.

The homosocial patroling may continue into adulthood, especially in the athletic arena. It has, for example, been discovered that in adult male figure skaters (Adams 1993), "kind of feminine" is a phrase used to police the boundaries of acceptable heterosexual behavior, and my research on collegiate heterosexual male cheerleaders finds both homosocial and institutional policing of men's behaviors designed to distance men from homosexuality. For example, in one cheerleading association, certain dance movements or stunts are considered too feminine and are therefore associated with the stigma of homosexuality (Anderson 2008b).

Because homophobic and misogynistic discourse is used to police masculine behaviors, the terms that are most commonly employed are "faggot," "fag," "pussy," and "wuss." None of this is to say, however, that these are the only derogatory terms males use in derision of each other; certainly, they use a variety of terms related to sex and biology. Michael Messner (2002) maintains that these forms of homophobic discourse are also connected to misogyny. In short, though children obviously do not intend it, through this sort of banter they teach each other that sex, whether of the homosexual or heterosexual kind, is a relational act of domination and subordination. The "men" are the ones who are on top, in control, doing the penetrating and fucking. Women, or penetrated men, are subordinate, degraded, and dehumanized objects of sexual aggression. This is just one manner in which homophobia also serves as a form of sexism (more on that in the next chapter).

Hegemonic Masculinity in Jock-ocratic School Cultures

The above section describes the use of athleticism and homophobic and sexist discourse in order to stratify men in a king-of-the-hill-style competition for the upper rungs of a masculine hierarchy. Much like the game, where the most dominant male occupies the top of the hill and physically pushes weaker boys down it, the contestation for masculine stratification is played out on flat sporting fields and courts in the institutions of both sport and public education where sport, through physical education, is made compulsory and those on sporting teams have their associations glorified publicly. This type of school environment is something I call a jock-ocracy, because the high school (and often university) culture is stratified around athletics, not academics.

In a jock-ocracy, boys that score the most touchdowns, goals, or baskets symbolically occupy the top of the hierarchy, and they often naturalize their status by marginalizing other males with homophobic and misogynistic discourse. Those who are softer, weaker, or more feminine are regarded as homosexual and are normally relegated to the bottom of the stratification, or cast out from masculine terrain altogether. Boys who reside at the top of the masculine hierarchy (that is, those with the most masculine capital) are required to maintain their social location through the continuous monitoring of masculine behaviors, in order to assure complicity with masculine expectations at nearly all times. As mentioned before, a continuous process of homosocial patrolling occurs by both self and others, as boys who deviate are routinely chastised for their aberrant behavior through homophobic and misogynistic discourse. Michael Kimmel (1994: 122) describes these processes by saying, "Masculinity must be proved, and no sooner is it proved that it is again questioned and must be proved again – constant, relentless, unachievable, and ultimately the quest for proof becomes so meaningless than it takes on the characteristics, as Weber said, of a sport."

The system of using athleticism to stratify men along an access of power is described as hegemonic because it is maintained not only through the real and symbolic forces of those who occupy the upper tiers, but through the willing participation of those who are subordinated. A high school jock-ocracy provides a clear understanding of the process of masculinity as hegemonic oppression because ancillary players (those possessing subordinated forms of masculinity) keep this volatile framework in place by lauding social merits onto the kings of the hill, literally cheering them on. Women, adult men, and other marginalized boys pay tribute to them by supporting them in the very arena that they struggle to maximize their influence – athletic competitions. The epitome of this is when women cheer for male athletes, relegating themselves to symbolic subservience, and when a student body votes a football player as homecoming king. The public celebration of masculine domination makes hegemonic masculinity a popular identity to adopt and therefore ensures compliance by other males seeking such admiration.

The praise of these kings by individuals and their institutions naturalizes and legitimizes the power of those who control the jock-ocracy. However, as an operation of hegemonic oppression, the system is not necessarily understood in this context. Rather, hegemonic processes conceal the legitimating of power upon athletes via myths of school pride. The subordinated members of school culture do not view their cheering as praise for the so-called elite and powerful men who dominate and subordinate. Rather they view it as cheering for "our school." Perhaps this system is also maintained because cheering for "our team" elicits hopes that the school's kings (in-group) will beat another school's kings (out-group). In this manner, even the marginalized can take solace in the fact that their institution is more masculine than the others, gaining them symbolic masculine capital via association with dominance.

Even if the home team fails to win, men symbolically align themselves with the athletic prowess of their heroes, by association as a spectator, and are encouraged to equate their own masculinity with that which devalues femininity and homosexuality. This association can be seen in the common language spectators use to describe an imagined affiliation with the athletes of a team: "my team lost" or "our team was amazing tonight." This is a process by which all men gain symbolic power over all women when *some* men beat all women at an athletic event or prevent women from competing against them in the first place. By associating with men, even men who cannot beat women gain power because their gender won. This, in essence, is one link between homophobia and sexism. Homophobia keeps all men in line, so that all men can benefit from the privileges of patriarchy.

Sporting Hegemony and Gay Athletes

The hegemony of sport as a necessary good for boys and men is so pervasive that it has even escaped critical examination by those who have been traditionally oppressed by it. In fact, many times these groups of people attribute their marginalization in sport not as a product of a dysfunctional social system but as a lack of individual effort to excel within sport, and they go on to espouse its virtues. Nowhere is this more obvious than with gay athletes.

Whereas one might suspect that gay athletes would maintain some distaste for sport, this was not the case in those I interviewed in my 2005 research on gay male athletes. Both openly gay and closeted gay athletes almost unanimously espoused the virtues of sport. Athletes of all levels expressed their desire to compete and excel in sport, many couching their affinity with terms of endearment, such as, "I love water polo," or arranging their social identities around it, "I'm a soccer player." Still others attributed sport to be more than a recreational activity: "I'd rather be playing football than doing just about anything else. I'm all about football: it's like a way of life for me." They attributed sport to having gained them friendships, self-esteem, and recreational enjoyment. Almost all of the athletes studied aspired to assimilate and excel in the institution, and few suggested structural changes that could make sport a more hospitable place for gay men.

Gay athletes are not consciously aware of their blind acceptance of the virtues of sport, they have merely embraced the orthodox model of sport because the hegemonic underpinnings of sport have prevented them from critically examining the effect sport has on society and on the stigmatization of homosexuality. For example, Marty, a gay football player, told me, "Yeah, I love football. It teaches you to be a team player. You really rely on others on the field, and the guys on the team have become like brothers to me." He continued to praise football, attributing to it the creation of many desirable social qualities, without once problematizing football for what seems to be some clear and highly problematic attributes, including the fact that the cohesion created on his team was structured in the antithesis of who or what he was – gay. Even after Marty experienced intense homophobic bullying from several of the coaches on his team (he remained closeted), he talked of his desire to return someday to coach football, with the very same coaches who frequently used violent discourse against homosexuality. When I asked him why he desired to return to such a situation he responded, "Well it's not like I was the only one whose been called a fag. The coaches call everyone fags. Well, fags or butt buddies. If everyone who got called a fag was really gay, we'd have an all-gay team."

Marty illustrates that sport, and its use in the production of masculinity, is so heavily inscripted, protected, and promoted by meta-myths that even those who are directly subjugated and marginalized by it ascribe to its values and maintain devotion to it. Hegemonic processes make sport one of the most cherished institutions in Western culture.

Given the homophobia thought to still exist within sporting culture, one would hardly expect gay athletes to report positive experiences after coming out to their teams. However, my extensive research into openly gay high school and university athletes shows just the opposite. For example, Ryan typifies some of the positive experiences my athletes report. A 19-year-old first-year student at a private university in Southern California, he came out to his crew team in a rather public manner. "The whole school knows about me, so from the first day of practice the team also knew about me" he said. Ryan, like the other athletes in my study, said that he had no difficulty with teammates. There was no homophobic taunting, and certainly none of the symbolic and literal violence that I faced when coming out in sport.

When I probed for situations that might make homophobia more salient, Ryan said, "I thought the real test would be when we were out on the road, when we had to share a bed. That was when it would come down to it." When the bedding configuration placed three athletes in a room with two beds, the rowers did not want Ryan to have one of the beds alone. They feared that not sharing a bed with him would send a message that they were homophobic. "We talked about it for a while, and we just pushed the two beds together and made one big one. That way nobody felt bad."

Perhaps not all of the athletes I interviewed felt as supported as Ryan, but most were unexpectedly pleased with their coming out experience, even those who played American football. I asked all of the informants, "If you could do it all over again, what, if anything, would you do differently?" to which almost all responded that they would have come out earlier. One athlete said, "It was so much easier than I thought. Now I look back and wonder why the hell I didn't do it sooner." Another said, "I forgot what I was supposed to be so worried about after I came out."

But some of these informants overgeneralized how well things were for them. For many, coming out highlights the reduction of cultural homophobia, but it also highlights the persistence of heterosexism. For example, Gabriel initially spoke of his coming out in glowing terms. He and two other of his fellow distance runners came out all on the same day, and Gabriel praised his coach for creating a supportive environment for them. However, because Gabriel attended a private Christian school, the team decided to keep their identities concealed from the rest of the school. This was justified because the school had kicked one of its students out the previous year simply for saying that he was gay. Highlighting how the homophobia of the institution still controlled his life, Gabriel talked about his state finals 1,600 meter relay race, and how he and his teammates enacted their agency to contest their subordination:

> My friend [also openly gay] and I were approached by our other two [hetero-sexual] teammates, right before the final race. They reached into their bag and pulled out two pairs of gay pride socks and said that they wanted us to wear them. We were really touched. And then they pulled out two more pairs and said that they were going to wear them in support of us.

Gabriel's experience was perceived as being positive to him. Together, he and his teammates symbolically stood against the school's homophobic policies. The glory of the story is unquestionable. Although I have repeated it many times now, it still brings tingles to my spine. But as enjoyable as those tingles are, there is a problem that they conceal. The athletes had to keep their identities secret in the first place.

Because I have been interviewing openly gay athletes (formally and informally) since 1998, I have seen a shift in the way athletes tell their stories. Collectively, what can be said from their experiences is that even though sport is still a macho enterprise, openly gay athletes *increasingly* exist within sporting spaces (even among football and basketball teams). Many of these athletes conform to all other mandates of orthodox masculinity, but increasingly many do not. Increasingly, they suggest that their heterosexual teammates also do not.

More recent stories of athletes to emerge from the closet, I argue, threaten the ability of sport to seamlessly reproduce orthodox masculinity. In doing so, they may help open the doors to increased acceptance of subjugated masculinities and perhaps even the acceptance of female athleticism.

While the culture of sport may not yet permit the creation of a formidable gay subculture, gay athletes are beginning to contest sport as a site of orthodox mascu-line reproduction. Their ability to perform on the pitch challenges orthodox notions of what it means to be "a man." This highlights that hegemony in the athletic arena is not seamless. Gay men are increasingly accepted within the belly of the beast.

Also, when I first published on 32/36 gay men in 2002, I found that virtually every openly gay athlete I could locate was not only good, but was truly outstand-ing. I even had 4 national champions (representing various sports). But by the time I published my updated research on gay athletes in 2005, I was able to locate dozens of lesser quality athletes. Although these are small numbers, they are also significant. The coming out of lesser athletes cannot be attributed to others blazing the path for them; they are individuals who made individual decisions to come out to their teams without having other openly gay athletes to lay the groundwork. If 32 out of 36 were extraordinary prior to 2000, but only 8 out of 22 were extraordinary after 2003, it highlights that individuals felt more confident in coming out due to a wider-spread phenomenon. Similarly, whereas I had a difficult time locating gay men to interview in the early parts of 2000, today they are much more accessible, and there is even a public registry for them on outsports.com.

Finally, supporting this decreasing homophobia in sport theory, a February 27,

2006 *Sports Illustrated* magazine poll of 1,401 professional teamsport athletes also shows that the majority (and 80 percent of those in the National Hockey League) would welcome a gay teammate, today.

Eric Anderson and Inclusive Masculinity Theory

In the years preceding my research on gay athletes, my research agenda has included multiple ethnographies about the experiences of straight men in sport, too. In my studies of white university rugby, cheerleading and soccer players (in both the US and the UK), as well as the members of a racially mixed university fraternity, I show that university-attending men are rapidly running from the hegemonic type of masculinity that has been privileged for the past twenty-five years.

Heterosexual men in these studies no longer physically assault their gay teammates, and heterosexual men increasingly refuse to symbolically wound gay men with homonegative discourse (Adams, Anderson and McCormack 2010). Instead, perhaps influenced by the decreasing rates of cultural homophobia of the broader society, many of these men are politically charged to change the landscape of masculinity. Others simply adopt an inclusive approach to masculinity because it is what their teammates are doing (McCormack 2010).

However, before discussing inclusive masculinity theory, it is important to note that the changes I see occurring among young men are not germane to gender alone. Recent decades have brought a lessening of orthodox views and institutional control of all types of gender, sexual, and relationship types, in North American and Western European cultures (Joyner and Laumann 2001). This is made evident in the growing percentage of people who engage in pre-marital intercourse (Laumann *et al.* 1994; Johnson *et al.* 2001), the social and legal permission for divorce, what some would suggest is a lessening of the traditional double standard for heterosexual intercourse (Tanenbaum 1999; Wolf 1997), and most important to inclusive masculinity theory, the expanded social and political landscape for gays and lesbians (Anderson 2005a, 2008; Barnett and Thomson 1996; Loftus 2001; McCormack 2010).

The impact of these shifting cultural attitudes – the increasing loss of our puritan sentiment – is perhaps best illustrated by examining teenagers. For example, whereas teenagers once traded baseball cards, today they trade digital pornography clips. The internet provides anyone the ability to instantly access a display of sexual variety. Here bodies fuck (predominantly for straight and gay men's pleasures) in all combinations, styles, mixtures, manners, and video quality. I am not necessarily critiquing this, instead, I think it provides what some feminists concerned with pornography have been calling for all along: not an abolition of pornography, but an explosion of the subjectivities of differing kinds of people in pornography (Ellis, *et al.* 1990). Gone is the expectation of heterosexual missionary sex (Segal 1994). The internet has sparked a sexual revolution. How this relates to decreasing stigma about homosexuality is a related matter (McCormack and Anderson in press).

Today's porntube.com generation see, early and often, sexual images that arouse or entertain them: whether accidentally or intentionally, my students tell me that they view video clips of gays, lesbians, and others once stigmatized by the Victorian cult of heterosexual boredom. Often a heterosexual cannot find his preferred images of heterosexual intercourse without filtering through the images of the acts once so socially tabooed. Curiosity of the other, or perhaps a desire to simply see what others enjoy, tempts the heterosexually minded young male into clicking on the link, watching what their fathers despised so much. The internet, I propose, has therefore been instrumental in exposing the forbidden fruit of homosexual sex, commodifying and normalizing it in the process. This, combined with a strategic and political bombardment of positive cultural messages about homosexuality through youth media, MTV, reality television, and other popular venues, has sent a message that while homosexuality is okay, homophobia is not.

Kids are not the only ones working at reducing homophobia, of course. In the years since my athlete was beaten we have seen tremendous cultural and institutional gains for gays and lesbians. Vermont passed Civil Unions in 2000, giving gays and lesbians all the state rights of marriage. In the summer of 2003, the US Supreme Court ruled that the 13 states with remaining sodomy laws could no longer enforce them. Just five months after this landmark ruling, the Massachusetts State Supreme Court granted gays and lesbians the right to marry, opening the door to constitutional challenges for gay marriage across the nation. In 2008, California and Connecticut followed.

Important changes have also occurred in Britain. In 2001, the UK's law (Section 28) prohibiting the discussion of homosexuality in schools was repealed. In 2006, it passed a domestic partnership act granting same-sex couples legal (but not cultural) equality with heterosexuals. And, in 2008, the UK published "best practice" guidelines for schools, stating that homophobic bullying is not to be tolerated, and recommending that schools include gay history in their curriculum, and introduce youth to gay role models.

These events, and myriad other legal municipal, state, national, and European Union rulings, have sparked public debates regarding the status of gays and lesbians in nearly every sector of American and British culture, including cherished American institutions like the Boy Scouts (which has come under increasing fire for their discriminatory practices), and most Judaeo-Christian churches (which frequently fracture over issues pertaining to homosexuality). Furthermore, gays and lesbians are increasingly gaining a normative, albeit mostly desexualized, representation on mainstream television, gaining popularity not only in a large number of shows with gays and lesbians, but also with shows *about* gays and lesbians. It seems that in the new millennium, Anglo-Americans are increasingly accepting of, perhaps even desensitized to, homosexuality.

All of this is crucial to the discussion of inclusive masculinity theory because my driving theoretical hypothesis is that homophobia directed at men has been central to the production of orthodox masculinity. Homophobia has been used as an ordering principle of valued or subjugated individuals in Western cultures (Plummer 1999). Homophobia made hyper-masculinity compulsory for boys, and it made the expression of femininity taboo. When one combines a culture of homophobia, femphobia, and compulsory heterosexuality, one has the make-up of what I call "homohysteria." Homophobic discourse has therefore been used as a weapon for boys and men to deride one another in establishing this hierarchy (Burn 2000). And because femininity was so deeply entwined with male homosexuality (Kimmel 1994), misogynistic discourse not only served to reproduce gender inequality among men, and between men and women, but it reproduced homophobia, too.

But what happens to the traditional, conservative, orthodox version of masculinity when our culture of homohysteria decreases? What implications might this have on men who were once forced into a narrow ascription of masculinity? I argue that the existence of inclusive masculinities means that there is an awareness that heterosexual men can act in ways once associated with homosexuality, with less threat to their public identity as heterosexual. This, I show, has socio-positive effects for straight men, gay men, and women as well.

Inclusive masculinity theory maintains that, in periods of high homohysteria, men's gendered terrains are severely limited, as is physical intimacy between men (cf. Ibson 2002). Accordingly, men's demonstrations of intimacy are generally relegated to the public sphere (such as playing sport), and soft tactility is prohibited. Thus, boys and men have traditionally been prohibited from holding hands, softly hugging, caressing, or kissing (Kaplan 2006). In such cultural moments, boys and men who *do* display physical or emotional intimacy are socially homosexualized and consequently stripped of their perceived masculinity.

However, inclusive masculinity theory argues that in cultures of diminishing homohysteria, two dominant (but not dominating) forms of masculinity will exist: one conservative and one inclusive. Because the conservative masculinity is not culturally hegemonic, I call this form "orthodox masculinity." Here, men remain homohysterical, and therefore tactically and emotionally distant from one another. Conversely, heterosexual men ascribing to an "inclusive masculinity" demonstrate emotional and physical homosocial proximity. They include their gay teammates, and are shown to value heterofemininity. Important in this cultural moment, however, is that neither form of masculinity retains cultural hegemony. In this stage, men who value orthodox masculinity might use homophobic discourse with specific intent to demonize homosexuals, while inclusive-acting men may use homophobic discourse but without intent to degrade homosexuals.

Finally, inclusive masculinity theory argues that in an Anglo-American culture of diminished homohysteria, homophobic discourse is almost entirely lost, or the meanings associated with it no longer maintain homosexualizing utility. In such a setting, the esteemed attributes of men will no longer rely on control and domination, thus intentional homophobic stigmatization will cease. Inclusive masculinity theory therefore highlights that there will be social inclusion of the form of masculinities that were once traditionally marginalized by hegemonic masculinity. Accordingly, inclusive masculinity theory maintains that, in such a zeitgeist, multiple masculinities will proliferate with less hierarchy or hegemony. There will also be an expansion of acceptable heteromasculine behaviors. In other words, when archetypes of inclusive masculinities proliferate, they do not seem to also "dominate."

Inclusive masculinity is therefore as much about the equal inclusion of gay men as it is about the inclusion of straight men's femininity. Moreover, there are other socio-positive variables that come from decreased homohysteria. I show that inclusive masculinities also lead to decreased sexism, and I suggest that this may help in the erosion of patriarchy. Inclusive masculinity theory also maintains that the gendered behaviors of boys and men will be less differentiated from girls and women in periods of diminished homohysteria. In other words, inclusive masculinity theory maintains that in periods of diminished homohysteria there will be a reversal of what gender scholars sometimes describe as the separation of gendered spheres (see Chapter 1). In such a culture, the differences between masculinity and femininity, men and women, gay and straight, will be harder to distinguish, and masculinity will no longer serve as the primary method of stratifying men.

Chapter Conclusion

This chapter examined the construction of a hegemonically dominant heterosexual masculinity, and how hegemonic processes of dominance and oppression are used in the process. It examined the relationship between homosexuality and masculinity, and the threat that homosexuality poses to the order of things. It clarified different forms of masculinity and highlights how they operate in the masculinized culture of teamsport. In doing so, it laid down the framework necessary to understand the relationship that gay male athletes maintain to both masculinity and the institution of sport.

It used the notion of hegemony in explaining how boys (gay or straight) are stratified according to a hegemonic model of masculinity, and how sport is primarily responsible for developing this model. However, this stratification is not always understood as boys being oppressed by more powerful boys. While a feature of hegemony is that there is often the threat of rules or force structuring a belief (such as the threat of pain, punishment, or death), that force cannot be the causative factor in order to elicit complicity. This is what separates hegemonic oppression (think contemporary sexism) from overt rule (think medieval Christianity). The key element to hegemony is that force cannot be the causative factor in order to elicit complicity. Rather, people must believe that their subordinated place is both *right* and *natural*. Sport, it would seem, has served well the principle for which it was designed (Chapter 1).

In this chapter, I showed that the social world created around men's power, physicality, and performance in sport subverts respect for women and gay men, who are not viewed as worthy participants in the sporting terrain. Rather, their social location frequently posits them as bodies to be pursued (for sex or for using to prove one's masculinity) and conquered by the rightful participants of the sporting terrain (more on this in the next chapter). Hegemonic processes have enabled sport to reproduce all of these socio-negative attributes because we have, as a culture, allowed sport to operate without critical examination. Sport largely escapes critical analysis, and empirical scrutiny goes unheard. This is a hegemonic process that reproduces the influence of sport on masculinity.

However, matters are changing. In my most recent research, I find university men are casting off hegemonic aspects of masculinity, instead replacing them with less homophobic, less sexist, less aggressive forms of masculinity. In these studies of soccer players, rugby players, and others, I find that heterosexual men today are more likely to open up and emotionally bond, even cry with one another. And, in the UK, men are even shown to kiss one another (on the lips) as a hetero-sexual bonding mechanism (Anderson 2009). Here, the kiss has been stripped of sexual significance. Symbolically, these kisses represent a new order for heterosexual men, one based on inclusion and compassion, instead of control and marginaliza-tion. This gives me hope that matters are changing.

6 Sport's Use in Marginalizing Women

Jenny's Story

I was a very young coach, maybe just 19, when the high school district I coached for decided that it made sense to have the boys' track team (coached separately) compete at the same time (in dual meets against other schools) with the girls' track team. Until this time, my high school's boys' team might stay at home to compete against the "Warriors" while the girls' team traveled to compete on the Warriors' home turf. Combining the competitions, so that they all took place on just one track at the same time, was thought a way of saving the school district money because it would cut transportation costs in half. There was, however, much outrage among the other coaches (all male) on my team.

The official rationale for my fellow coaches' anger was that competing both teams simultaneously would slow the meet down, adding perhaps two extra hours per meet. However, this logic failed me. While it was true that the meet would last longer, it would also cut in half the amount of meets that we had to prepare for. Setting up the track, organizing the officials, the timers, setting up tarps, tents, a public address system, etc, took far more than two hours per meet. According to my logic, having the girls combined with the boys either meant that there would be twice as many coaches to help, or we would only have to set up for a meet half as often. This seemed a smart idea.

I sensed that my colleagues' resentment came instead from having to compete with girls. Proving my point, one coach finally said, "It will kill boys' track. Nobody wants to watch a fat girl struggle around the 3,200." Although I was a young coach, something went off in my head. *That's not right*, I thought. From my perspective, not only should the two teams compete together, but they should train together as well.

A few years later, several of my athletes were accepted into one of the most prestigious high school track meets in the US. Here, I was surprised to see that Jenny, who ran for our girls' team, was admitted into the mile. I knew she was a fairly good miler, but she was not in the same comparative league as my boy runners. Still, on this day, Jenny improved dramatically, dropping her mile time down to 5:26. After her race, one of the boys on my team said, "Imagine how good she could be, if she could be coached by you?"

The women's distance coach was not an expert, and fortunately for Jenny, he was therefore open to doing whatever it took to help Jenny improve. When I approached this coach with the suggestion that Jenny train with the guys, he was open to it. The following week Jenny's coach asked the other girls on his team what they thought of it. While some thought it was good for Jenny (therefore supporting it), most did not. To them, Jenny was a girl. They therefore maintained that she should train with the girls. Eventually, a compromise was struck so that Jenny could train with my boys two days a week. After a few weeks of running with the guys, Jenny was one of the fastest milers in the nation.

Jenny's success was amazing, and Stanford University was interested in her. If she could run this fast the following year (her last year of high school) Stanford indicated that they would give Jenny a full scholarship. Jenny was ecstatic, her parents were elated, and all seemed in place for Jenny to earn a scholarship to one of America's most prestigious universities. Unfortunately, matters soon changed.

The following cross-country season, the school hired a new coach for the girls' distance running team. Although she came with very little history of success, she did not permit Jenny to train with my team. I tried to negotiate with her, couching my arguments not in the weakness of her coaching, but instead suggesting that there were no girls on Jenny's team to push her, and that Jenny needed to be with the boys for this. The new coach did not see matters this way. She maintained that she had a responsibility to keep Jenny with the other girls, so that Jenny could force them to run faster. I tried to explain to her that in distance running, talent is the most important factor; that the other girls were just so much slower than Jenny that it was impossible for them to catch her. I stressed that Jenny had much at stake here. Her parents could not afford to send her to Stanford, and that in the best interest of the athlete, Jenny belonged with the boys.

Refusing to allow Jenny to train with the boys even one day a week, we took the matter to the school's principal. His response, "The girls' team has a coach, and it is not you." We took the matter to the school district, but they sided with the principal. Jenny's parents even threatened to sue the school district, arguing that their child had special needs because of her exceptional abilities. They argued that there was a highly successful coach, with fast male runners that could help her with those needs. They lost, and Jenny was forced to train with the girls' team.

However, because she had fought to run with the boys, she was marginalized by the other girls on the team. Now, Jenny had no training partners, and a well below-mediocre coach. She got slower, and Stanford stopped calling.

I'm not much one for rules, particularly when they inflict harm upon an athlete. I therefore volunteered to coach Jenny privately, at a location away from the school, after my team had finished their practice. The plan was simple, because the workouts Jenny's coach gave her were far below her abilities: later that night we would meet under cover of darkness to train. I would not be able to have her train with my boys, because they did a hard workout during school practice, but I would run with Jenny myself. Jenny began to improve and all was working well. Until her coach found out.

In response (vengeance), her coach upped Jenny's training, so that she would be too tired to train with me. She also encouraged the other girls on the team to shun Jenny. Jenny, one of the best milers in the nation, became so marginalized and disenfranchised that she ended up transferring schools. She never earned that scholarship.

Jenny's story is not unique. Women all over the country are denied the opportunity to improve their performance because they compete on gender-segregated sporting teams. These women are, however, denied more than just the ability to perform better. They are also denied the ability to befriend men in ways they may not otherwise be able to. It strikes me as odd that we tout teamsport as worthy pursuits because they build team spirit and teach the skills necessary in modern life. Last I checked, modern universities, workplaces, and families are usually comprised of both men and women. If sport teaches us teamwork, does it not make sense to learn the type of teamwork that will be required in "real life"; the kind of teamwork where both men and women work together?

Jenny's story points out that women can be as insistent on sex-segregation in sport as men are. In this case, Jenny was welcomed by the boys' team; the sexism came from the female coach and female teammates. This highlights that sport is a mutually agreed upon system of discrimination. Ultimately, however, it is a system that benefits men as a collective more than it does women. As long as women believe that feminism is about separatism, we all miss out on a vital opportunity to bring the genders closer together.

Sex Segregation in Sport

The hidden process of gender segregation has been documented from early childhood (Thorne 1993) throughout adulthood (Williams 1995), but is it something made much more *visible* in sport. Largely a product of both men's and women's socialized desires, men and women occupy separate spaces in the sporting world (Hargreaves 2002). Few other institutions naturalize the segregation of men and women so near perfectly as do teamsport (Davis 1990). While occupational sex segregation is declining in other institutions (Rotolo and Wharton 2004), formal and traditional reasoning has left teamsport a largely unexamined arena of gender segregation (Caudwell 2003). While this segregation has *many* male-driven purposes, it is important to note that feminist separation also occurs in sport.

One can certainly understand feminist desire to play sport away from men, particularly because women are protected from the violence of male athleticism in gender-segregated sport (Kreager 2007; Smith 1983). Female-only settings also appear to empower women and to provide them with female solidarity in a setting free from men's intimidation and harassment (Fielding-Lloyd and Meân 2008). But the ethos surrounding separate sporting programs is much more institutionalized than simply a matter of women desiring to play separately. In the wider context, Fielding-Lloyd and Meân (2008: 37) suggest that separatist policies "can hinder gender equity as they re/produce difference." This is the product of men producing and reproducing their own privilege over women. And the privilege men maintain from segregated sport extends far beyond the institution of sport.

When boys are socialized into sport for the perceived "character-building" benefits, they also construct a language specific to sport; language that earns them human capital. Boys and men learn to bond, relate to each other, work and solve problems all without the presence of girls and/or women in sport. And, because sport is gender segregated, it means that women are excluded from the domain in which this language and way of relating is learned. Women therefore have a harder time acquiring the cultural codes and behavioral conducts deemed necessary to impress masculine gatekeepers in other social institutions that are dominated by men (Cameron 1998). This is something gatekeepers (those who do the hiring) code as "skills." Additionally, it has been suggested that in learning mutually shared characteristics, backgrounds, interests, experiences or knowledge, co-membership is established between the gatekeeper (male) and the job candidate (also male), instigating a comfort level for both parties and enhancing solidarity and positive feeling towards one another. In accordance with this interaction, it is perceived that gatekeepers (particularly within the sports industry) seek out candidates with similar sporting backgrounds, experiences and knowledge to themselves, as they believe that their own sporting careers have prepared them well for their job and assume those who display similar levels of social and masculine capital would be best suited to the job they have on offer.

Thus, men's gender segregation (and dominance) in sport helps translate into men justifying their privilege in the work world. This is even true of the work world that relates to sport (presented later in this chapter).

I argue that the separation of the sexes in sport maintains a hegemonic stranglehold on our abilities to think differently, to imagine a better model of gender integration in sport (Anderson 2008c). This is because sport is naturalized through notions of "opposite" phenotypes (Davis 1990; Messner 2002), and myths about boys' elevated levels of innate aggression and athletic advantage over girls (Butterfield and Loovis 1994). Thus, collectively, sex segregation in sport, as Messner describes (2002: 12), is "grounded in a mutually agreed-upon notion of boys' and girls' 'separate worlds.'"

But there are serious costs associated with gender segregation other than career progression. In the gender-segregated arena of sport, men are not introduced to the athletic abilities and sexual/gendered narratives of women. Instead, in the homosocial world of men's teamsport, males are socialized into an ethos in which women are devalued as athletes and valued as sexual objects. Bereft of alternative gender narratives, hegemonic masculinity remains predicated in anti-feminine, sexist, and (frequently) misogynistic thinking. Without having women as teammates, men fail to learn of women's sexual narratives, they fail to learn of their athletic abilities, and they fail to learn of women's leadership capabilities. This later leads to men's advantage in employment in corporate life.

I've spent a good part of my academic career examining the socio-negative aspects of gender segregation in sport. But perhaps the most illuminating research I have conducted on this considers male ex-high school football players; men who were not able to make their university football teams because of the decreasing opportunity structure upon which sport is built (Chapter 4), and ended up competing for their university's coed cheerleading team, instead. Findings from this research lead me to suggest that, in the gender-segregated arena of sport, the extreme regimentation and inordinate amount of time required to excel often deprives men of experiences outside of the athletic arena, where they might otherwise be introduced to the athletic abilities and sexual/gendered narratives of women. Instead, in the homosocial world of men's teamsport, males are socialized into an ethos in which women are valued as sexual objects and devalued as athletes (Curry 1991; Schacht 1996). This is made more possible because there are no women to contest these narrow understandings, and also because coaches are recruited from a pool of ex-athletes who matriculated through the same system.

Essentially, I suggest that because teamsport are nearly compulsory for American youth, young boys are indoctrinated into a masculinized, homophobic, and sexist gender regime from early childhood – an institution they cannot easily escape. Even if boys are fortunate enough to enter a gender-integrated sports team when young, by the time they reach high school, gender segregation is the norm, as it was for Jenny and the boys on my team. Additionally, the demands of competitive sport often consume such quantities of time that it also structures men into off-the-field social networks of teammates – positioning them into a near-total masculine institution (as discussed in Chapter 3).

Bereft of alternative gender narratives, and desiring social promotion among their peers, boys and men are more willing to subject their agency to orthodox masculinity – which remains predicated in anti-feminine, sexist, and (frequently) misogynistic thinking. In this aspect, segregation on the field is complicated by the effect of a near-total institution off the field. But data from my cheerleading research clearly shows that when these same men become familiar with the experiences of women (in the gender-integrated sport of cheerleading), almost all adopt a new gender strategy that looks more favorably upon women (none downgraded their position on women). While some of this change may occur because of the liberalizing attitudes of university life in general (Ohlander *et al.* 2005), I attribute much of their reconstruction to the gender-integrated sport of cheerleading.

In coed cheerleading, the time constraints of training and travel structures athletes into mixed-sex social networks, at least part of the time. Here, men are likely to have conversations with women about sex, gender, sport, and life – the kind of conversations they were often unable to have in a homosocial culture such as football. In partaking in these conversations, informants not only open themselves to hearing of the multiple narratives of women, but they also learn to see them as worthy and competent athletes, teammates, coaches, and leaders. In cheerleading, even men who were once highly sexist are able to socialize and develop cohesion with women as participants of equal agency and responsibility for team performance and outcomes – something that works against gender stereotyping. Coupled with a more inclusive institutional and organizational setting (something I was not able to achieve with Jenny's coach), these men are led to undo much of their separatist, sexist thinking.

The findings of my cheerleading research, however, stand out as odd compared to other research showing that the integration of men and women does not always deter gender stereotyping (Jackson and Warren 2000; Harvey and Stables 1984).

I, however, suggest that teamsport may be uniquely effective in reducing gender stereotypes precisely because they necessitate that men and women work together for the accomplishment of victory. In other words, for once, I am highlighting a way that sport *could* (but does not) help promote virtue.

My argument makes logical sense: men relying upon women to obtain their athletic goals will look more favorably upon women. The findings of my cheerleading research indicate that the gender-integrated nature of cheerleading may therefore help *disrupt* the reproduction of orthodox masculinity among men in gender-segregated teamsport.

I do not claim gender integration to be a panacea for the sexual, social, ethical, and gender-related problems associated with sport; men's teamsport is far too entwined with other masculinist systems and institutions for that. Furthermore, my research does not address what effect gender-desegregating teamsport might have on female athletes, particularly considering that women have been shown to be subordinated by men within other integrated terrains (Britton and Williams 1995). Nor does my research address how gender-integrated teamsport might impact upon the number of socio-positive attributes that Sabo and his colleagues (2004) correlate with women's sporting participation. But whereas dominant ideology maintains that gender segregation is valuable because it shelters women from men's violence, I question whether violence against women might instead be promoted through sporting segregation. If gender segregation in sport is even *partially* responsible for men's violence against women then my research should serve as a call for further academic inquiry into the effects of gender-integrating sport.

Still, it is recognized that gender-desegregating sport is a politically charged proposition, and I am aware that among traditionalists of sport the potential implications of these findings may not be received favorably. But only by examining both sides of this question might we come to a better understanding of the impact gender segregation has on athletic culture. Hegemonic perspectives that value gender segregation in sport – whether they be masculinist or feminist in origin – should not stop us from academically examining a counter-proposition. As Frye (1999: 361) says, "If you are doing something that is so strictly forbidden by the patriarchs, you must be doing something right." One thing is certain, without gender integration competitive, organized, teamsport continues to benefit men, in their cultural, patriarchal, rule over women.

Pierre Bourdieu and Patriarchy

Patriarchy (men's cultural and institutional dominance over women) is the norm in most societies. Although a few, rare, matriarchal societies have existed – including some Native American societies – the power and privilege that men maintain over women is ubiquitous, profound and mundane. Men take up more space in coed settings, and they are often thought smarter, more competent, funny, or generous. Men's rule gives them elevated wages over women, a faster route to promotion, and a better piece of the pie. Patriarchy, of course, runs all the way to the top of the power structures, as men dominate and control all-important institutions for creating both policies and cultural beliefs: thus, men control politics, religion, education, entertainment, news, etc.

Women sometimes maintain strength in the institutions that clean up after men's doings, like childcare, teaching, social work, nursing, and other care-providing occupations (Williams 1995). Women also take notes for powerful men; they do their shopping and wash their clothes and homes. But what is interesting about patriarchy in contemporary society, despite the fact that women now attend college/university at the same rate as men, is that women continue to vote for men. Thus, women contribute to their own oppression. This means that patriarchy is not just overt (forced) rule, it is (as we discussed in the previous chapter) hegemonic oppression.

Illustrating this, with each new class of students I have (and my classes are equally representative of men and women) I try a simple experiment. I rush into class late, and loudly announce, "Sorry I'm late. Listen up, I need you to quickly divide yourselves into groups of five, and elect a leader." By instructing my students to configure themselves into groups of five, I assure that the gender split cannot be equal. And because men almost always sit next to men, and women with women, the chances are that most of the teams will be strongly gendered one way or another. What is interesting about this exercise is that when a team is comprised of all men, they almost always pick the tallest male in the group to be the leader; when the team is mixed (to any degree) they almost always pick a male to be the leader. Occasionally, if there is only one male in the group of five, they will pick a female leader, but the general rule is that men and women almost exclusively pick tall men to be their leaders. This highlights the embeddedness of patriarchy. I gave them no clue as to what qualities this leader might need to possess for the "game." Accordingly, if picking a leader were a random process, one would expect 50 percent of the leaders to be men and 50 percent of the leaders to be women. But it's not. This highlights the hegemonic aspects of patriarchy: men and women mutually agree that men are to lead women, and not the other way around.

In the 1970s, several general theories addressing patriarchy (men's institutional privilege and cultural domination over women) were advanced (Rubin 1975) concerning domination of one group by another via economic, social, and cultural hierarchies. But the origins of men's dominance are multifaceted.

Pierre Bourdieu (now deceased) was one of the most influential social theorists of his generation. Trained mainly as an anthropologist, he suggested that patriarchy is likely produced by an interlocking system of cognitive oppositions and social patterns in families, schools, and the state, all of which are grounded in the opposition of the dominant male and submissive female (Bourdieu 2001). It is the interlocking system of cognitive categories and objective social differences that produce the (false) perception that there are deep-seated differences between the sexes. This is something that Mariah Burton-Nelson (1994) aptly points out in her book *The Stronger Women Get, the More Men Love Football*.

Connell's (1987) notion of hegemonic masculinity (Chapter 5) addresses the issue of patriarchy, too. She suggests that the purpose of having one hegemonic archetype of masculinity is not just about stratifying men along a continuum of diminishing returns. She suggests that the current hegemonic form of masculinity contains sexist and misogynistic tenets in order to help men maintain their patriarchal privilege over *all* women. Non-hegemonic men may pay (or lose out) for not maintaining the characteristics associated with the elite form of masculinity, they may even be harassed, bullied, or exploited because of it. Nonetheless, with everyone looking "up" to the dominant version of masculinity, simply *being* male permits all men to benefit from the marginalization of all women. This is something Connell calls the "patriarchal dividend."

In other words, all men invest in their symbolic (hegemonic) form of dominating masculinity, so that they might hold up this version as symbolic proof of their right to rule. This is why Connell does not develop a process of hegemonic femininity. Instead, she suggests that because men are collectively positioned over women in society, the elite form of femininity is best described as *emphasized femininity*.

Hegemonic masculinity helps maintain patriarchy, because while all men are stratified below "hegemonic masculinity," all women are stratified below all men. Men's rule over women is maintained by the few elite dominants who essentially show that men's dominance over women is natural, and right. Because some men (the pros) beat all women (in, say, football) it sets up the illusion that all men are superior. This, I suggest, is one reason that men do not want women playing in the same teams as them, and is why sport remains one of the most segregated institutions in Western culture (not even the military is as gender segregated). By preventing women from playing with men, we maintain the illusion that all men are better than all women (Burton-Nelson 1994). By segregating women away from men, women cannot establish leadership positions (think team captain) over men.

Bourdieu (2001) describes the need to highlight how a social movement committed to "symbolic subversion" can erode men's privilege. Bourdieu suggests that gay men (who are so marginalized in Connell's theorizing that they are hardly considered within the terrain of masculinity) possess the unique circumstances necessary toward undermining masculine orthodoxy. Bourdieu beleives that the gay male maintains the ability to invisibly gain access to male privilege, so that he can then become visible (as gay) with full citizenship. In other words, Bourdieu saw the gay male as being able to penetrate masculinized terrains while closeted, to raise their worth among men, and then to come out as gay, exposing the fallacy upon which the system is built. Thus, he thought the gay male was uniquely positioned to align with feminists in a terrain or progressive coalition politics to attack male dominance materialistically, symbolically, and domestically.

While this may have real saliency in sport, Bourdieu's point seems to ignore the actual history of gay liberation politics. The connection between masculinity and sexism has been trumpeted since the 1970s, yet the alliance between gay and feminist groups has been tenuous, at best. The potential for gay liberationist ideas of undermining patriarchy, I argue, has also passed. This is because, by the mid- to late 1970s, much of the radical impulse in gay liberation had been eclipsed by a more pragmatic approach to the obtainment of civil rights, that focused on individual rights and lifestyle alternatives – an assimilationist approach. Gay marriage (which I favor) serves as a perfect example.

This, however, is not to suggest that gay men do not still pose a threat to heteromasculine dominance. I suggest that one arena in which gay men maintain considerable agency is in sport. Accordingly, I agree with Connell (1987, 1995) in that hegemonic masculinity helps reify and reproduce patriarchy. I also agree with Burton-Nelson (1994) that sport symbolizes and legitimates this dominance. And I agree with Bourdieu (2001), in viewing male dominance from a historical materialist (radical feminist) perspective. Ultimately, however, I think that patriarchy is just much more complex than can be addressed with any one single theory. Oppression comes in many forms, and has many different etiologies.

Bourdieu (2001) suggests that males also suffer under a patriarchal culture. This is because they have to respond to collective expectations of being male. Thus, males become mastered by their own dominance. New (2001: 729) adds that, "Men may have conflicting interest in relation to the gender order. While men are frequently agents of the oppression of women, and in many senses benefit from it, their interests in the gender order is not pre-given, but constructed by and within it." She adds, "Since in many ways men's human needs and capacities are not met within the gender orders of modern societies, they also have a latent 'emancipatory interest' in their transformation." Yet, Bourdieu implies that even if men wished to reject their lot, they would be inhibited from doing so. This is because of their deeply socialized gender patterns.

Women's Status in Sport

In 2009, the Women's Sport and Fitness Foundation (WSFF) published their first paper as part of the commission on the future of women's sport. This paper was entitled "Trophy Women? Why a balanced business board is good business for sport." The paper provides the most recent figures on gender proportions in sports leadership from the WSFF's yearly Sports Leadership Audit, the most accurate and extensive of its kind in the UK. The results of this audit suggest that at present there exists "a leadership crisis" (WSF 2009: 3) in the sports sector. The WSFF therefore states that "sport is failing in its core business: performance." Under-representation of women at a senior level means that sport is ill-equipped to understand and engage with 51 percent of the population.

In the US, women's sporting participation *has* increased since the 1972 passage of Title IX (McDonagh and Pappano 2008). Today, women are well represented as participants at the lower levels of sport. However, women's representation dramatically decreases in the professional ranks; particularly among the sport that captures media interest (Burstyn 1999). Also since the passage of Title IX, the percentage of women that coach women's teams has decreased to 42.4 percent. Acosta and Carpenter (2006) show that less than 2 percent of men's collegiate teams are coached by women.

In the UK, Sportcoach research (2004, as cited in Claringbould and Knoppers 2008) shows that 81 percent of all qualified coaches (at all levels of sporting participation) are men, and shows that women are far less likely to have a presence at higher levels of sports organizing bodies, too. For example, they show that in the Netherlands Olympic organizing body, just 14 percent of the employees are women. Even when women do make it into sport management, they are likely to be placed in marginalized positions (Whisenant *et al.* 2002).

Similarly, Lapchick and colleagues (2006) have also shown that sport media is run mostly by and for men. For example, they surveyed more than 300 US daily newspapers, finding that men comprised 95 percent of sports editors in newspaper sports departments, 87 percent of assistant sports editors, 93 percent of columnists, 93 percent of reporters, and 87 percent of copy editors/designers. David Nylund (2007) found that 80 percent of sports talk radio hosts are men. Accordingly, Farred (2000: 101) describe sports talk radio as "overwhelmingly masculinist," and Smith (1983: 1) calls it "an audio locker room."

What this suggests, is that despite the gains of feminism and the mandates of Title IX, there has been little change to the gatekeeping practices of the occupations within the sport industry (Fielding-Lloyd and Meân 2008). Accordingly, Knoppers and Anthonissen (2005: 1) write, "Despite at least thirty years of research and policy making directed primarily at women ... and regardless of changes in the way managers do their work, senior management [in sport] is still primarily a male preserve, numerically and culturally." Moreover, the literature on sport, coaching, and members of the sport media complex highlight that not only are members of these occupations over-represented by men, but that they are occupied by highly *masculinized* men (Bruening and Dixon 2008).

However, the sexual and gendered composite of sport and its ancillary organizations is of more than just academic interest. The manner in which people are recruited and retained in sports stakeholders' positions is a matter of political and social concern (Cunningham 2008; Fielding-Lloyd and Meân 2008). Burstyn (1999) and others (Bryson 1987; Messner and Sabo 1990) argue that while sport is widely regarded as being outside the dominant political and social Western institutions, the masculinist account of power and patriarchy that it promotes is also central to the constitution of political power. Accordingly, sport as an idealized practice of masculine power and privilege has profound social consequences outside the sporting arena (Sage 1990). This, perhaps, is why men and women in my classes (who are all athletes) choose men to lead. One cannot help but wonder whether if these women (trained to have higher self-esteem through sport) elect men, non-sporting women would, too? And if they elect them in my class, would they not also elect them in the working world?

Teamwork, discipline, hard work, and sacrifice are characteristics that are thought synonymous with business, too. Thus, the self- and forced segregation of females from males in sport means that men and women are schooled in different institutions. Here, one sex is left severely lacking in valued training and social networking. Clearly, women have a hard time competing with the type of masculine and social capital that sport yields, not because they lack male genitalia, but because they are formally segregated from boys and men in sport. In this manner, what is learned in sport is reproduced outside of sport: people who learn homophobia, sexism, and conservative forms of masculinity in sport learn cognitive patterns and leadership styles that then spill over into other institutions. Those who do not learn the cultural codes and behavioral conducts of sport (women, openly gay men, and others) do not impress upon the masculine gatekeepers their worthiness of occupational performance. Water-cooler questions are organized around, "What sport did you play" and not "What differing voice can you bring to this institution?" This helps explain patriarchal dominance and the over-representation of heterosexual men in positions of power, aside from willing homophobia and misogyny.

Supporting this, Howe's (2001) research into the professionalization of rugby highlights how institutional norms are highly influential in recreating identities among players on *and off* the pitch. Similarly, Parker (2001: 61) suggests that everyday routines construct masculine identities through official and unofficial norms, including a "professional attitude." These studies illustrate the power of social capital in constructing a certain type of valued individual for the leadership market. They signify the social connections and norms of relational cooperation that are embedded in trustworthiness of cooperation for mutual benefit of orthodox achieving men (Putnam 1995).

What I am suggesting here is that some senior managers *may* strategize to keep women and openly gay men out of positions of power themselves, but it is much more likely that the institutionalization of sexism and homophobia operates in a more insidious manner. I suggest that even well-minded, gay-friendly feminist men can unwillingly reproduce the culture of masculine privilege in sport and other institutions: sexism occurs not just because heterosexual men decide that they do not wish women to join their club. We must instead look to the micro-, meso-, and macro-layers of the social institutionalization of men's privilege in sport if we are going to understand how men's privilege is reproduced elsewhere.

In other words, while *some* might strategize to keep women and gay men out, it is more likely that the gatekeepers choose individuals that have social and masculine capital – factors that they assume will make a *heterosexual and sporting man* "the best man" for the job. Gatekeepers (often ex-sportsmen) are likely to consider that their former sporting histories have well prepared them for their current occupation. Accordingly, New (2001: 736) suggests that, "The best 'man' could be anyone who might not threaten the ways of being and doing with which they are comfortable." Women and openly gay men might actually come to the workforce with a different perspective.

Further Marginalizing Women through Homophobia, Sexual Harassment, and Abuse

For decades, women's sport has been trivialized and marginalized by a sexist culture, and women who participate in it are often socially ostracized (Coakely 2004). Today, through legislation, the advocacy of the Women's Sports Foundation, and declining cultural homohysteria, millions of girls and women play competitive, organized sport. However, women are still subject to multiple types of abuse, much of it by their coaches.

For example, the high percentage of men coaching women often leads to sexual harassment and sexual abuse. The Women's Sports Foundation suggests that sexual harassment, and even sexual assault, is a significant problem in school and open amateur sport settings, and that it often goes unreported because athletes are afraid that either their complaints will not be taken seriously, or that they will hinder their careers by making a report.

Sexual harassment occurs among both male and female athletes, partially because coaches have immense control over their athletes' lives, inside and outside of sport. Coaches control their athletes, grow to take on important roles in their athletes' lives, and this makes it more difficult for athletes to report harrassment. Brackenridge and Kirby (1997) suggest that sub-elite athletes are most at risk for this, because they have spent years climbing the sporting ladder, but have not yet made it. Novices can drop out with more ease, and highly successful professional athletes develop more independence, but it is the sub-elite group that is most vulnerable.

Perhaps a more common type of sexual harassment, however, is the homophobia and masculine-phobia that comes with women's sport, from male and female coaches, as well as female players. Almost all females participating in sport find that their sexuality is called into question (Kwiatkowski 1998), particularly in sport that is associated with more roguish pursuits, like rugby. In fact, a 1994 NCAA survey found that 53 percent of women's college athletes and 51 percent of women's coaches and administrators were concerned that their involvement in sport would lead others to assume that they were lesbian.

In an attempt to distance themselves from lesbianism, heterosexual female athletes often express their gender in hyper-feminine ways. This is something Felshin (1974) calls the "apologetic," and it has remained largely unchanged for as long as women have been competing in sport. Griffin (1998) categories eight ways in which women perform the apologetic: 1) silence; 2) denial; 3) promotion of a feminine heterosexual image; 4) promotion of a heterosexy image; 5) search for heterosexual-only space; 6) attacks on lesbians; 7) preference for male coaches; 8) acknowledgement of but disassociation from lesbians. Accordingly, although it is lesbians who largely created the legal and social space for women to play sport, heterosexual teammates often (not always) show antipathy toward them (Sykes 1998). Lesbian athletes can find themselves othered in an already othered group (for more on othering see Chapter 7), stigmatized for being both female and lesbian. This environment leads coaches to use negative recruiting (in which high school recruits are warned against competing for another college team because of the "high rates of lesbians" on it), and this creates a hostile environment for all involved.

Clearly then, there are many similarities between gay male and lesbian athletes: the most significant is the compulsory heterosexuality required of each. Heteronormativity sets up clear demarcations as to how men and women are supposed to act, who they are allowed to love, and what sexual subjects they are permitted to speak of publicly. If an individual transgresses these scripts, punitive measures are enacted; namely, one's sexual orientation is called into question, whether it be as lesbian or gay. In this manner, homophobia polices gender roles (Griffin 199; Messner 1992; Pronger 1990).

But there are additional difficulties for lesbian athletes. In men's sport, when a gay male athlete comes out, it does not generally homosexualize the others on his team (Anderson 2005a). For example, there is currently an openly bisexual rugby player at my university (on the top team), but nobody assumes that other men on the team are gay or bisexual because one is. Conversely, one of my other heterosexual female students plays for the women's rugby team; yet she reports that although there are less than 10 percent lesbians, all of the women are perceived as being lesbian because of their involvement with the sport. This can create extra hostility toward lesbian athletes.

For example, I was once listening to a master's degree student talking about how she and her three friends were "victimized" by homophobia when she was younger. "Everyone was wondering if we were lesbian, and we were not." The student then said, "So when we won our trophy, we went up to the front and said, 'and by the way, we are not lesbian.'" This poor graduate student did not know how to react when I stood and told her that she had committed a sick act of homophobia. From her perspective, she was victimized by those assuming she was lesbian. From my perspective, she was defensively denouncing lesbianism, further silencing and stigmatizing an already othered group. The situation clearly highlights how homophobia in sport hurts both gay and straight women.

Not all teams are homophobic, however. There are many teams that embrace their lesbian players. Teams in which straight and lesbian women live together, play together, and compliment each other's lives. Griffin (1998) suggests some variables that make a team more inclusive. She suggests that the attitude of the institution for which the athletes play is important. She also suggests that an increased emphasis on winning will result in a decreased acceptance of gay athletes on a team, as increased pressure seems to call for increased homophily. Still, the attitudes of the coach are likely to be important.

Interestingly, while one might expect the presence of a gay or lesbian coach on a team to help legitimate lesbian athleticism, openly lesbian coaches seem to find themselves victimized by a silencing of their sexual orientation, and they in turn, by complying to the culture's heteronormative mandates, continue to propagate their own silence. It is also quite common for younger lesbians (who are more out and proud with their identity) to face hostility by their closeted lesbian coaches (who act out aggression in their frustration). Sadly, these coaches fail to recognize that keeping lesbian sexuality in the closet is vitally important to normative heterosexuality, which reproduces discrimination against lesbian women.

Chapter Conclusion

In this chapter, I hope to have shown that the system of reproducing the masculinized nature of sport and its ancillary occupations and organizations is much more than just culturally hegemonic, it is also structural. Not just structural in the sense of a social, historical and institutionalized pattern, but literally structured by codified rules of segregation, reminiscent of the same rules that once formally segregated blacks from whites. It is a resilient system, which, despite the gains of second wave feminism that characterize the broader culture, reproduces multiple forms of discrimination against women.

Sex segregation in sport helps the entire institution of sport to reproduce itself as an extremely powerful gender regime. Because almost all boys are socialized into this institution in their formative years, they learn cognitive patterns and gendered behaviors that they carry with them into their adult years and into other institutions as well. Here, they discriminate against women in hiring practices and other social matters of equality.

I described men's rule over women as patriarchy, and used Bourdieu to theorize how men have continued to dominate women in most of the important institutions in our culture. But it is important to remember that the system by which men reproduce their dominance in sport (or any other social institution) is not seamless. Women continue to make grounds at undoing formal sexism and the institution-alization of men's privilege. In sport, women have made considerable progress in gaining the right to play, albeit in their own segregated sporting spaces.

I propose that sport is instrumental in maintaining cultural patriarchy. It is a place where boys and men still "learn" to symbolically dominate women. Although women have made great progress gaining access to playing sport, it is time for the next step. I propose that it is time to gender-integrate community, youth, and school sporting teams. This is a proposal I further address in the final chapter.

7   Sport's Use in Excluding, Reproducing Stereotypes, and Othering

CJ's Story

My best friend CJ and I share one very common trait. We are both perpetually coming out of the closet. For me, whenever I meet someone new, the question is how/when do I come out as gay? Every time I meet a new guy, for example, it is only a matter of time until they try to bond with me by pointing out a sexually attractive woman, or asking if I am married. For CJ, it is different. He wonders whether this new person will detect that he walks with a slight limp, and if he is wearing shorts he knows that until he comes out, the other person will be wondering what happened to him. This is because of the obvious metal foot that is suctioned on from just below his right knee. You see, my friend CJ lost a foot to bone cancer. And just as I will have to come out to new people until the day I die, so will he have to tell people how he lost his foot.

I first met CJ when I was teaching at the University of California, Irvine. Here, I befriended many of the distance runners on the team. I would have loved to run with them, to serve as a volunteer assistant coach; and judging by the number of athletes on the team who came to me for running-related advice, I would have been very well received among the athletes on the team. There was only one problem. One day, I happened to be traveling on the same airplane as the runners, when one of my favorite students, Jules, said to the head running coach (in the airport lounge) "Hey, Eric Anderson is here." The coach responded, "I sure hope that faggot isn't sitting next to me." This answered my question as to why the coach did not want my voluntary assistance with his team. Thus, my involvement with the runners on the U.C. Irvine cross-country team consisted of contact with the players away from their official training.

I had advised runners on many issues for several years, and whether their coach liked it or not, a good number of them signed up for my classes. One day, Jules came to me to tell me a story about a freshman named CJ. "He was a good runner in high school," Jules said about his teammate, "and we all love him. The only problem," he went on to tell me, "is that CJ went undiagnosed with bone cancer for quite some period of time."

The only way an athlete at U.C. Irvine could be excused from official training was to have the team's doctor examine him. This particular team's doctor missed a telltale sign of bone cancer (a star shaped pattern on the X-ray) and instead continued to tell CJ that his pain was caused by a stress fracture. His coach, more interested in winning than seeing his athlete healthy, urged CJ to run races on this stress fracture, despite the obvious pain that it caused. By the time CJ realized his problem was worse than his coach or doctor accounted for – seeking the help of a more qualified physician – it was too late. The new physician recognized the star-shaped pattern immediately, and within a few days CJ had his lower left leg cut off. Months of chemotherapy, and several surgeries later, CJ was (and remains) cancer-free.

This story (and it is not over yet) immediately highlights several problems with orthodox thinking in sport. First, it clearly makes salient that the coach's homophobia prevented him from having a well-qualified volunteer coach. This same homophobia also caused serious tension with Jules that same year when he came out as bisexual. However, the story also highlights the problem of a total institution. Because the athletes were required to see a physician within the system (an individual who undoubtedly feels pressure to pass athletes into playing), CJ's condition went undiagnosed. Meanwhile the cancer spread. Yet, the problem with sport for CJ doesn't end here. The exclusivity of competitive, organized sport would generate yet another shocking turn in CJ's story.

CJ was immediately fitted with an artificial running leg. Although CJ knew that his dream of being a top-notch university distance runner was over, he nonetheless desired to remain part of the team – to continue to compete for and train with his friends. The only problem was that CJ's coach never returned his calls. The coach symbolically told him that he was not interested in having him on his team anymore.

Now, I certainly do not intend to convey, with this story, that all coaches are this blatantly evil. They certainly are not. However, I do intend to relate that many of the socio-positive aspects of sport we espouse (team cohesion, developing a sense of loyalty to sport, etc.) are often traits that are valued because they help the coach win. And, when a coach wins, he/she is socially, emotionally, and sometimes professionally (including financially) rewarded. So, although CJ's loyalty to his team influenced him to endure extreme pain in several races, the loyalty was not returned. Once CJ was no longer a top-notch performer he was discarded by his coach – like a racing greyhound who has no use to its owner after his racing days are over.

Fortunately for CJ, however, there is something of a happy ending to his story. Jules was crushed by CJ's rejection. He therefore asked if I would be interested in meeting CJ, with the aim of having me coach him. I told Jules that I would love to, and that I liked CJ the moment I met him. I found him bright, funny, liberal, and passionate about continuing with the sport he loved. Together, he and I began the long process of learning to run on an artificial leg.

There were, of course, many setbacks (including the fact that his stump was severely swollen), however, exactly one year from the day CJ was diagnosed, we managed to run a mile race on the track, in front of his cheering family and friends. By the end of the second year, CJ was beating me in road races, and he broke a few world records for his particular division of Paralympic running as well. Perhaps

CJ's running chapter was best summarized when he finished his first marathon in 3:23. I have coached hundreds of athletes to win major championship meets, but I have never been more proud of anyone than I was of CJ that day. In the final meters he outkicked me and I saw him stop at the finish line, take his artificial foot off, and hold it up for the cheering crowed to see. He then hopped across on one foot.

Today, CJ teaches high school in inner-city Los Angeles. I have had the pleasure of seeing my runner become an amazing and inspiring teacher.

On one hand, CJ's story highlights the ugliest side of organized, competitive teamsport. Here, men and women are excluded based on group membership categories of all types. When CJ was part of the able-bodied group (with sufficient athletic talent) he competed for the men's grouping of other able-bodied athletes. But when CJ lost a leg and became a member of a disabled male group, there was no place for him to compete at U.C. Irvine. He would have been a competitive runner on the women's team, but his possession of a penis somehow prevented this from happening. CJ was shut out of this level of organized, competitive sport. His bodily characteristics no longer aligned with the manner in which athletes are categorized and included.

On the other hand, CJ's story also shows how less organized sport, in this case road racing, can be used to build confidence, repair lives, and bond people of different life histories.

Categorizing and Dividing

Like race, gender and sexuality, *dis*ability is a socially constructed paradigm, as one cannot say just where disability begins or ends. CJ is technically disabled, but he is still a faster runner than most. Highlighting the difficulty in problematizing what a disability is, CJ once ran a disability race in New York. He finished the 5 kilometer race around Central Park in second place; behind a runner who was missing three fingers. While that might outrage you, it brings up the question of where a disability begins. If CJ's competitor was missing four fingers, five, his hand, the lower part of the arm? Where does a disability begin? And is one is able-bodied but less naturally talented, is this a disability? Today, my 41-year-old body has a hard time keeping up with CJ. Am I disabled because my heart won't pump as fast, and my muscles fatigue quicker than his?

The same categorization/classification difficulties emerge with race. Is Tiger Woods black? His heritage is a mixture of white, African American, Native American, and Chinese. So what is he? And while this may only be a question of interest to us when sporting teams were segregated by race, Tiger Woods might have found himself rejected by both white- and black-run sporting organizations fifty years ago. This classification system also relates to gender. Quite simply put, there is no such thing as male/female. Instead, multiple types of gendered humans exist (Fausto-Sterling 2000).

In August of 2009, 18-year-old Caster Semanya won gold in the track and field in the World Athletics Championships in Berlin. However, a "sex" test later "confirmed" that she is both a man and a woman (a hermaphrodite). At the time of writing, it is not clear what the official governing body of the sport will do with her. She identifies as a woman, but maintains biological advantages (including three times the elevated testosterone levels of the female average) that give her advantage compared to other women. But don't all elite female runners have an advantage over non-elite? Who, I ask, should she be able to run with? Is it fair to put her with other "women," or with "men"?

What about a male who has genital surgery and takes hormones to become female (MTF)? Like Thai champion kick boxer Parinya Charoenphol/Nong Toom who underwent surgery to become a female (MTF), but is still better than all the men. Which division does she belong? Would you change your mind if after the surgery and hormones she was only as good as the average woman?

These artificially constructed categories affect more than just one's sporting performance. The history of the way we have treated sexual minorities, racial minorities, women, and those whose bodies that don't look "normal" is horrific. For example, a century ago in the US it was not uncommon for sports clubs to deny access for individuals with a disability. Public bathrooms, theaters, swimming pools, and other facilities were segregated by race, gender *and* disability (Faye and Wolfe 2009).

Unfortunately, many governing bodies and sports systems continue to perpetuate the false premise that separate, segregated opportunities for sport, leisure, and cultural activities by persons with a disability are both desirable and equitable. We (of course) do the same for gender, but there is less outrage about this. This is not to suggest that there is not great joy to be had in sport that is exclusively designed for people with disability, or even joy for gays and lesbians to compete in their own organized competitions – certainly women enjoy competing in their own segregated space – but it is to suggest that the artificial boundaries of inclusion and exclusion are socially constructed. In the case of disability sport, questions of eligibility concerning what type of disability a participant must have, and whether or not it is substantially different in rules and practice from so-called able-bodied are open to many different perspectives (Faye and Wolfe 2009). In the case of gender, it asks questions (without definite answer) about one's psychological identity, body parts, hormone levels, and chromosome configuration. So where does CJ compete? Clearly he was no longer "fast" enough to help the men's team win, but (unlike with sex segregation in sport) should he then be permitted to run with the women?

Questions of how one divides teams are seriously complex. And I do not have all of the answers. However, keeping Jenny from running with the boys simply because she was a woman is the same as denying CJ the right to run with the girls, simply because he is a boy. My argument is designed to critically interrogate sport for dividing people based on artificially constructed categories of male/female, ability/disability, race and/or sexuality. Yet this, sadly, is the history of sport – it is also the history of modern humanity.

In this chapter I examine how competitive, organized teamsport are used to create a sense of "other," in order to artificially boost the perception that people fit into neat categories. I also examine how sport pits groups against each other.

This sense of "in-group" and "out-group" serves to divide communities and reify stereotypes of those we perceive as being different. Thus, this chapter examines how sport takes our cultural penchant for in-group and out-group and builds on this to produce or reproduce stereotypes and hate – all based on team affiliation. It describes how sport teaches us to out-group (and therefore often hate) members of other teams, simply because of their sporting affiliation. Sport, I argue, is an arena in which it becomes acceptable to generalize about the character, ability, or morality of others.

Tajfel and Turner's Social Identity Theory

Social identity theory, developed by Tajfel and Turner (1979) was originally developed to understand the psychological basis of inter-group discrimination. It has its roots in Tajfel and colleagues' earlier desire to identify the minimal conditions necessary to lead members of one group, an in-group, to discriminate against another, an out-group. According to social identity theory, we all maintain a personal sense of self (so I have an idea of who Eric Anderson is), but we also maintain other personal identities, which correspond to our group memberships. So, when I ran track for my high school I identified at one level as Eric Anderson, but at another level I identified as a member of the Huntington Beach High School track team, as an American and (privately) as gay. Different social contexts therefore trigger us to think (and therefore feel and act) on other group memberships, whether they be team, work, family, religion, sexuality, race or national origin. Thus, we all have multiple social identities; we all have internalized group memberships.

Social identity theory asserts that group membership creates a sense of in-group self-categorization, which leads to an enhancement of a sense of our group's worthiness. However, this enhanced self-image comes at the expense of the out-group. Turner and Tajfel (1986) show that the mere act of individuals categorizing themselves as group members is sufficient enough to lead them to display in-group favoritism. In other words, all people need to do is be randomly placed in a group, and they begin to take on an in-group/out-group mentality.

Highlighting this, in 2005, I was on an American reality television program, *The Real Gilligan's Island.* At the start of the filming, in Cancun, Mexico, the 14 contestants were forced to endure a three-day camera-operator strike (Marxism in action). While we waited for more camera-operators to be flown in from Los Angeles, we spent 24 hours a day with each other, isolated in an area no bigger than a basketball court.

Subgroups (cliques) began to form. They were based in mutual interest and/or sexual attraction. However, once the new camera crews showed up, and the "game" officially began, the producers divided us into two teams. The teams began to compete, and within just a few hours animosity toward the other team developed. The friendships gained in the old cliques helped stay off an othering for a while, but ultimately alliances became solidified based on the artificial selection of team membership. It seemed we were learning to hate each other for no apparent reason other than the fact that we were divided into two teams.

There are of course more scientific studies than my reality TV experience, but I had to somehow gloat that I have done reality television! In one study Tajfel (1982) assigned schoolboys to meaningless groups. In dividing the students, care was taking to account for history of conflict, personal animosity or interdependence. The schoolboys were then asked to assign "points" to anonymous members of both their own group and the other group. In other words, this was not a competition; no team would emerge as a winner. Boys were simply asked to assign "points" (the higher the better) to other boys. The conclusion: boys awarded more points to people who were identified as "in-group members," even though these categories were artificially constructed and meaningless. In other words, they displayed in-group favoritism.

Tajfel and Turner (1979) suggest that in-group favoritism occurs because, after being categorized by a group membership, individuals seek to achieve positive self-esteem by positively differentiating their in-group from a comparison out-group. We feel better about ourselves when we feel good about our social groups, and the way we get to feel good about our groups is by negatively judging other groups.

According to Tajfel and Turner, prejudice is therefore a strategy for achieving and maintaining a high self-esteem.

Because of this, we pay more attention to criteria that make our group look better than the other group, ignoring evidence to the contrary. This quest, for what Tajfel and Turner call *positive distinctiveness*, means that people's sense of who they are is defined in terms of "we" rather than "I." We look for faults in others, without examining our own. On the reality television show, this manifested when my team began to look for problems, character faults, or disagreeable behaviors with members of the other team – and the other team did the same.

I lost a crucial competition (raft building) and was kicked off the island (you can see the video clip on my website, www.ericandersonphd.com), rather early into the show (you can also see me do drag – and I look fab). But when, for the Hollywood premier, we were reunited some months later, I found that my joy in the reunion was not matched by the other contestants. This is because I left the show before the teams really began to pick each other apart, and thus the majority of memories I retained were from our three days before the games began. However, the longer the other contestants battled team-to-team, the more entrenched their hatred toward each other grew. The "reunion" was characterized by group infighting, shunning, and even threats of lawsuits. The question I therefore ask is, *if this can occur among individuals who were previously friends one must ask what might occur in sport, where groups battle for precious few goods (victory and prestige)?*

One sport-related study (Levine *et al.* 2005), found men who strongly identified as fans of one particular English football (soccer) team and subjected them (without their knowledge) to an experiment in which they witnessed a runner fall and hurt his ankle. When the runner (an actor) was wearing the T-shirt of the same football team the test subject supported, they were more likely to help than when they were wearing the T-shirt of another football team.

However, social interaction theory also highlights that competing groups can become cohesive, if they face a larger, outside threat. If the cast of my reality television show were to suddenly find themselves involved in a hurricane, they would likely forget about their group membership and help each other survive (they might go back to squabbling later). Highlighting this, the same researchers tried their football jersey/injury test slightly differently. Before exposing the football fan to the injury scene, the researchers asked them to fill out a questionnaire about football in general. They were told that the researchers were examining the good sides of sport, suggesting that other researchers only examine the bad aspects of football fandom. Thus, the researchers attempted to reduce inter-group conflict between football fan groups by posing a larger threat. When these men were exposed to the same injury scenario, they helped men who were wearing the T-shirt of the opposing team in higher rates. The authors of this study (Levine *et al.* 2005: 451) conclude:

> In the first study, recognizing the signs of common group membership in a stranger ... leads to the increased likelihood that bystanders will intervene to help those in distress. However, they also show that group memberships are not fixed or inevitably salient. In [the second study] previous intergroup rivalries become submerged within a more inclusive or common categorization. Those who were previously identified as out-group members are now extended the benefits of group membership.

Tajfel and Turner (1979) identify three variables whose contribution to the emergence of in-group favoritism is particularly important. The first is the extent to which individuals identify with an in-group; the second is the extent to which the prevailing context provides ground for comparison between groups; and the third is the perceived relevance of the comparison group, which itself will be shaped by the relative and absolute status of the in-group. Individuals are likely to display favoritism when an in-group is central to their self-definition and a given comparison is meaningful or the outcome is contestable. In subsequent studies of in-group bias, others have shown that the tendency to favor in-group members is likely culturally specific, and it should also be highlighted that maintaining in-group bias is not necessarily the same thing as maintaining prejudice.

What I am interested in, however, is how in-group/out-group processes might be enhanced in sport and transferred outside of sport. Explicating this, in an example of two girls who share many in-group features (race, age, and gender), is Ellen's story. Ellen and her best friend Kathi were childhood friends – at least until they were picked to play on opposite soccer teams at age 13. Until this time, the girls had played several years together as teammates.

Sadly, as each girl's team accelerated toward their championship meet, they grew to view each other as "others." This was influenced by teammates who saw their opposition through lens of "the enemy." Their coaches contributed to the erosion of their friendship as well. As a university student today, Ellen mourns the loss of her friend. Even though they still live in the same town, she feels there is too much animosity between them to reach out and redevelop the friendship. Essentially, sport broke them apart. If sport can do this for two friends, what might sport be able to do for athletes of differing color? Here, racialized beliefs (regardless of how false) can be intensified.

Racism in Anglo-American Sport

Prior to the end of slavery in 1863, black sport participation was severely limited. Slaves played games amongst themselves (Wiggins 1977, 1980a, 1980b), and were selected to participate in boxing matches against fellow slaves for the pleasure of the white audience, or to serve as jockeys for white-owned horses (Sage 1990), but there was little status and no pay for these positions. After slavery's abolition in 1863, prevailing racist attitudes made it difficult for blacks to participate in the white-owned professional sporting leagues. For example, white boxers refused to fight black boxers, and although black athletes had begun to make progress by playing in major league baseball in the 1880s, that progress was stifled by an 1888 "gentleman's agreement" amongst major league club owners not to sign black players.

In response, during the 1920s and 30s black athletes began to organize and compete in their own "Negro" leagues in the sports of baseball, football, and basketball. By the end of the 1930s, "Negro" leagues spread to boxing and track, and participant numbers in these leagues grew dramatically (Ashe 1988). Perhaps the most eventful moment was the signing of the first black baseball player, Jackie Robinson, to the Brooklyn Dodgers in 1945. But a more important milestone came in 1954 with the United States Supreme Court decision of Brown vs. the Board of Education. That same year Gordon Allport wrote his book about prejudice (discussed in the next section). The landmark decision prohibited racial segregation in America's educational facilities. This, combined with the growing commercialization of sport, led white schools to recruit talented black athletes.

In the 1960s, black athletes were vital to the operation of the black social revolution in the US. Perhaps no better an example of the revolt of the black athlete can be found than Harry Edward's orchestrated demonstration during the 1968 Mexico Olympics, in which gold medallist Tommie Smith and bronze medallist John Carlos offered the now-famous clenched fist salute. This event heightened America's awareness to the racial issues that pervaded our society.

Today, an initial examination of professional sport appears to show little discrimination against black athletes. In fact, blacks are overly represented in football, baseball, and basketball. However, there is much research to suggest that racism still pervades American sport. In 1967, Harry Edwards coined the term "stacking" to refer to the racial segregation that occurs in sport. This is not the same type of segregation that keeps women from playing with men, but it is a cultural segregation that maintains that blacks and whites (or other races) are overly represented in certain playing positions. Blacks, for example, are only represented in any real numbers in just a very few sports. Stacking suggests that black athletes may need to be better than their white counterparts in order to make team selections. In other words, there are few black benchwarmers. If one is a mediocre player in professional sport, you can count on the fact that he is white.

Much of stacking is theorized to occur via an underlying assumption that black athletes are not such intelligent players as white athletes. They are therefore not awarded roles that hold a high responsibility for the outcome of the game, such as quarter-back, goalie, or pitcher/bowler.

Because of the under-representation of black athletes in these central positions, young black athletes playing the central positions in their formative years often choose to try out for other positions in college, in order to maximize their chances of making the team. This is a process known as "self-stacking." Furthermore, black athletes are less likely to be hired to management positions, because they have not provided the same opportunity as whites to prove their intellect and leadership in the central positions as players. Hence, blacks are seriously absent in coaching and managerial positions in most professional sport.

Rimer (1996) found that African Americans and Latinos who do get hired as coaches have had longer, and better, careers than white coaches, suggesting that they have to be significantly better than their white counterparts to be hired. If one is a mediocre coach, he/she is probably white. Thus, the tenets of stacking occur in both players and those who coach/manage the players.

Further evidence of discrimination in sport comes from Richard Majors' (1990), description of "cool pose." Majors proposes that black men in the US have accepted the dominant definition of masculinity in America, but have limited success in most institutional spheres. Whereas white men are provided the opportunity to prove their masculinity in the institutions of education, politics, and business, blacks are not. These social conditions have, over the years, produced frustration that has resulted in "black men channelling their creative energies into the construction of unique, expressive, and conspicuous styles of demeanor, speech, gesture, clothing, hairstyle, walk, stance, and handshake" (Majors 1990: 111).

I add to this discussion, however, that while decreasing cultural racism has led to increased sporting integration in sport, black sporting prowess might also help reproduce stereotypes of black citizens as overly aggressive. In other words, sport might, at one level, help reduce prejudice among teammates (see the next section), while at the same time reproducing racist thinking at a societal level.

I am particularly concerned about sport and its ability to other. It is one thing to have two split groups of white kids overvaluing their own members (when they are artificially split), but sport teaches us to view the opposing team as the enemy, and it teaches us to look for differences or faults with other teams, or to create them if they do not exist. Thus, in sport, we teach kids that it is okay to judge others via group affiliation. How then, does this play into demographic group affiliation when a team that is mostly black plays a team that is mostly white?

This also plays out in national rivalries – soccer wars. In 1970, following a World Cup match, 2,000 people were killed in a war between Honduras and El Salvador, a war begun by rivalries of fans (Eitzen 2003). The point is that sport builds cohesion among a group or nationality of citizens, but this has a cost. I argue that the development of cohesion is often more about the out-grouping (the development of hatred) of others than it is about learning to love members of your own group.

Evidence of this was found in my research on the Navajo (Chapter 4). Recall that these athletes (and their community) took particular pride in beating white teams. But how do they feel about white teams when they lose to one? And how do white teams feel about Navajo teams when they lose to one? This might even expand into notions of ethnocentrism: we learn not to like "their type," because their type is preventing us from achieving our goals.

In other words, we expect people not to make or reproduce stereotypes about others in work, family, education, and other social settings, yet we accept the generalizing of others when involved in sport. Does this then mean that the Olympic Games promote ethnocentrism, instead of unifying the world?

Although outside the scope of this book, this (quickly) brings us to the concepts of CORF (casting off reflected failure), and BIRG (basking in reflected glory). In short, sport fandom provides us an opportunity to associate with the dominants. Because unlike sports participation, in fandom we can choose who we "support." Thus, when a team is winning, people wear the shirts and proudly proclaim themselves, say, Manchester United fans. But when Arsenal is winning, things change. Sport permits us to change our allegiance, to always shift our loyalties and our identities so that we can associate with the winners, so that we can identify with the in-group and feel better about our (make-believe) category membership. If a team wins, we bask in that glory, feeling proud of our team association. If they lose, we cast them off, "they are not my team." John F. Kennedy said this best – "Victory has a thousand fathers, but defeat is an orphan."

The message I present here is complicated. This is because prejudice runs at the personal (self), organizational (team), and cultural (societal) levels. The development of prejudice, and even simple racial thinking, is a highly complex process. At one level, sport might be useful for breaking down prejudice (as when white and black members compete together in pursuit of a common goal), but on another level, it might also reproduce prejudice.

Gordon Allport and Contact Theory

The question of othering (and the potential for reifying stereotypes and engendering hatred) that sport brings is influenced by research that suggests that sport might be useful in helping reproduce prejudice between groups. Key to this theory, however, is that members of these groups must work together, on the same team.

In 1954 Gordon Allport wrote *The Nature of Prejudice*. It remains one of the most influential publications in the field of inter-group relations, being called a "brilliant and accurate statement of the eclectic causes and possible cures of prejudice" (Aronson 1978), and a work that presents "a lasting paradigm" for the study of this topic (Pettigrew 2008). Allport's work receives this praise because it provides a balanced, clearly organized, and integrative account of the extensive but conceptually fragmented research on ethnic hostility in the US during the first half of the twentieth century. Allport's emphasis is on multiple causations of prejudice, suggesting that it would be a serious error to ascribe prejudice and discrimination to any single, "taproot, reaching into economic exploitation, social structure, the mores, fear, aggression, sex conflict, or any other favored soil. Prejudice and discrimination … may draw nourishment from all these conditions, and many others" (1954: xviii).

Allport's interpretations of diverse findings of prejudice framed the analysis for later advances in theory concerning prejudice. His ideas on explaining how stereotypes are acquired and maintained anticipated constructs that are currently guiding research. It was (as stated in the last section) written during a time in which it was believed that racial tensions were fuelled primarily by prejudice, most of which was "a product of the fears of the imagination" rather than a realistic competition between groups resources (1954: xv). The implication until then was that prejudice was the central problem of majority-minority relations, the fundamental cause of social, political, and economic inequalities between groups and the most formidable barrier to change in the status quo. Allport, however, argued that discriminatory behavior was more often a matter of individuals conforming to group or social customs, and that it was not normally an expression of ingrained hostility or deep personal conviction shaped by prejudice. Thus, one's discriminatory behavior might change when new rules of conduct are introduced by a legitimate authority.

Emerging as a social theory during the civil rights era, the primary notion of Allport's contact theory is that, under the right conditions, contact between groups in conflict diminishes inter-group prejudice. The theory was initially applied to issues of race and racial integration; consequently, numerous early studies utilized contact theory to demonstrate the positive effects of inter-group contact across racial categorizations (Kephart 1957). More recently, empirical studies have also found that contact theory can apply to homosexuality as well (Eskilson 1995; Herek 2002; Herek and Capitanio 1996). McCann *et al.* (2009), for example, suggest that among the numerous ways social attitudes toward homosexuality are socially upgraded, social contact with sexual minorities plays an important role. These studies suggest that, when the homosexuality of a friend is revealed, homophobic men are forced to quickly re-evaluate their impressions of someone they had previously viewed positively. In other words, once they understand that a friend is gay, they experience an "awakening of new ideas," which challenges the preconceptions they had of homosexuality (McCann *et al.* 2009: 211).

I argue that contact theory was at play in the cheerleading research I earlier described (Jeff's story). When men played only against other men, they maintained views about women that were challenged (and changed) after competing in a sport that was gender-integrated.

Contact theory is, however, more complex than it might first appear. Allport (1954) proposed four necessary conditions for inter-group contact: 1) equal status among groups within the situation; 2) common group goals; 3) cooperative interaction; and 4) authoritative support. According to Allport, without these conditions, social contact might actually have the undue effect of reinforcing social prejudices and stereotypes. Thus, he argued that positive contact (incorporating elements of the four optimal conditions) is required to negate social distance and challenge stereotypes.

More recently, however, Pettigrew and Tropp (2006) postulate that not all of these conditions are *essential* for reducing prejudice. While they suggest that these conditions might form a "package" that best facilitates the effect, socio-positive effects *can* also be achieved with just one condition. Also, in 2008, Pettigrew added a fifth variable: the importance of self-disclosure in cross-group relationships. When applied to homosexuality, for example, this means that it is not just about knowing a homosexual that counts in reducing homophobia; what is really important is the ability to talk to the individual about sexuality (self-disclosure). Again, I found this important in men's unlearning of their sexism in befriending female cheerleaders, too.

But whereas contact between members of one group (say race) may vary under one team, it more often reproduces hatred than reduces it. This is because, more often than not, when races mix in sport, they oppose each other. The Navajo team is made almost exclusively of Navajo players, and the white teams they play are made almost exclusively of white players. Thus, not only are the conditions that Allport suggests are necessary for reducing racial tensions not met, but they are exacerbated. I argue that one race prevents another race from acquiring their goals. Coaches and athletes frequently express ill feelings toward one's competitor, as they have been socialized into an in-group/out-group perspective that is predicated upon establishing the other team as the enemy. Rather than viewing competitors as agents in cooperation to bring out the best in individuals and groups, other teams are viewed as obstacles in the path of obtaining cultural and economic power. In order for me to win, you must lose.

This makes sense when the distribution of goods is predicated upon one's victory. Sport is political because it is about the distribution of the power that comes with winning, and politics rarely makes for cohesion between disparate groups. Worse, in order to tap into this power, sport, especially contact teamsport, teaches us that it is okay to commit violence against another. Violence in the name of victory is acceptable because victory is the symbolic method by which masculinity (particularly) is distributed in a postindustrial culture. When this violence (physical or symbolic) is used against another team, we easily generalize that "all" of the members of a team are deviant. On the reality TV program I took part in, because the seven members of the opposing team were unhappy with the actions of just one of my team members, we were all cast in the same, deviant, light.

Ultimately, I suggest that when sport is structured so that people of various colors, abilities, sexualities, or gender play together (on the same team), it might reduce prejudicial thinking through Allport's notion of contact theory, but when teams of differing demographic backgrounds play against each other, it has the opposite effect.

Chapter Conclusion

Perhaps the most pervasive myth about teamsport is that it teaches athletes to work together, "as a team." This sense of common strife is thought to unite players in team cohesion. This cohesion and struggle is then thought to reduce prejudices among players. The primary purpose of this chapter, however, was to highlight that in order for members of one sporting team to unite, they must be united in opposition to the players of another team. While this struggle might temporarily unite players of a particular team in competition, it is often the case that a team's demographics represent the demographics of the locations from which they are comprised. Thus, it is more likely that white teams will end up competing against Navajo teams, or black teams will end up competing against Hispanic teams, than whites and Navajos, blacks and Hispanics, will play together on the same team.

Worse, because of positive distinctiveness, individuals end up making generalizations about the "character" of the entire other team. When two teams compete, all it takes is for one member of the opposing team to cheat, for the entire opposing team to be brandished "cheaters." Sport, therefore, maintains the ability to reinforce rather than break down stereotypes. If, for example, a stereotype exists that men of one particular race are violent, and one member of that race commits violence in the sporting context, it reproduces this stereotype for all those on his team (and often by extension, to his race).

This chapter did not discuss much sport at the international level, and how international games, particularly the Olympics, also divide nations. However, I suggest that if we were serious about the Olympics bringing nations together, athletes would march in to the Olympic venue according to their sport, not their nation. What the Olympics really reflects is symbolic warfare.

Collectively, whether we are discussing youth or Olympic sport, it seems to me that the in-group/out-group nature of sport (something we as human beings already fall too easily into) makes it more likely that teams will end up hating each other, rather than appreciating each other's contribution to the sporting competition. Sport is unique in this aspect. I therefore suggest that two teams of youth, posed to battle in a teamsport, should instead lower their weapons (bats and balls) and organize a musical instead.

8   Changing Sport

The primary purpose of this book has been to critically examine sport, and to put forth empirically supported, theoretically based arguments that highlight the ways in which sport reproduces a great deal of social harm. Throughout the chapters, I have aimed to demonstrate that:

1   Sport does not build character (at least not in the way we assume that it does).
2   Sport does not promote substantial educational or socioeconomic attainment for the underpriviledged.
3   Sport does not reduce prejudice.
4   Many types of competitive, organized sport not only fail to promote one's health, but can also cause a great deal of injury, disease, and early death.
5   Sport is an arena in which youth are trained to follow the instructions of elders without thinking for themselves. This opens them up to emotional and physical abuse.
6   The structure of sport influences coaches to abuse their athletes (through too much training and risking of their athletes' health) in order to win.
7   Sport teaches participants to sacrifice their health, education, and other life chances for the sake of moving up through its ranks.
8   In sport, we learn to commit violence not only against ourselves, but we learn to accept that violence committed against others is an acceptable "part of the game."
9   Because sport remains a socially valued institution (which nearly compels all youth to participate) they "learn" that the sexes are not equal enough to compete together.
10   Men (particularly) learn the attitudinal positioning of homophobia, sexism, and anti-femininity.
11   Gender segregation in sport helps symbolically reproduce patriarchal privilege.
12   Gender segregation in sport also provides men with social capital and formal networks that help them (and not women) gain occupations within and outside of the sporting industry.
13   Sport reproduces a "good old boys" network that privileges white, heterosexual, able-bodied men in many capacities.

14 Sport teaches us to hate our competitors, to view them as standing in the way of our success.

15 Sport discriminates against those who do not fit the athletic mold, and it sometimes (formally or informally) excludes those with disability or those who come out as sexual minorities.

16 Sport helps reproduce class inequality, particularly by offering false hope for those in economic disparity.

17 Sport is used to teach a modern (lower-class) workforce the requirements that employers wish of their employees in a capitalist economy. In sport, these same youths are also being trained to value the attributes of soldiering.

18 There are a plethora of other arguments against sport that I have made in this book. And I could have critiqued professional sport harshly, too – the commercialism of it, the way it exploits many of its players, the way it promotes a masculinized, warrior-like nation.

19 I might equally have examined international competitions and the Olympics for not only bankrupting the cities that host them, but for (re)producing nationalism as well.

Accordingly, the exercise so far has been largely an academic investigation into the problems of sport in society. However, it was also my aim to teach social theory in the process. It is my hope that this book might attract students to an interest in social theory, students who might not otherwise have previously cared or thought much about social theory.

However, because I consider myself a *public sociologist*, I cannot feel good about myself if I leave this book as just a critique of sport. I feel compelled to also use my understanding of the way sport operates in society in order to postulate ways upon which we can improve the socio-positive outcomes of sport, and reduce the socio-negative. I do not have answers for all of the problems that plague sport, and I am aware that our culture's obsession with sport will prevent this from happening. However, only in speaking about the ways we can improve sport will my voice be heard. In the sections that follow, I therefore suggest ways we can make sport a more positive institution.

Revise How Coaches Are Recruited, Trained and Evaluated

Coaching as a profession stands out as unusual in that a bachelor's degree is not required. One cannot counsel patients without an MA or PhD, one cannot practice medicine without an MD, and one cannot cut hair without a state-certified license. Without a similar institutionalized system of training, measurement and accreditation for coaches, there is little opportunity to evaluate or reform coaching practices outside of team victories. Thus, if a coach is a good technical coach, and wins meets, there is little reason for him to alter his coaching style, even if he is abusive. In fact, the structure of sport promotes abuse. Accordingly, sport is *full* of men and women who predicated their identities as athletes, and who were therefore drawn to coaching as a mechanism to remain within the field. Here, they are provided with a phenomenal amount of power.

As described in Chapter 2, these powers are legitimate, coercive, reward, expert and referent. Few occupations offer all five powers. And while it is not absolutely necessary to understand exactly what and how each of these powers operates, it is important to understand that few other occupations/professions offer individuals the ability to associate with all five types (Jones *et al.* 2004).

Clearly coaches use reward power by offering players social promotions, more playing time, or public praise, and they use coercive power in punishing athletes with the opposite. Coaches establish their legitimacy in the eyes of their athletes primarily through having "come up" through the system, often as a successful player first, and then by producing quality athletes. This legitimacy, coupled with the title "coach," is then thought (often erroneously) to make one an expert, as coaches are assumed to possess the technical knowledge beneficial to advancing athletes. In other words, a person does not need to be an expert in order to maintain expert power, they only need be perceived as an expert. As I have discussed, coaches most often lack the qualifications, knowledge and skills to be a safe and effective coach. Finally, coaches sometimes gain the respect of their athletes through referent power because athletes desire to accomplish the same feats, times, or levels of play, or because they look to the coach as a mentor or parental figure. This is the, "Look what sport did for me" attitude. Unfortunately, with young athletes looking up to the coach, the coach maintains a great deal of power in socializing individuals into a particular belief system. Thus, as gatekeepers, coaches maintain a great deal of sway in determining the social outcomes of sport. The combination of these five powers quite nearly gives a coach *absolute* power. When one adds these powers to the institutional autonomy coaches are given, it is a recipe for danger.

This absolute power leads to a plethora of coach-related problems, including sexual, emotional, and physical abuse. In their study of abused professional athletes, Kelly and Waddington (2006: 153) found that "no matter how abusive or violent the manager's [coach's] behavior may be, his authority was not to be questioned and those who did question it were punished, in this case by being withdrawn from the games." Jones and colleagues (2004) suggest that a coach's power surpasses any other profession, which ultimately encourages conformism (Hughes and Coakley 1991), obedience (Tomlinson and Yorganci 1997) and dependence (Cense and Brackenridge 2001). In his study of adult athletes physically abused by their coaches (1997), Phil Doorgachurn (www.coachabuse.com) finds that the adult male athletes he studied suggested that their coaches believed that they were more qualified in diagnosing and curing injuries than registered health professionals (c.f. Toftegaard-Nielsen 2001). He gives an example of how one coach undermined medical professionals, by stating that they were wrong, and that the athlete needed to return to training despite severe medical warnings not to. Athletes are compelled to follow these directions, even against the advice of professionals, because if they do not, they lose favor in their coach's eyes and may lose valued playing positions and time.

Summarizing this, within competitive teamsport – and from a very early age – athletes are only selected to the next level of play if they adhere to the orthodox tenets of sport, where they are influenced by the top-down modeling of the near-total institution. Finally, the institution itself excludes input from those not within its dominant framework. Thus, this system is more than just culturally hegemonic, it is also structural. Not just structural in the sense of a social, historical and institutionalized pattern, but literally structured by codified rules of segregation, reminiscent of the same rules that once formally segregated blacks from whites.

Changing the system will not be easy. This is because there needs to be a requirement to obtain a bachelor's degree qualification in coaching. At my university we offer just such a degree. However, although we take in 70 students a year, very few go on to coach. This is because the vast majority of coaching positions do not provide a subsistence level of income, let alone enough to pay a mortgage and have the occasional vacation. Thus, the vast number of coaches come from an army of volunteers. And although these volunteers may be well-meaning, they are not necessarily capable of understanding the complex ways in which sport can cause a great deal of social damage. Most do not maintain training in behaviorism, counseling, small group dynamics, and other topics that are necessary in order to effectively, and positively, lead a group of athletes into a healthier, happier, and more confident existence.

Without the ability to train coaches (and pay them what teachers earn), we cannot expect them to have a bachelor's degree in coaching education. This means that we normally rely upon weekend certification courses. These courses are far too insubstantial. Most tend to focus on "how not to get sued." I suggest that we need to implement a standardized way of objectively, anonymously, and fairly evaluating coaches. At the moment, if a coach applies for a paid coaching position, he/she is evaluated on two basic merits: 1) their performance accomplishments as an athlete, and 2) their team's win/loss record. There is no systematic way of evaluating the graduation rates of a coach's athletes, the level of socio-positive impact the coach had on the players, or any other socio-positive measurement. But if we had, perhaps at each unique level of coaching, a standardized form for coaching assessment, measured and cumulated by an independent body, we could ask to view a coach's "report card." Just like a student graduates with a grade point average in the US, or a degree classification in the UK, coaches should also have a user-rating.

But this is not the only measurement of a coach's ability. Another problematic situation with coaching is that coaches are relatively unsupervised. For the most part they operate alone, without independent observation. Even if they have an assistant coach, it is more likely that the two will collude on their behaviors and approaches to coaching rather than critically reflect upon each other's performance.

My thesis is that coaches need to be observed and monitored. Thus, having (for example) a paid official, trained in coaching education (or a sport psychologist or sociologist) supervise a coach for a week's training, might help identify problems and promote solutions. This is not designed to just police coaches for their errant behaviors (although it would also do that) but it is also designed so that the coach might have a hands-on professional with which to discuss his or her particular coaching styles. In other words, what we need are "super coaches" – men and women who are not concerned with whether a coach trains a team to victory, but one that examines how a coach trains his or her players for life. This would at least partially address the problem. If we believe strongly in the socio-positive aspects of sport, than we should also be willing to pay for it.

Contesting Gendered Binaries through Gender Integration

As a gay, pro-feminist sociologist, allow me to indulge in just a moment of hyperbolic stereotyping. You are walking down the street, alone, where you see coming from the opposite direction either a) ten men; b) ten women; or c) five men and five women. Considering possibility of fear, which group scares you the most? Statistically speaking, of course, you would be wise to fear the group of ten men the most.

Now, consider a scuffle breaks out over a call on the pitch, which group arrangement above is most likely to result in individual violence, or even a team brawl? Again, the choice is that of all men. It is partially for these reasons (and so many more) that I, and others, suggest we need to gender-integrate sport (McDonagh and Pappano 2008).

The results of my research lead me to some general conclusions concerning the gender-segregated arena of sport. Here, I suggest that the extreme regimentation and inordinate amount of time required to excel at sport often deprives men of experiences outside of the athletic arena, where they might otherwise be introduced to the sexual/gendered narratives of women. Instead, in the homosocial world of men's teamsport, males are socialized into an ethos in which women are valued as sexual objects, devalued as athletes, and masculinity is predicated in opposition to femininity. This is made more possible because there are no women (or openly gay men) to contest these narrow understandings. But it is also made possible because coaches are recruited from a pool of ex-athletes who moved up through the same system (discussed above). Essentially, I argue that because teamsport is near compulsory for youth, young boys are indoctrinated into a masculinized, homophobic and sexist gender regime from early childhood – an institution they cannot easily escape. Even if boys are fortunate enough to enter a gender-integrated sports team when young, by the time they reach high school, gender segregation is the norm.

Additionally, the demands of competitive sport often consume such quantities of time that it also structures men into off-the-field social networks of teammates – positioning them into a near-total masculine institution. Bereft of alternative gender narratives, and desiring social promotion among their peers, boys and men are more willing to subject their agency to orthodox masculinity, which remains predicated in anti-feminine, sexist, and (frequently) misogynistic thinking. In this aspect, segregation on the field is complicated by the effect of a near-total institution off the field.

Data from my research on male cheerleaders (who compete alongside female cheerleaders in the coed division of cheerleading) show that when men become familiar with the experiences of women, almost all adopt a new gender strategy that looks more favorably on women. I suggest that in gender-integrated sport, the time constraints of training and travel structures athletes into mixed-sex social networks, at least part of the time. Here, men are likely to have conversations with women about sex, gender, sport, and life – the kind of conversations they were often unable to have in a homosocial culture. I find that, in partaking in these conversations, men not only open themselves to hearing the multiple narratives of women, but they also learn to view women as worthy and competent athletes, teammates, coaches, and leaders.

I therefore suggest that gender-integrating teamsport may be the required crack in the system to help undo patriarchy. Gender-integrating sports teams is more valuable than gender-integrating men and women in other masculinized terrains (like firefighting or the police force) because virtually all boys play organized sport. Thus, I maintain that gender-integrating sport should be a starting point for an "opposing [gender] strategy" (Foucault 1984: 101) that erodes at patriarchy.

But my idea of gender-integrating sport is to do more than just reform men; it would also provide women the same social training, the same access, and the same symbols that men currently have associated with their formal participation in sport. If women are to compete, equally, with men for social power and prestige, they must break up the boys' network where it is formulated – sport.

I do not, however, wish to claim that gender integration is a panacea for the sexual, social, ethical, and gender-related problems associated with men's sport or even our society; men's teamsport is far too intertwined with other masculinist systems and institutions for that. Furthermore, I do not analyze how gender-desegregating teamsport might negatively impact on female athletes, particularly considering that women have been shown to be subordinated by men within other integrated terrains (Britton and Williams 1995; Reskin and Roos 1990). Nor do I know how gender integration might impact upon the number of socio-positive attributes that Sabo and his colleagues (2004) correlate with women's sporting participation.

However, there is another reason for further investigating my gender integration proposition. Where the dominant ideology maintains that gender segregation is valuable to women because it shelters women from men's violence in sport, I question whether violence against women off the field might instead be promoted through sporting segregation. We know that male teamsport athletes have elevated rates of violence against women compared to non-athletes and non-teamsport athletes (Kreager 2007). Accordingly, if gender segregation in sport is even *partially* responsible for men's violence against women, then the socio-positive results of what I found in the sport of cheerleading should serve as a call for further academic inquiry into the effects of gender-integrating other/all sport.

Still, the notion of gender-integrating sport (and changing the rules of sport to facilitate this) is met with great resistance. Whenever I speak about the subject, I find opposition. For example, I recently debated the issue with athletes in a class in New York. The class (comprised of equal numbers of men and women) was wholly resistant to the idea of gender integration. Men had a plethora of reasons and rationales why women should not play with men: 1) they might get hurt at the hands of overly muscled men; 2) they might not want to play on men's teams; and 3) it would be impossible to change the structure of sports to permit this as the purists of sport would never permit such. When I then pointed out that 1) a 100-pound male can try out and play rugby for a man's team, but a 300-pound woman cannot; 2) women should have the choice to play with men; they did not yield. Instead they came up with a host of new reasons why women "simply" should not be allowed to play with men.

Interestingly, not a single woman spoke during the entire hour. Although I begged and pleaded with them, "Women, how can you let these men say this about you? Where are your voices? Why are you so complicit to the men's complaints?" not one spoke up. In the end, it helps us realize that this is not only a problem of men trying to protect their sacred terrain, but it is a problem of women having been so subordinated, and being so complicit with what they have been given, that they fail to enact their agency to bring about gender parity.

So why do most people protest the gender integration of sport? More important is the question of why it is socially permissible to say that women should not play on men's teams, but it is not permissible to say that gays should not play on straights teams, or that blacks should not play on white teams? Exemplifying this, when I ask my students how many think that black men have an advantage over white men in the hundred-meter dash, every student raises their hand. "So why not then have a black men's 100 meter race, and a white men's 100 meter race?" The students object to my proposition, "That would be racist." So why, I ask, is it not sexist to suggest that woman should have their own finals? After all, it is quite possible that gay men may be better served by being formally excluded from heterosexual men's sport, instead being given their own sporting spaces. It is also possible that black athletes might benefit from playing in racially segregated teamsport. Therefore (according to this faulty logic) they should be provided their own space. But each of these suggestions is readily met with charges of homophobia and racism. This of course is the power of hegemony: it prevents women from seeing their own oppression.

One can argue that professional sports differs from school sports, or community sponsored sports, because they are private organizations and they therefore should not be forced to integrate. But, professional sports are also places of work and occupation; if it can be shown that they intentionally or deliberately deny women sporting occupation who are otherwise qualified, they should be sued. However, where tax-payer money is concerned, we should all call for gender integration in sport. Thus, at the youth, high school, recreational, and university levels of play, sport should be integrated.

I suggest that if you are creative enough, matching weights, abilities, requiring the ball to pass through the hands of a woman first, etc., you can figure out how to effectively gender-integrate any sport. And, although I cannot spell out here exactly how gender integration might occur in all sport (as each sport is unique in the structures and rules that govern it), I might highlight, however, that we can easily change the rules of sport. Whenever the capitalists desire to change sport for their profits, sport changes. For example, when basketball wanted to speed up the game, adding a shot clock, or to improve the risk-taking of the game, adding a three point line, they did it. So too can they gender-integrate sport.

In my sport, cross-country, the top five men from each team to cross the finish line are scored. But if we were to simply change the rules to say that the top five men and the top five women across the finish line were to score, we would success-fully integrate the sport. The men's and women's teams would come together as one, and the men would learn to rely upon, train with, and desire the promotion of their female teammates in order that they might win. Even if the top five finishers from my team are men, they would finish their race, turn right back around, and cheer their female teammates on.

Other sports, like American football, are more difficult to gender-integrate. First, we need to remove the head banging from this sport. For the health and safety of all who play, this sport needs to be turned into flag football. We can then safely line men and women up into positions where they are valued, and where their competition is fair. For example, we can line women against women on the offensive and defensive line. We can, if we desire, switch these positions around as necessary. Perhaps in the first quarter women play quarter-back, and in the second quarter men play quarter-back. In other sports, we simply need to match people up according to weight, or ability, and not according to the possession of a penis. And there is absolutely no reason to have gender segregation in sports like volleyball, or baseball.

For a more in-depth analysis of gender-integrating sport, I suggest you read Eileen McDonagh and Laura Pappano's (2008) *Playing with the Boys: Why Separate is not Equal in Sport*.

Changing the Purpose of Sport by Changing Sport Structures

The current function of most organized sporting programs remains that of win-ning. But if we can reorganize sport so that the primary purpose is to teach moral responsibility, we might have a better outcome. For example, in one experiment on a group of juvenile delinquents (Bredemeier *et al.* 1986), the researchers assessed students on measures of aggression, and divided them into three groups to be equally matched. One group received training in martial arts with the philosophical component of maintaining responsibility, and emphasizing respect for others, as well as the building of self-esteem. The second group did the same fighting, but they did not have these values stressed to them as they learned the skills. After the trial, the boys in the first group scored lower on aggression and higher on self-esteem, while the boys in the second group scored even higher on measures of delinquency than before their martial arts training. This is a philosophical approach to change, but because winning is what most value it is unlikely that philosophy alone will bring about this change.

However, this is not the philosophical approach that most coaches maintain. It may be on their list of "the purposes of sport," but what is on their immediate minds is to win. This is because winning is what is easily measurable, and winning is what those not involved with our sport can readily see. Exemplifying this, coaches and athletes frequently express ill feelings toward their competitors, as they have been socialized into an in-group/out-group perspective that is predicated upon establishing the other team as the enemy (Chapter 7). Rather than viewing competitors as agents in cooperation to bring out their best, others (often even members from the same teams) are viewed as obstacles in the path of obtaining cultural and economic power. "In order for me to win, you must lose." Violence (conscious or not, intentional or unintentional) becomes an acceptable tool in achieving this victory. Hence, the structure of the sport produces the culture of the sport.

There are, however, other ways to structure sport. Sport can, for example, be restructured to determine that both teams must reach parity within an allotted period of time while still playing their best, or both lose. Alternatively, if teams were given a task that must be accomplished together in an allotted period of time, athletes from both teams would win or lose together – minimizing the in-group/out-group process (my alternate suggestion is to give up sport and instead take up theater). Unfortunately, the existing sport competition structure is so powerful in its influence, basked in decades of "tradition," that many maintain that without winning, there is no purpose to sport. This ethos moves sport further from the field of leisure and recreation, and closer to the act of war.

However, it is possible to keep the precise same structure of sport, but remove the competitive emphasis of coaching for victory. Let me explain. Your town's little league probably works something like this. Parents sign their kids up to play, and the kids either try out for or are randomly selected for one particular team. Here they are to play for the duration of their season. At the conclusion of the season, the team disbands, and the next year, new teams are picked. However, during the course of the season there exists one, coherent, team. This team has one coach, and perhaps some assistant coaches. This necessarily means that when that team wins, that particular coach has won. I propose to change the system.

In my little league world, during the first day kids come to a field where, let us pretend, 200 of them sign up. These kids are randomly divided into ten teams (20 kids per team). These boys and girls are then randomly assigned one of ten coaches. For that week, each coach is assigned to teach a basic skill. At the end of the week, the teams come together and play a competition against another team. However, when that competition is over, the kids' names are put into a hat and they are randomly picked again to be part of a team the next week. A coach is randomly assigned to each randomly picked team, and for the duration of the next week, all the coaches teach the kids the second skill. This process occurs throughout the season of play.

In my system of play we retain competition (and I agree that competition is fun), but I remove a sense of winning/losing history. With my system, no team emerges as the victor at the end of the season of play. Statistically speaking, each kid will win half of their matches, and each kid will lose half of their matches, too. Thus, if you think there is something to be learned from wins and losses (I do not) each kid will have the opportunity to experience both. Hopefully, they will learn that the win or loss is not important. To further this idea that it's about the journey, not the victory, there is no banquet to celebrate one team's dominance.

Furthermore, in my system, coaching power is decentralized. No individual coach has the power to promote or hinder an athlete's career. They might maintain the power to do such for the course of a week, but each kid will eventually be exposed to a number of different coaches. This means that if the coaches are of mixed sex, and come from a variety of racial and sexual minority backgrounds, we can also expose each kid (in just one season of play) to learn from members of other demographics.

My system also prevents the development of in-group and out-group. One cannot hate the "Wildcats" because the Wildcats change every week. Finally, because coaches and assistant coaches are randomly assigned and selected, it means that coaches and assistant coaches do not also maintain a win/loss record. When they are evaluated, they are then evaluated for their coaching, not their win/loss record. The system prevents many of the types of abuse that occur with youth sport.

Make Well-Rounded Athletes, Regulate Them, and Make It Safe

Considering that some positions in professional American football (admittedly choosing the most violent sport) will take 130,000 full-speed hits in their lives, leaving two-thirds (or more) with permanent disabilities (Eitzen 2003), likely sending a good number to drug dependency to deal with the pain, and a good number to early graves, there is no doubt that "this" type of sport is not healthy. The point is that the benefits of sport often severely outweigh the physical abuse sport brings. However, I understand that professional athletes are adults. I understand that they (like soldiers) compete voluntarily. While I still maintain that these adults are heavily socialized/influenced into their decisions – the same cannot be said for youth. Youth sport is not adult sport, and youth should not play like adults.

Yet there is currently an escalation of services, consulting, coaching, private instruction, sport psychology services, training camps, speed camps – and pressure – on young athletes, all geared to treat them as if they were professionals. The rules of sport haven't changed much since they were adopted over a hundred years ago (and perhaps the pressure on kids to become world-class athletes has not changed much either), but the professional "services" offered to keep those broken young bodies going, have. Hyman (2009: 18) says that, "All these changes are dangerously lifting the temperature, contributing to a perverse global warming of youth sports." Parents are convinced that if they want their kids to succeed at sport, they must begin training – now. Specializing in sport is thought to prepare a kid for success in that sport. Tiger Woods and the Williams sisters have driven this point home. However, talent is also talent. Let me explain.

When I was in high school, my coach was excited to have an individual, Jon, join our team as a freshman, because he held dozens of national age-group records as a kid. He had been training and racing hard since he was young, and he was without question a talented high school runner as a freshman. However, Jon was not the best. Far from it, he was nowhere close to being the best. He certainly was not destined to become the world-class runner his dad thought he would be. This is because there is a law of diminishing returns concerning training. Jon had simply done his work early. His improvement therefore came in small increments, whereas I had just begun my running career. My improvement therefore came in leaps and bounds. By the time I was a senior, I was as fast as he was. The point is, one does not need to waste their youth specializing in a sport in order to make it in a sport. Accordingly, we should not be training kids in just one sport when they are young.

If I were to tell students in a fourth grade class that they are expected to write a research article, with twenty-five references, that contributes to the body of knowledge in whatever subject they are taking, I would be thought crazy. Assigning this task is what PhDs do, not fourth grade students. However, we fail to make this same "level of ability" realization with youth sport. Here, we readily expect kids to perform like adults. We expect youth to act like professionals when it is not an age- (or ability-) appropriate task. If we are willing to understand that a kid should not spend eight hours a day writing a PhD dissertation, then we should also understand that a kid should not be practicing sport eight hours a day.

This means that we need to regulate the amount of time kids can play competitive sport in organized sporting leagues. This also means that we need to regulate how much high school athletes can also train, as well as university athletes. The way to do this is within organizing bodies of that particular sport. I am not advocating that we should say that kids can only legally play sport three hours a day. I am saying that organizing bodies should determine, "If you want to compete in this organizing body, your athletes can only do this much." This is the way the NCAA handles matters for its athletes, and it is only fair that youth baseball leagues or high school teams do the same. The consequences of permitting our kids to focus on just one sport, to practice until it hurts, are simply too great. Hyman (2009: 66) says, "Children entertaining themselves at their own pace, in their own way, simply did not play sports until it hurt" . We need to return to this ethos.

It is not, however, just how much kids play that we need to regulate. We also need to regulate what they can do. I have already suggested that sport that requires using the head as a weapon should be changed: American football needs to become flag football. But the same is true of soccer. Heading the ball needs to be banned from the game. This would prevent not only the microtrauma that's (potentially) caused by the ball bouncing off one's skull, but it would reduce the collision of skulls in pursuit of that ball. In soccer (and other sports), goal posts also need to be lined with pads, and players should be required to wear thinly protective helmets in many sports where head-to-head collisions occur.

Similarly, baseball (at all levels) needs to ban the curve ball. There is just too much evidence that the motion required to throw the ball places undue stress on the arm. In wrestling, athletes need to be prevented from attempting crash weight-loss programs that occasionally stop some of their hearts. Thus, they need to be weighed not just the day of their match, but three, six and nine days before each match in order to discourage losing massive amounts of water weight in just a few days. These are the types of regulations we need to protect kids from their overly zealous parents, coaches, and selves. I'm sure you can think of more.

Disentangling Competitive Sport from School Systems

Influential sport sociologist Jay Coakley summarizes the current model we run competitive organized sport under as the *power and performance model.* Here, he (2004) suggests that sport emphasizes the use of strength to push human limits, dominate opponents, and strive for victory. Accordingly, sporting excellence is defined through competitive success, and intense dedication is thus required. This type of sport privileges record-setting and it sees the body as a machine in order to do such. In order to operate, it requires a hierarchical authority structure in which athletes are subordinate to their coaches and it engenders antagonism between players as they compete for precious resources. However, there is another model for sport.

Coakley describes the *pleasure and participation model* as emphasizing an ethic of personal enjoyment, making connections to other players (from one's own and other teams), empowerment of players, respect for the body, inclusive participation, and democratic decision-making (Mahiri 1998). In this approach one views "competitors" as agents necessary to bring out one's personal best, and opponents are therefore respected. I suggest that one good way to promote the participation model (particularly in the US) is to disentangle school sport programs from competitive sport.

Gerdy (2002) suggests that America is unique in its conflation of sport and school cultures. Indeed, I have now lived and coached in both the US and the UK, and here, in the UK, sport is not so ingrained into school systems. Instead, sport is run though community organizations. By doing this, we help disassociate sporting popularity from peer culture dominance. In other words, the "jocks" do not receive the same institutional support that leads them to dominate social worlds in school settings (Bissinger 1990).

There are other advantages in running sport through community systems. First, kids join the community clubs from all schools, and they socialize with players from various ages. This has the latent effect of reducing inter-school tensions. It also helps kids learn to socialize with and relate to adults (and vice-versa). Furthermore, in this system, a player can stay with a coach or transfer to compete with another coach. They are not institutionally bound to play in just one team as they are in school-run sport in the US. Abusive coaches will therefore find themselves short of players to field a team.

Disentangling sport from university systems is also a good idea. In the UK, sport are run as student clubs, and most are student coached. While there are some competitive university competitions, they are not as intense, nor does sport involve the money, scholarships, or eligibility wars, which US sport does. Having university sport being student-led also leads to more democratic play: coaches are not making careers off the backs of their athletes.

Even if we cannot untangle sport from education in the US, we should at least make sure that coaches are part of the educational team. By requiring coaches to also be teachers, you first assure that coaches have some training in teaching. When coaches are also educators, they are more likely to be cautious in their approach to coaching, as their entire livelihood depends on it. Furthermore, schools and universities need to have a counselor or psychologist serve as an intermediary between the school's athletic department and the students. Students should not have to complain about a coach to another coach, or an athletic director. Coaches should fall under the same human resource managers that teachers do.

Emphasize Play over Sport

If we believe that playing sport has something valuable to offer our citizens, then we should particularly want our children to be involved in it. As a society, we certainly encourage them to play sport, promising them that it will be fun. However, kids, and adults alike, soon learn that sport is only fun for those who excel at it. Kids drop out of sport for lots of reasons that make it "not fun": not getting playing time, being repeatedly out-matched, sadistic coaches, parental pressure, stress of winning, and an over-organization of their "play" by adults. You see, most kids don't "play" sport; instead, they compete in sport.

Play contrasts with competition in several ways. The most obvious is that with play, there is no notion of win or lose. Even if one were playing cops and robbers, and one were to shoot the other first, this "loss" is not categorized, scored, or reported, in any systematic way. Generally, the one acting out the dying is just as happy to play this role as to be the gun-toting sheriff. However, more important to my thesis is that play requires "reciprocal typification" (Berger and Luckmann 1967: 31–4). Play requires one to put oneself into another's shoes. Now, games still require rules, but they are more fluid, they serve to keep the balance of play – or to make the play more "real." But what is key about play is that it is more socially democratic. Rules recognize the needs of others, in making the play more democratic, more socially inclusive.

Because play tends to be more democratic than organized sport, we are first likely to pick teams that we maintain are fairly balanced. This is because we recognize that in play the primary purpose is to have fun; compared to the primary purpose of winning. In play, rules can be changed in order to facilitate the fun, so if one team is winning by a majority, we are free to switch around team members. Conversely, sport rules remain rigid obstacles that prevent this type of creativity and spontaneity. In play, people tend to stop when they feel an impending injury, as there is no need to push oneself through pain for the sake of victory. Also, when we play, we tend not to draw a crowd, so there is no additional pressure to perform. In play, we tend not to engage in acts of violence. This is because, in play, nothing is really "on the line," so there is no real reason to foul a player. Also, in playing a pick-up game of soccer, no coach has power. One's future success is not related to pleasing the coach.

My argument is that playing instead of competing brings fewer socio-negative outcomes. Yet playing soccer, for example, instead of competing in it, still requires one to run back and forth for 90 minutes. Playing soccer is more likely to teach cooperation than when one competes in it; and when one makes a mistake while playing soccer, one does not feel as awful as with failure while competing. Play is just much more democratic.

If you watch kids playing a sport (as opposed to competing in a sport) you will notice that their idea of what is fair varies from the adult perspective. Kids on a playground might be playing a game of basketball, five kids on one team, and five on the next. Perhaps one team is winning, by a lot. Just then, another kid, the eleventh, comes and asks to play. This kid will not only be consumed into the game, but he will be added to the weaker side. And if the team with five players continues to beat the team with six, the next kid wishing to play will also be added to the larger team, making it 7 to 5. Alternatively, if the team with five continues to run the score up, the kids will soon swap players, adding a better player to the weaker side.

In baseball, kids naturally permit younger players to take more swings at the ball, or they pitch the ball in more of an arch, giving them a greater chance of making contact with it. In soccer, boundaries are made smaller, a goal is marked out by two backpacks, instead of the giant expanse of the "official" goal size. If one goalie is better than another, he may have a larger goal area to cover.

The point is that kids play a sporting game (even competing) but they do so under a set of rules, that is: 1) inclusive; and 2) fair. Adults, however, come along with a different notion of what it means to be "fair." Here, they say that what is fair is to have just five players on each team. From the adult perspective it is fair to have five on five, regardless of the imbalance in abilities.

Kids, on the other hand, know that sport is more fun when it is competitive. Somewhere between early childhood and adolescence, however, they have this sense of fairness (of fun) stripped away from sport. They learn the adult rules, the institutionalized perspectives of sport – and that is firmly camped in determining a winning team from a losing one. Highlighting this, I bring a balloon to my class, blow it up, and select a student from the class to come to the front. I do not say what we are doing, and I give the student no instructions. Instead, I hit the balloon up in the air, and call off "one." She hits the balloon back and I call off "two." This continues until after the twenty-second return where I miss the balloon, it bounces off the floor and I hit it back, calling off "23." The class moans. I stop and ask why. "You cheated," they proclaim.

But have I cheated? Is it not possible that I was playing this balloon bounce game for fifty tosses to see how few times the balloon might hit the floor? Or perhaps I was playing the game with the idea that you are allowed "three strikes" (so to speak) before it's over? Or maybe I was timing it, hoping to get to 100 balloon hits in a faster time than last year's class? The point is, if my students have been so structured by the "official rules" of something like a balloon game, how firmly might they stand by the rules of an organized sport like baseball? This highlights that sporting recreation loses its democratizing flexibility, becoming instead a rigid, iron cage that we call sport. Sport robs not just children of play, it robs us all of play.

One of my favorite classroom exercises is to ask my students to put their book down for a moment, to close their eyes, and remember back to a time when they were happily playing a sporting game with their friends in childhood. I ask them to visualize the location, remembering their emotions. If you were to also do this, like my students, you would likely recall a time when you were young, perhaps playing a ball game in the street or park near your house. Maybe it was summer, the sun was setting, mom was calling you in for dinner, and you were begging for five more minutes. So I now ask, "Who won?" Chances are, you cannot remember. This is because the victory was not the important part of your play. You remember this time fondly, because it was fun. We need to return to a state of sporting play.

References

Acosta, V. R. and Carpenter, L. J. (2006). "Women in intercollegiate sport: A longitudinal study twenty nine year update 1977–2006." Unpublished manuscript, Brooklyn College, New York.

Adams, A., Anderson, E. and McCormack, M. (2010). "Establishing and challenging masculinity: The influence of gendered discourses in football (soccer)." *Journal of Language and Social Psychology, 29*(3), in press.

Adams, M. L. (1993). "To be an ordinary hero: Male figure skaters and the ideology of gender." In T. Haddad (ed.), *Men and Masculinities* (pp. 163–181). Toronto: Canadian School Press.

Allan, E. J. and De Angelis, G. (2004). "Hazing, masculinity, and collision sports: (Un)becoming heroes." In J. Johnson and M. Holman (eds), *Making the Team: Inside the World of Sport Initiations and Hazing* (pp. 61–82). Toronto: Canadian Scholars Press.

Allan, E. J. and Madden, M. (2008). "Hazing in view: College students at risk. Initial findings from the national study of student hazing." Paper presented March 11, 2008, College of Education and Human Development.

Allport, G. (1954). *The Nature of Prejudice*. Cambridge, MA: Addison-Wesley.

Anderson, E. (2000). *Trailblazing: America's First Openly Gay High School Coach*. Fountain Valley, CA: Identity Press.

Anderson, E. (2002). "Openly gay athletes: Contesting hegemonic masculinity in a homophobic environment." *Gender & Society, 16*(6), 860–877.

Anderson, E. (2005a). *In the Game: Gay Athletes and the Cult of Masculinity*. Albany, NY: State University of New York Press.

Anderson, E. (2005b). "Orthodox and inclusive masculinities: Competing masculinities among heterosexual men in a feminized terrain." *Sociological Perspectives, 48*, 337–55.

Anderson, E. (2006). "Using the master's tools: Resisting colonization through colonial sports." *International Journal of the History of Sport, 26*(2), 247–266.

Anderson, E. (2007). "Coaching identity and social exclusion." In J. Denison (ed.), *Coaching Knowledges: Understanding the Dynamics of Sport Performance*. London: A&C Black.

Anderson, E. (2008a). "Being masculine is not about who you sleep with …: Heterosexual athletes contesting masculinity and the one-time rule of homosexuality." *Sex Roles, 58*(1–2), 104–115.

Anderson, E. (2008b). "Inclusive masculinity in a fraternal setting." *Men and Masculinities. 10*(5), 604–620.

Anderson, E. (2008c). "'I used to think women were weak': orthodox masculinity, gender-segregation, and sport." *Sociological Forum, 23*(2), 257–280.

Anderson, E. (2009). *Inclusive Masculinity: The Changing Nature of Masculinities*. London: Routledge.

Anderson, E. (2010). "Why some men cheat." *Journal of Social and Personal Relationships*, in press.

Anderson, E. and McCormack, M. (2010). "The re/production of homosexually-themed discourse in organized sport." *Journal of Language and Social Psychology*. Article under review.

Aronson, E. (1969). "A theory of cognitive dissonance: A current perspective." In L. Berkowitz (ed.), *Advances in Experimental Social Psychology* (pp. 1–34). New York: Academic Press.

Aronson, E. (1978). "Reconsiderations: The nature of prejudice." *Human Nature, 1*, 92–94.

Asch, S. (1951). "Effects of group pressure upon the modification and distortion of judgments." In H. Guetzkow (ed.), *Groups, Leadership and Men* (pp. 177–190). Pittsburgh, PA: Carnegie Press.

Ashe, A. (1988). *A Hard Road to Glory: A History of the African-American Athlete*. Vol. 1. New York: Warner Books.

Barnett, S. and Thomson, K. (1996). "Portraying sex: The limits of tolerance." In R. Jowell, J. Curtice, A. Park, L. Brook, and K. Thomson (eds), *British Social Attitudes, the 13th Report*. Aldershot, Hants: Social and Community Planning Research.

Baum, A. (2006). "Eating disorders in the male athlete." *Sport Medicine, 36*, 1–6.

Becker, G. (1964). *Human Capital*. Chicago, IL: University of Chicago Press.

Bem, D. J. (1967). "Self perception: An alternative interpretation of cognitive dissonance phenomena." *Psychological Review, 74*, 183–200.

Berger, P. L. and Luckmann, T. (1967). *The Social Construction of Reality: A Treatise in the Sociology of Knowledge*. New York: Anchor.

Bissinger, H. G. (1990). *Friday Night Lights: A Town, a Team, and a Dream*. Boston, MA: Addison-Wesley.

Blass, T. (2000). *Obedience to Authority: Current Perspectives on the Milgram Paradigm*. Lawrence Elbraum Associates, New York.

Bloom, G. A. and Smith, M. D. (1996). "Hockey violence: A test of the cultural spillover theory." *Sociology of Sport Journal, 13*(1), 65–77.

Bourdieu, P. (2001). *Masculine Domination*. Stanford, CA: Stanford University Press.

Brackenridge, C. H. (1995). "Think global, act global: The future of international women's sport." *Journal of the International Council for Health, Physical Education, Recreation and Dance, 31*(4), 7–11.

Brackenridge, C. H. (2000). "Harassment, sexual abuse, and safety of the female athlete." *Clinics in Sports Medicine, 19*(2), 187–198.

Brackenridge, C. H., Bringer, J. D. and Bishopp, D. (2005). "Managing cases of abuse in sport." *Child Abuse Review, 14*(4), 259–274.

Brackenridge, C. and Kirby, S. (1997). "Playing it safe: Assessing the risk of sexual abuse to elite child athletes." *International Review for the Sociology of Sport, 32*, 407–418.

Brannon, R. (1976). "The male sex role: Our culture's blueprint for manhood, and what it's done for us lately." In R. Brannon and D. David (eds), *The Forty-Nine Percent Majority* (pp. 1–40). Reading, MA: Addison-Wesley.

Bredemeier, B. and Shileds, D. (1995). *Character Development and Physical Activity*. Champaign, IL: Human Kinetics.

Bredemeier, B. J., Weiss, M. R., Shields, D. L. and Shewchuk, R. M. (1986). "Promoting moral growth in a summer sport camp: The implication of theoretically grounded instructional strategies." *Journal of Moral Education, 15*, 212–220.

Britton, D. M. and Williams, C. (1995). "Don't ask, don't tell, don't pursue: Military policy and the construction of heterosexual masculinity." *Journal of Homosexuality, 30*(1), 1–21.

Brophy, I. N. (1946). "The luxury of anti-Negro prejudice." *Public Opinion Quarterly, 9*, 456–466.

Bruening, J. E. and Dixon, M. A. (2008). "Situating work-family negotiations within a life course perspective: Insights on the gendered experiences of NCAA Division I head coaching mothers." *Sex Roles, 58*, 10–23.

Bryshun, J. (1997). *Hazing in Sport: An Exploratory Study of Veteran/Rookie Relations.* Unpublished Masters Thesis, University of Calgary.

Bryshun, J. and Young, K. (1999). "Sport related hazing: An inquiry into male and female involvement." In P. White and K. Young (eds), *Sport and Gender in Canada* (pp. 269–293). Don Mills, Ontario: Oxford University Press.

Bryshun, J. and Young, K. (2007). "Hazing as a form of sport and gender socialization." In K. Young and P. White (eds), *Sport and Gender in Canada* (2nd edn) (pp. 302–327). Don Mills, Ontario: Oxford University Press.

Bryson, L. (1987). "Sport and the maintenance of masculine hegemony." *Women's Studies International Forum. 10*, 349–360.

Burn, S. M. (2000). "Heterosexuals' use of 'fag' and 'queer' to deride one another: A contributor to heterosexism and stigma." *Journal of Homosexuality, 40*, 1–11.

Burstyn, V. (1999). *The Rites of Men: Manhood, Politics and the Culture of Sport.* Toronto: University of Toronto Press.

Burton Nelson, M. (1994). *The Stronger Women Get the More Men Love Football.* New York: Avon Books.

Butterfield, S. A. and Loovis, E. M. (1994). "Influence of age, sex, balance, and sport participation in development of kicking by children in grades K–8." *Perceptual and Motor Skills, 79*, 121–138.

Byrne, S. and McLean, N. (2001). "Eating disorders and athletes: A review of the literature." *Journal of Science and Medicine in Sport, 4*, 145–159.

Cameron, D. (1998). "Is there any ketchup, Vera? Gender, power and pragmatics." *Discourse and Society, 9*, 437–455.

Cancian, F. M. (1987). *Love in America: Gender and Self-development.* Cambridge: Cambridge University Press.

Carlson, D., Scott, L., Planty, M. and Thompson, J. (2005). "What is the status of high school athletes 8 years after graduation?" Report released by the National Center for Educational Statistics, United States Department of Education.

Caudwell, J. (2003). "Sporting gender: Women's footballing bodies as sites/sights for the (re)articulation of sex, gender, and desire." *Sociology of Sport Journal, 20*(4), 371–386.

Cense, M. and Brackenridge, C. H. (2001). "Temporal and developmental risk factors for sexual harassment and abuse in sport." *European Physical Education Review. 7*(1), 61–79.

Chase, J. H. (1909). "How a director feels." *Playground, 3*(4), 13.

Claringbould, I. and Knoppers, A. (2008). "Doing and undoing gender in sport governance." *Sex Roles, 58*, 81–92.

Coakley, J. (2004 [1998]). *Sport in Society: Issues and Controversies* (8th edn) Boston, MA: McGraw-Hill.

Cockerill, I. M. (1996). "Exercise dependence and associated disorders: A review." *Counselling Psychology Quarterly, 9*, 119–129.

Collie, A., McCrory, P. and Makdissi, M. (2006). "Does history of concussion affect current cognitive status?" *British Journal of Sports Medicine, 40*, 550–551.

Colvin, A. C., Mullen, J., Lovell, M. R., West, R. V., Collins, M. W. and Groh, M. (2009). "The role of concussion history and gender in recovery from soccer-related concussion." *American Journal of Sports Medicine, 37*(9), 1699–1704.

Connell, R. W. (1987). *Gender and Power*. Stanford, CA: Stanford University Press.

Connell, R. W. (1995). *Masculinities*. Cambridge: Polity.

Crosset, T. (1986). "Male coach/female athlete relationships." *First Interdisciplinary Conference for Sport Sciences*, Sole, Norway, 15–16 November.

Crosset, T. (2000). "Athletic affiliation and violence against women: Toward a structural prevention project." In J. McKay, M. Messner and D. Sabo (eds), *Masculinities, Gender Relations, and Sport* (pp. 147–161). Thousand Oaks, CA: Sage.

Crosset, T., Benedict, J. and MacDonald, M. (1995). "Male student athletes reported for sexual assault: A survey of campus police departments and judicial affairs offices." *Journal of Sport and Social Issues, 19*, 126–140.

Cunningham, G. B. (2008). "Creating and sustaining gender diversity in sport organizations." *Sex Roles, 58*, 136–145.

Curry, T. (1991). "Fraternal bonding in the locker room: A profeminist analysis of talk about competition and women." *Sociology of Sport Journal, 8*, 119–135.

Cushion, C. and Jones, R. (2006). "Power, discourse and symbolic violence in professional youth soccer: The case of Albion football club." *Sociology of Sport Journal, 23*(2), 142–161.

Davis, L. (1990). "Male cheerleaders and the naturalization of gender." In M. Messner and D. Sabo (eds), *Sport, Men and the Gender Order* (pp. 153–161). Champaign, IL: Human Kinetics.

Delaney, J. S., Al-Kahmiri, A., Drummond, R. and Correa, J. A. (2008). "The effect of protective headgear on head injuries and concussions in adolescent football (soccer) players." *British Journal of Sports Medicine, 42*, 110–115.

Deutsch, M. and Gerard, H. B. (1955). "A study of normative and informational social influences upon individual judgment." *Journal of Abnormal and Social Psychology. 51*, 629–636.

Donnelly, P. and Young, K. (1988). "The construction and confirmation of identity in sport subcultures." *Sociology of Sport Journal, 5*, 223–240.

Doorgachurn, P. (1997). Personal correspondance with the author, November.

Drummond, M. J. N. (2001). "Boys' bodies in the context of sport and physical activity: Implications for health." *Journal of Physical Education New Zealand, 34*, 1343–1350.

Drummond, M. J. N. (2002). "Men, body image, and eating disorders." *International Journal of Men's Health, 1*, 89–98.

Eccles, J. S. and Barber, B. L. (1999). "Student council, volunteering, basketball, or marching band: What kind of extracurricular involvement matters?" *Journal of Adolescent Research, 14*, 10–43.

Edwards, T. (2006). *Cultures of Masculinity*. London: Routledge.

Eitzen, D. S. (2001). *Sport in Contemporary Society: An Anthology*. New York: Paradigm Publishers.

Eitzen, D. S. (2003). *Fair or foul: The Dark Side of American Sport*. New York: Rowman and Littlefield.

Ellis, K., O'Dair, B. and Tallmer, A. (1990). "Feminism and pornography." *Feminist Review 36*, 15–18.

Eskilson, A. (1995). *Trends in Homophobia and General Attitudes: 1987–1993*. Paper presented at Annual Meeting of the Amateur Sociological Association, 90th, Washington, DC.

Ewald, K. and Jiobu, R. M. (1985). "Explaining positive deviance: Becker's model and the case of runners and bodybuilders." *Sociology of Sport Journal, 2*, 144–156.

Farred, G. (2000). "Cool as the other side of the pillow." *Journal of Sport & Social Issues. 24*(2), 96–117.

Fausto-Sterling, Anne (2000). *Sexing the Body: Gender Politics and the Construction of Sexuality*. New York: Basic Books

Faye, T. and Wolf, E. (2009). "Disability in sport in the twenty-first century: Creating a new sport opportunity spectrum." *Boston University International Law Journal, 27*, 231–224.

Felshin, J. (1974). "The triple option … for women in sport." *Quest, 21*, 36–40.

Feist, D., Shenton, B. and de Souza, T. (2004). *Induction Ceremonies in University Sport in the UK*. Paper presented on February 2, 2004 to the British University Sports Association.

Festinger, L. (1957). *A Theory of Cognitive Dissonance*. Stanford, CA: Stanford University Press.

Fielding-Lloyd, B. and Meân, L. J. (2008). "Standards and separatism: The discursive construction of gender in English soccer coach education." *Sex Roles, 58*, 24–39.

Filene, P. G. (1975). *Him/Her/Self: Sex Roles in Modern America*. New York: Johns Hopkins University Press.

Filiault, S. (2009). "Playing with the natural body: Gay athletes, body image, and the hegemonic aesthetic." Doctoral thesis-by-publication. Adelaide: University of South Australia.

Finkel, M. A. (2002). "Traumatic injuries caused by hazing practices." *American Journal of Emergency Medicine, 20*(3), 228–233.

Foucault, M. (1975). *Discipline and Punish: The Birth of the Prison*. New York: Random House.

Foucault, M. (1984). *The History of Sexuality, Volume 1: An Introduction*. Trans. by Robert Hurley. New York: Vintage.

French, J. R. P. and Raven, B. (1959). "The bases of social power." In D. Cartwright (ed.), *Studies of Social Power*. University of Michigan Press.

Freud, S. (1905). "Three essays on the theory of sexuality." *Complete psychological works* (vol. 7). London: Hogarth.

Freud, S. (1929). *Civilization and its Discontents*. London: Penguin.

Frye, M. (1999). "Some reflections on separatism and power." In J. Kourany, J. Sterba and R. Tong (eds), *Feminist philosophies* (pp. 359–366). New Jersey: Prentice Hall.

Gerdy, J. (2002). *Sports: The All American Addiction*. University Press of Mississippi.

Gervis, M. and Dunn, N. (2004). "The emotional abuse of elite child athletes by their coaches." *Child Abuse Review, 13*(3), 215–223.

Giddens, A. (ed.) (2001). *The Global Third Way Debate*. Cambridge: Polity.

Girginov, V., Papadimitrious, D. and Lopez De D'Amico, R. (2006). "Cultural orientations of sport managers." *European Sport Management Quarterly. 6*(1), 35–66.

Gladwell, M. (2009). "Offensive play: How different are football and dogfighting?" *The New Yorker*, 22 November.

Goffman, E. (1961). *Asylums: Essays on the Social Situation of Mental Patients and Other Inmates*. New York: Doubleday.

Gough, B. and Edwards, G. (1998). "The beer talking: Four lads, a carry out and the reproduction of masculinity." *Sociological Review, 46*(3), 409–435.

Graham, K. and Wells, S. (2003). "Somebody's gonna get their head kicked in tonight: Aggression among young males in bars – a question of values?" *British Journal of Criminology, 43*, 546–566.

Gramsci, A. (1971). *Selections From the Prison Notebooks*. New York: International Publishers.

Greendorfer, S. (1992). "A critical analysis of knowledge construction in sport psychology." In T. Horn (ed.), *Advances in Sport Psychology* (pp. 201–215). Champaign, IL: Human Kinetics.

Griffin, P. (1998). *Strong Women, Deep Closets: Lesbians and Homophobia in Sport.* Champaign, IL: Human Kinetics.

Grogan, S. (2007). *Body Image: Understanding Body Dissatisfaction in Men, Women, and Children* (2nd edn). New York: Routledge.

Grogan, S. and Richards, H. (2002). "Body image: Focus groups with boys and men." *Men and Masculinities, 4*, 219–232.

Hamilton, V. L. and Sanders, J. (1999). "The second face of evil: Wrongdoing in and by the corporation." *Personality and Social Psychology Review 3*(2), 222–233.

Hanson, M. E. (1995). *Go! Fight! Win! Cheerleading in American Culture.* Bowling Green, OH: Bowling Green State University Popular Press.

Hargreaves, J. (1986). *Sport, Power and Culture: A Social and Historical Analysis of Popular Sports in Britain.* Cambridge: Polity.

Hargreaves, J. (1995). "Gender, morality and the National Curriculum." In L. Lawrence, E. Murdoch and S. Parker (eds), *Professional Development Issues in Leisure, Sport and Education.* Eastbourne: Leisure Studies Association.

Hargreaves, J. (2002). "The Victorian cult of the family and the early years of female sport." In S. Scraton and A. Flintoff (eds), *Gender and Sport: A Reader* (pp. 53–65). London: Routledge.

Hardy, J., Eys, M. A. and Carron, A. V. (2005). "Exploring the potential disadvantages of high team cohesion in sports teams." *Small Group Research, 36*(2), 166–187.

Harvey, T. J. and Stables, A. (1984). "Gender differences in subject preference and perception of subject importance among third year secondary school pupils in single-sex and mixed comprehensive schools." *Educational Studies, 10*(3), 243–253.

Herek, G. M. (2002). "Heterosexuals' attitudes toward bisexual men and women in the United States." *The Journal of Sex Research, 39*(4), 1–18.

Herek, G. M. and Capitanio, J. P. (1996). "Some of my best friends: Intergroup contact, concealable stigma, and heterosexuals' attitudes toward gay men and lesbians." *Personality and Social Psychology Bulletin, 22*, 412–424.

Hoch, P. (1972). *Rip Off the Big Game.* New York: Doubleday.

Holman, M. (2004). "A search for a theoretical understanding of hazing practises in athletics." In J. Johnson and M. Holman (eds), *Making the Team: Inside the World of Sport Initiations and Hazing* (pp. 50–60). Toronto: Canadian Scholars Press.

Hoover, N. C. (1999). "National survey: Initiation rites and athletics for NCAA sports teams." Available online at: www.alfred.edu/news/html/hazing (accessed November 3, 2008).

Howe, D. (2001). "An ethnography of pain and injury in professional rugby union: The case of Pontypridd RFC." *International Review for the Sociology of Sport, 36*, 289–303.

Hughes, R. and Coakley, J. (1991). "Positive deviance among athletes: The implications of overconformity to the sport ethic." *Sociology of Sport Journal, 8*, 307–325.

Hyman, M. (2009). *Until it hurts: America's obsession with youth sports and how it hurts our kids.* New York: Beacon Press.

Ibson, J. (2002). *Picturing Men: A Century of Male Relationships in Everyday American life.* Washington and London: Smithsonian Institution Press.

Jackson, C. and Warren, J. (2000). "The importance of gender as an aspect of identity at key transition points in compulsory education." *British Educational Research Journal 26*(3), 375–388.

Jeziorski, R. (1994). *The Importance of School Sports in American Education and Socialization*. New York: University Press of America.

Johnson, A., Mercer, C., Erens, B., Copas, A., McManus, S. and Wellings, K. (2001). "Sexual behavior in Britain: Partnerships, practises, and HIV risk behaviors." *The Lancet, 358*(9296), 1835–1842.

Johnson, C., Powers, P. S. and Dick, R. (1999). "Athletes and eating disorders: The National Collegiate Athletic Association study." *International Journal of Eating Disorders, 26*, 79–88.

Jones, R. L., Armour, K. M. and Potrac, P. (2004). *Sports Coaching Cultures: From Practice to Theory*. London: Routledge.

Joyner, K. and Laumann, E. (2001). "Teenage sex and the sexual revolution." In E. O. Laumann and R. T. Michael (eds), *Sex, Love, and Health in America: Private Choices and Public Consequences* (pp. 41–47) University of Chicago Press.

Kaplan, D. (2006). "Public intimacy: Dynamics of seduction in male homosocial interactions." *Symbolic Interaction, 28*(4), 571–595.

Kelly, S. and Waddington, I. (2006). "Abuse, intimidation and violence as aspects of managerial control in professional soccer in Britain and Ireland." *International Review for the Sociology of Sport 41*(2), 147–164.

Kelman, H. C. and Hamilton, V. L. (1989). *Crimes of Obedience: Toward a Social Psychology of Authority and Responsibility*. New Haven, CT: Yale University Press.

Kephart, W. M. (1957). *Racial Factors and Urban Law Enforcement*. Philadelphia: University of Pennsylvania Press.

Kimmel, M. S. (1994). "Masculinity as homophobia: Fear, shame, and silence in the construction of gender identity." In H. Brod and M. Kaufman (eds), *Theorizing Masculinities*. London: Sage.

Kininham, R. B. and Gorenflo, D. W. (2001). "Weight loss methods of high school wrestlers." *Medicine & Science in Sport & Exercise, 33*, 810–813.

Kirby, S. L. and Wintrup, G. (2002). "Running the gauntlet: An examination of initiation/hazing and sexual abuse in sport." *Journal of Sexual Aggression, 8*(2), 49–68.

Kivel, P. (1999). *Boys Will be Men: Raising our Sons for Courage, Caring, and Community*. Gabriola Island, BC: New Society Publishers.

Kleiber, D. A. and Roberts, G. C. (1981). "The effects of sport experience in the development of social character." *Journal of Sport Psychology, 3*, 114–122.

Knoppers, A. and Anthonissen, A. (2005). "Male athletic and managerial masculinities: Congruencies in discursive practices." *Journal for Gender Studies, 14*, 123–135.

Krause, J. and Priest, R. (1993). "Sport value choices of US military cadets – a longitudinal study of the class of 1993." Unpublished manuscript, Office of Institutional Research, U. E. Military Academy, West Point, NY.

Kreager, D. (2007). "Unnecessary roughness? School sports, peer networks, and male adolescent violence." *American Sociological Review, 72*, 705–724.

Kwiatkowski, M. (1998). *Sporting Femininity: Perceptions of Femininity and Homophobia within the Sport and Recreation Experiences of Women*. Unpublished dissertation, University of Tennessee.

Lapchick, R., Brenden, J. and Wright, B. (2006). *The racial and gender report card of the associated press sports editors*. Orlando: Institute for Diversity and Ethics in Sport.

Latane, B. (1981). "The psychology of social impact." *American Psychologist. 36*(4), 343–356.

Latane, B. and Bourgeois, M. J. (2001). "Successfully simulating dynamic social impact." In J. Forgas and K. Williams (eds), *Social Influence: Direct and Indirect Processes* (pp. 61–78). London: Taylor and Francis.

Laumann, E., Gagnon, J., Michael, R. and Michaels, S. (1994). *The Social Organization of Sexuality: Sexual Practices in the United States.* Chicago, IL: University of Chicago Press.

Laurson, K. R. and Eisenmann, J. C. (2007). "Prevalence of overweight among high school football linemen." *Journal of the American Medical Association, 297*, 363–364.

Levine, M., Prosser, A., Evans, D. and Reicher, S. (2005). "Identity and emergency intervention: How social group membership and inclusiveness of group boundaries shape helping behavior." *Personality and Social Psychology Bulletin, 31*, 443–453.

Lindeman, A. K. (1999). "Quest for ideal weight: Costs and consequences." *Medicine & Science in Sport & Exercise, 31*, 1135–1140.

Loftus, J. (2001). "America's liberalization in attitudes towards homosexuality, 1973 to 1998." *American Sociological Review, 66*, 762–782.

Lyle, J. (2002). *Sports Coaching Concepts: A Framework for Coaches' Behaviour.* London: Routledge.

Madison, J. and Ruma, S. (2003). "Exercise and athletic involvement as moderators of severity in adolescents with eating disorders." *Journal of Applied Sport Psychology, 3*, 213–222.

Mahiri, J. (1998). *Shooting for Excellence: African American Youth Culture in New Century Schools.* New York: Teachers College Press.

Majors, R. (1990). "Cool pose: Black masculinity in sports." In M. Messner and D. Sabo (eds), *Sport, men and the gender order: Critical feminist perspectives* (pp. 109–115). Champaign, IL: Human Kinetics.

Marsh, H. (1992). "Extracurricular activities: Beneficial extension of the traditional curriculum of subversion of academic goals." *Journal of Educational Psychology, 84*, 553–562.

Marsh, H. (1993). "The effects of participation in sport during the last two years of high-school." *Sociology of Sport Journal, 10*, 18–43.

Marx, K. and Engels, F. (1967). *The Communist Manifesto.* New York: Penguin.

Mathisen, J. A. (1990). "'Reviving 'muscular Christianity': Gill Dodds and the institutionalization of sport evangelism." *Sociological Focus, 23*(3), 233–249.

McCann, P. D., Minichiello, V. and Plummer, D. (2009). "Is homophobia inevitable? Evidence that explores the constructed nature of homophobia, and the techniques through which men unlearn it." *Journal of Sociology, 45*(2): 201–220.

McCaughey, M. (2007). *The Caveman Mystique: Pop-Darwinism and the Debates over Sex, Violence, and Science.* New York: Routledge.

McCormack, M. (2010). "The declining significance of homohysteria for male students in three sixth forms in the south of England." *British Educational Research Journal*, in press.

McCormack, M. and Anderson, E. (in press). "'It's just not acceptable anymore': The erosion of homophobia and the softening of masculinity at an English state school." *Sociology.*

McCrea, M., Hammeke, T., Olsen, G., Leo, P. and Guskiewicz, K. (2004). "Unreported concussion in high school football players: Implications for preventions." *Clinical Journal of Sport Medicine, 14*(1), 7–13.

McDonagh, E. and Pappano, L. (2008). *Playing with the Boys: Why Separate is Not Equal in Sports.* Oxford: Oxford University Press.

McGuffey, C. S. and Rich, B. L. (1999). "Playing in the gender transgression zone: Race, class, and hegemonic masculinity in middle childhood." *Gender and Society*, *13*(5), 608–627.

McGuigan, B. (1995). *Queering the Pitch: The Experiences of Gay Athletes in Mainstream Sport and Gay Games V.* Unpublished Dissertation, Exeter University.

Messner, M. (1987). "The meaning of success: The athletic experience and the development of identity." In H. Brod (ed.), *The Making of Masculinities: The New Men's Studies* (pp. 193–209). Boston, MA: Allen and Unwin.

Messner, M. (1992). *Power at Play: Sports and the Problem of Masculinity.* Boston, MA: Beacon Press.

Messner, M. (2002). *Taking the Field: Women, Men and Sports.* Minneapolis, MA: University of Minnesota Press.

Messner, M. and Sabo, D. (1990). *Sport, Men and the Gender Order: Critical Feminist Perspectives.* Champaign, IL: Human Kinetics.

Michener, J. (1976). *Sports in America.* New York: Fawcett Crest.

Milgram, S. (1974). *Obedience to Authority: An Experimental View.* New York: Harper and Row.

Miller, W. C. and Jacob, A. V. (2001). "The health at any size paradigm for obesity treatment: The scientific evidence." *Obesity Review*, *2*, 37–45.

Miller, K., Melnick, M., Barnes, G., Farrell, M. and Sabo, D. (2005). "Disentangling the links among athletic involvement, gender, race, and adolescent academic outcomes." *Sociology of Sport Journal*, *22*(2), 178–193.

Miller Lite (1983). *Miller Lite Report on American Attitudes Toward Sports.* Milwaukee: Miller Brewing Company.

Miracle, A. W. and Rees, C. R. (1994). *Lessons of the Locker Room: The Myth of School Sports.* Amherst, NY: Prometheus Books.

Monaghan, L. (2001). *Bodybuilding, Drugs and Risk.* London: Routledge.

Mrozek, D. (1983). *Sport and American Mentality, 1880–1910.* The University of Knoxville, TN: Tennessee Press.

Muir, K. and Seitz, T. (2004). "Machismo, misogyny, and homophobia in a male athletic subculture: A participant observation study of deviant rituals in collegiate rugby." *Deviant Behavior*, *25*, 303–327.

Nardi, P. (1999). *Gay Men's Friendships.* Chicago, IL: University of Chicago Press.

Neimark, J. (1991). "Out of bounds: The truth about athletes and rape." *Mademoiselle*, *97*(5), 196–199, 244–246.

New, C. (2001). "Oppressed and oppressors? The systematic mistreatment of men." *Sociology*, *35*, 729–748.

Nuwer, H. (2004). *The Hazing Reader.* Bloomington, IN: Indiana University Press.

Nixon, H. (1994). "The relationship of friendship networks, sports experiences, and gender to expressed pain thresholds." *Sociology of Sport Journal*, *13*, 78–86.

Nylund, D. (2007). *Beer, Babes, and Balls: Masculinity and Sports Talk Radio.* New York: State University of New York Press.

Ohlander, J., Batalova, J. and Treas, J. (2005). "Explaining educational influences on attitudes toward homosexuality." *Social Science Research*, *38*, 781–799.

Oxendine, J. (1988). *American Indian Sport Heritage.* Champaign, IL: Human Kinetics.

Parker, A. (2001). "Soccer, servitude and sub-cultural identity: Football traineeship and masculine construction." *Soccer and Society*, *2*, 59–80.

Pascoe, C. J. (2005). "'Dude, you're a fag': Adolescent masculinity and the fag discourse." *Sexualities*, *8*, 329–346.

Peralta, R. (2007). "College alcohol and the embodiment of hegemonic masculinity among European American men." *Sex Roles, 56*, 741–756.

Pettigrew, T. F. (2008). "Future directions for intergroup contact theory and research." *International Journal of Intercultural Relations, 32*, 187–199.

Pettigrew, T. F. and Tropp, L. R. (2006). "A meta-analytic test of intergroup contact theory." *Journal of Personality and Social Psychology, 90*(5), 751–783.

Plummer, D. (1999). *One of the Boys: Masculinity, Homophobia and Modern Manhood*. New York: Harrington Park Press.

Pollack, W. (1998). *Real Boys: Rescuing our Sons from the Myths of Boyhood*. New York: Henry Holt and Company.

Pope, H., Phillips, K. A. and Olivardia, R. (2000). *The Adonis Complex: The Secret Crisis of Male Body Obsession*. New York: Free Press.

Pronger, B. (1990). *The Arena of Masculinity: Sports, Homosexuality, and the Meaning of Sex*. New York: St. Martin's Press.

Putnam, R. (1995). *Bowling Alone: The Collapse and Revival of American Community*. New York: Simon & Schuster.

Ransome, P. (1992). *Antonio Gramsci: A New Introduction*. London: Harvester Wheatsheaf.

Raphael, R. (1988). *The Men from the Boys: Rites of Passage in Male America*. Lincoln, NB: University of Nebraska Press.

Reskin, B. and Roos, P. (1990). *Job Queues, Gender Queues: Explaining Women's Inroads into Male Occupations*. Philadelphia, PA: Temple University Press.

Rigauer, B. (1981). *Sport and Work*. New York: Columbia University Press.

Rimer, E. (1996). "Discrimination in major league baseball: Hiring standards for major league managers, 1975–1994." *Journal of Sport and Social Issues, 20*, 118–133.

Robidoux, M. (2001). *Men at Play: A Working Understanding of Professional Hockey*. Montreal and Kingston: McGill-Queen's University Press.

Robinson, L. (1998). *Crossing the Line: Violence and Sexual Assault in Canada's National Sport*. Toronto, ON: McClelland & Stewart.

Rotolo, T. and Wharton, A. (2004). "Living across institutions: Exploring sex-based homophily in occupations and voluntary groups." *Sociological Perspectives, 46*(1), 59–82.

Rotundo, E. A. (1993). *American Manhood: Transformations in Masculinity from the Revolution to the Modern Era*. New York: Basic Books.

Rubin, G. S. (1975). "The traffic in women: Notes on the "political economy" of sex." In R. R. Reiter (ed.), *Toward an Anthropology of Women* (pp. 37–85). New York: Monthly Review Press.

Rudd, A. and Stoll, S. (2004). "What type of character do athletes possess? An empirical examination of college athletes versus college non-athletes with the RSBH Value Judgement Inventory." *The Sport Journal, 7*(2), 1–10.

Russell, B. (1938). *Power: A Social Analysis*. London: Allen & Unwin.

Ryan, J. (1996). *Little Girls in Pretty Boxes: The Making and Breaking of Elite Gymnasts and Figure Skaters*. New York: Doubleday Books.

Sabo, D., Miller, M., Melnick, M. and Heywood, L. (2004). *Their Lives Depend on it: Sport, Physical Activity, and the Health and Well-being of American Girls*. East Meadow, NY: Women's Sports Foundation.

Sabo, D., Melnick, M. and Vanfossen, B. (1989). *The Women's Sports Foundation Report: Minorities in Sport*. New York: Women's Sports Foundation.

Sage, G. (1990). *Power and Ideology in American Sport: A Critical Perspective*. Champaign, IL: Human Kinetics.

Salkeld, L. (2008). "University golf society students kept score as fresher drank himself to death on pub crawl." Available online at: www.dailymail.co.uk/news/article-519094/University-golf-society-students-kept-score-fresher-drank-death-pub-crawl.html (accessed November 28, 2008).

Schacht, S. (1996). "Misogyny on and off the 'pitch': The gendered world of male rugby players." *Gender & Society, 10*, 550–565.

Segal, L. (1994). *Straight Sex: Rethinking the Politics of Pleasure.* Berkeley, CA: University of California Press.

Shields, D. L., Bredemeier, B. J., Gardner, D. E. and Bostrom, A. (1995). "Leadership, cohesion, and team norms regarding cheating and aggression." *Sociology of Sport Journal, 12*, 324–336.

Silva, J. (1983). "The perceived legitimacy of rule violating behavior in sports." *Journal of Sport Psychology, 5*, 438–466

Smith, M. (1975). "The legitimation of violence: Hockey players' perceptions of reference group sanctions for assault." *Canadian Review of Sociology and Anthropology, 12*(1), 72–80.

Smith, M. (1983). *Violence in Sport.* Toronto: Butterworths.

Smith-Rosenberg, C. (1985). *Disorderly conduct: Visions of gender in Victorian America.* New York: Oxford University Press.

Spencer, C. (1995). *Homosexuality in History.* Orlando, FL: Harcourt Brace.

Spring, J. (1974). "Mass culture and school sports." *History of Education Quarterly, 14*, 483–499.

Sundgot-Borgen, J. and Torstveit, M. K. (2004). "Prevalence of eating disorders in elite athletes is higher than in the general population." *Clinical Journal of Sport Medicine, 14*, 25–32.

Sutton, N. (2008). *Initiations: Why I Took Part in One.* Available online at: http://news.bbc.co.uk/1/hi/uk/7646891.stm (accessed June 15, 2009).

Sykes, H. (1998). "Turning the closets inside out: Towards a queer-feminist theory in women's physical education." *Sociology of Sport Journal, 15,* 154–173.

Tajfel, H. (1982). "Social psychology of intergroup relations." *Annual Review of Psychology, 33*, 1–39.

Tajfel, H. and Turner, J. (1979). "An integrative theory of intergroup conflict." In W. G. Austin and S. Worchel (eds), *The Social Psychology of Intergroup Relations.* Monterey, CA: Brooks-Cole.

Tajfel, H. and Turner, J. C. (1986). "The social identity theory of inter-group behavior." In S. Worchel and L. W. Austin (eds), *Psychology of Intergroup Relations.* Chicago, IL: Nelson-Hall.

Tanenbaum, L. (1999). *Slut!: Growing up Female with a Bad Reputation.* New York: Seven Stories Press.

Thompson, J. K. and Cafri, G. (2007). *The Muscular Ideal: Psychological, Social, and Medical Perspectives.* Washington, DC: American Psychological Association Press.

Thompson, J. K., Heinberg, L. J., Altabe, M. and Tantleff-Dunn, S. (1999). *Exacting Beauty: Theory, Assessment, and Treatment of Body Image Disturbance.* Washington, DC: American Psychological Association.

Thorne, B. (1993). *Gender Play: Girls and Boys in School.* New Brunswick, NJ: Rutgers University Press.

Toftegard-Nielsen, J. (2001). "The forbidden zone: Intimacy, sexual relations and misconduct in the relationship between coaches and athletes." *International Review for the Sociology of Sport, 36*(2), 165–182.

Tomlinson, A. and Yorganci, I. (1997). "Male coach/female athlete relations: Gender and power relations in competitive sport." *Journal of Sport & Social Issues*, *21*(2), 134–155.

Trota, B. and Johnson, J. (2004). "Introduction: A brief history of hazing." In J. Johnson and M. Holman (eds), *Making the Team: Inside the World of Sport Initiations and Hazing* (pp. x–xvi). Toronto, ON: Canadian Scholars Press.

Vaz, E. (1972). "The culture of young hockey players: Some initial observations." In A. W. Taylor (ed.), *Training Scientific Basis and Application* (pp. 222–234). Springfield, IL: Charles Thomas Press.

Wacquant, L. J. (1995). "The pugilistic point of view: How boxers think and feel about their trade." *Theory and Society*, *24*, 489–535.

Whisenant, W., Pedersen, P. and Obenour, B. (2002). "Success and gender: Determining the rate of advancement for intercollegiate athletic directors." *Sex Roles*, *47*, 485–491.

Wiggins, D. K. (1977). "Good times on the old plantation: Popular recreations of the black slave in Antebellum south, 1810–1860." *Journal of Sport History*, *7*(2), 21–39.

Wiggins, D. K. (1980a). "The play of slave children in plantation communities of the old south, 1820–1860." *Journal of Sport History*. *7*(2), 21–39.

Wiggins, D. K. (1980b). "Sport and popular pastimes: Shadow of the slave quarters." *Canadian Journal of History of Sport and Physical Education*, *11*(1) 61–68.

Williams, C. (1995). *Still a Man's World: Men Who Do "Women's" Work*. Berkeley, CA: University of California Press.

Wolf, N. (1997). *Promiscuities: The Secret Struggle for Womanhood*. New York: Random House.

Woodward, R. (2000). "Warrior heroes and little green men: Soldiers, military training, and the construction of rural masculinities." *Rural Sociology*, *65*(4), 6–40.

WSF (Women's Sports Foundation) (2009) http://www.womenssportsfoundation.org/ Issues-And-Research/Research-And-Policy-Institute/Research-Reports.aspx.

Yeager, K. K., Agnostini, R., Nattiv, A. and Drinkwater, B. (1993). "The female athletic triad: Disordered eating, amenhorrhea, and osteoporosis." *Medicine & Science in Sports & Exercise*, *25*, 775–777.

Yelland, C. and Tiggemann, M. (2003). "Muscularity and the gay ideal: Body dissatisfaction and disordered eating in homosexual men." *Body Image*, *4*, 107–116.

Young, K. (1983). "The subcultures of rugby players: A form of resistance and incorporation." Unpublished Master's Thesis, McMaster University, Hamilton, ON.

Index